**SAGE** was founded in 1965 by Sara Miller McCune to support the dissemination of usable knowledge by publishing innovative and high-quality research and teaching content. Today, we publish more than 750 journals, including those of more than 300 learned societies, more than 800 new books per year, and a growing range of library products including archives, data, case studies, reports, conference highlights, and video. SAGE remains majority-owned by our founder, and after Sara's lifetime will become owned by a charitable trust that secures our continued independence.

Los Angeles | London | Washington DC | New Delhi | Singapore | Boston

# CARING

## *for the*

# ELDERLY

Thank you for choosing a SAGE product!
If you have any comment, observation or feedback,
I would like to personally hear from you.
*Please write to me at* **contactceo@sagepub.in**

**Vivek Mehra,** Managing Director and CEO,
SAGE Publications India Pvt Ltd, New Delhi

## Bulk Sales

SAGE India offers special discounts
for purchase of books in bulk.
We also make available special imprints
and excerpts from our books on demand.

*For orders and enquiries, write to us at*

Marketing Department
SAGE Publications India Pvt Ltd
B1/I-1, Mohan Cooperative Industrial Area
Mathura Road, Post Bag 7
New Delhi 110044, India

*E-mail us at* **marketing@sagepub.in**

## Get to know more about SAGE

Be invited to SAGE events, get on our mailing list.
*Write today to* **marketing@sagepub.in**

This book is also available as an e-book.

# CARING
## — *for the* —
# ELDERLY

Social Gerontology in the Indian Context

*Edited by*
**Tattwamasi Paltasingh**
**Renu Tyagi**

 **SAGE** www.sagepublications.com
Los Angeles • London • New Delhi • Singapore • Washington DC • Boston

*First published in 2015 by*

**SAGE Publications India Pvt Ltd**
B1/I-1 Mohan Cooperative Industrial Area
Mathura Road, New Delhi 110 044, India
*www.sagepub.in*

**SAGE Publications Inc**
2455 Teller Road
Thousand Oaks, California 91320, USA

**SAGE Publications Ltd**
1 Oliver's Yard, 55 City Road
London EC1Y 1SP, United Kingdom

**SAGE Publications Asia-Pacific Pte Ltd**
3 Church Street
#10-04 Samsung Hub
Singapore 049483

Published by Vivek Mehra for SAGE Publications India Pvt Ltd, typeset in 10.5/12.5pt Bembo by Diligent Typesetter, Delhi, and printed at Chaman Enterprises, New Delhi.

**Library of Congress Cataloging-in-Publication Data Available**

**ISBN:** 978-93-515-0263-0 (HB)

**The SAGE Team:** Supriya Das, Saima Ghaffar, Kritika Vashist, Nand Kumar Jha and Rajinder Kaur

# Contents

## SECTION V
## Positive Ageing: Outlook and Approaches

# List of Tables

# List of Figures

# List of Abbreviations

| | |
|---|---|
| ACA | Additional Central Assistance |
| ADL | Activities of Daily Living |
| AISCCON | All India Senior Citizens' Confederation |
| ANOVA | Analysis of Variance |
| ATIS | Advanced Traveller Information Systems |
| AVCSS | Advanced Vehicle Control and Safety Systems |
| BCI | Brain-Computer Interface |
| BIMARUO | Bihar, Madhya Pradesh, Rajasthan, Uttar Pradesh and Odisha |
| BKPAI | Building knowledge base on Population Ageing in India |
| BPL | Below Poverty Line |
| BSNL | The Bharat Sanchar Nigam Limited |
| CBOs | Community-Based Organizations |
| CBR | Community-based Rehabilitation |
| CCRA | Certified Credit Research Analyst |
| CDC | Centres for Disease Control |
| CED | Chronic Energy Deficiency |
| CEDAW | Convention on the Elimination of All Forms of Discrimination against women |
| CHI | Consolidated Health Initiative |
| CI | Confidence Interval |
| CNCDs | Chronic Non-communicable Diseases |
| CPRC | Chronic Poverty Research Centre |
| CSO | Central Statistics Office |
| CSR | Corporate Social Responsibility |
| CVD | Cardio vascular diseases |
| DBP | Diastolic Blood Pressure |
| DFID | Department for International Development |
| DMCI | Downtown Moncton Centre-ville inc. |
| DRDA | District Rural Development Authority |

| DST | Department of Science and Technology |
|---|---|
| EAA | European Anthropological Association |
| ESIS | Employees' State Insurance Scheme |
| GESS | Group for Economic and Social Studies |
| GIS | Geographical Information System |
| GoI | Government of India |
| HACC | Home and Community Care services |
| HALE | Health Report-Estimated Healthy Life Expectancy |
| IADL | Instrumental Activities of Daily Living |
| IANS | The Indo-Asian News Service |
| ICSSR | Indian Council of Social Science Research |
| ICT | Information and Communication Technology |
| IDPM | The Institute for Development Policy and Management |
| IFA | International Federation on Ageing |
| IGNDPS | Indira Gandhi National Disability Pension Scheme |
| IGNOAPS | Indira Gandhi National Old Age Pension Scheme |
| IGNWPS | Indira Gandhi National Widow Pension Scheme |
| IIPA | Indian Institute of Public Administration |
| ILO | International Labour Office |
| ITS | Intelligent Transportation Systems |
| JNC | Joint National Committee |
| KSERA | Knowledgeable Service Robots for Ageing |
| LIC | Life Insurance Corporation of India |
| LICHFL | Life Insurance Corporation Housing Finance Ltd |
| LTC | Long-term Care |
| MBPY | Madhu Babu Pension Yojana |
| MDG | Millennium Development Goals |
| MIPAA | The Madrid Plan of Action on Ageing |
| MoSJE | The Ministry of Social Justice and Empowerment |
| MPF | Maldives Partnership Forum |
| NCAER | National Council of Applied Economic Research |
| NCRB | National Crime Record Bureau |
| NCT | National Capital Territory |
| NECIWG | National Economic Council Interagency Working Group |
| NFBS | National Family Benefit Scheme |
| NGOs | Non-governmental Organizations |
| NICE | National Initiative on Care for Elderly |

| NIHCE | National Institute for Health and Clinical Excellence |
|---|---|
| NIHFW | National Institute of Health and Family Welfare |
| NISD | National Institute of Social Defence |
| NMT | Nightingales Medical Trust |
| NOAPS | National Old Age Pension Scheme |
| NPHCE | National Programme for Healthcare for the Elderly |
| NPOP | National Policy for Older Persons |
| NPSC | National Policy for Senior citizens |
| NSAP | National Social Assistance Programme |
| NSAPAP | National Social Assistance Programme and Associated Programmes |
| NSSO | National Sample Survey Organization |
| OAP | Old-age Pension |
| OATS | Older Adults Technology Services |
| OBC | Other Backward Class |
| OECD | Organisation for Economic Co-operation and Development |
| PACS | Poorest Areas Civil Society |
| PCME | Per Capita Monthly Expenditure |
| PF | Provident Fund |
| PIB | Press Information Bureau |
| PWD | Persons with Disabilities |
| QoL | Quality of Life |
| SAP | Special Assistance Programme |
| SBP | Systolic Blood Pressure |
| SC | Scheduled Castes |
| SCA | Senior Citizens Associations |
| SCOFCA | Scarcity of Family Care |
| SCSS | Senior Citizens Savings Scheme |
| SEARO | South-East Asia Regional Office |
| SHGs | Self-help Groups |
| SMS | Short Message Service |
| SOAPS | State Old Age Pension Scheme |
| SOC | Selective Optimisation with Compensation Theory |
| SPSS | Statistical Package for the Social Sciences |
| SRS | Shadow Robotic System |
| SSC | Social Security Cell |
| ST | Scheduled Tribes |
| TBS | The Benevolent Society |

| | |
|---|---|
| TIE | Technology Interventions for Elderly |
| TNN | The Nashville Network (News Channel) |
| U3A | Universities of Third Age |
| UGC | University Grants Commission |
| UN-DESA | United Nations Department of Economic and Social Affairs |
| UNESCAP | United Nations Economic and Social Commission for Asia and the Pacific |
| UNFPA | United Nations Population Fund |
| USSP | Union for the Scientific Study of Population |
| WHO | World Health Organization |
| WSSR | World Social Security Report |

# Foreword

In line with many other countries in the world, India has made considerable strides towards achieving its long-cherished objective of transforming its demographic landscape. Despite significant regional and intra-regional variations, there is improvement, over the past three decades, in indicators such as replacement level fertility, low mortality and a steady increase in life expectancy—both at birth and later years of life. The recent data available from the Sample Registration System[1] reveal that several states have either achieved the desired fertility level or are about to achieve it soon; only a few Indian states, including Uttar Pradesh, Bihar and Madhya Pradesh, lag behind. The data also reveal impressive progress in longevity and mortality rates. Obviously, with every successive year, these changes are likely to become more intense, causing several far-reaching consequences for the economy and society—one of the most significant being large-scale changes in the age composition of the country's population.

Interestingly, due to its perpetuating demographic changes, India is already in the process of experiencing a bimodal (or double-humped) population growth. The shares of both younger (15-plus) and older (60-plus) populations in the country are increasing simultaneously; the former because of the momentum generated by past fertility, and the latter because of sustained improvements in major demographic parameters and growing longevity. Analysts from both academia and institutions engaged in population planning and management must pay attention to both of these trends and their socio-economic repercussions. With a growing bulge in working-age populations (the first hump), there may, inter alia, be a fast growing pool of labour market participants, with very high pressure on the labour market clearance mechanism. How far this pool may be used gainfully within the framework of productive and decent employment is an issue

---

[1] *SRS Bulletin*, Vol. 47, No. 2, October, 2012.

paramount to overall policymaking. In contrast, a growing bulge in the size of the elderly population (the second hump), particularly those over 75 or 80, poses somewhat different but equally compelling sets of issues; a few of the more critical emanate from the income and health security requirements of the elderly.

With most projections suggesting a spectacular increase in the size of the elderly population over the coming decades, that is, from more than 103 million in 2011 to about 296 million in 2050, India appears to be falling short in its realization and preparedness to deal with major geriatric issues. Besides a somewhat apathetic attitude displayed so far by the state, media and major civil society organizations, there are many other factors that make this happen. One of them perhaps is the dearth of scientific literature to describe psycho-social processes of ageing, societal attitude towards the older persons, feminization of ageing, dominance of widowhood, inequalities in old-age health and care, functional autonomy, elderly well-being, etc. With some of these underpinnings, this excellent and timely book has exclusively been devoted to a range of neglected issues and engages its readers with a variety of illuminating discussions on ageing and the aged in a country which is yet to see through more carefully the challenges linked with the second hump of its population growth.

Gerontology, which remains the main plank of this book, deals with both social as well as physiologic aspects of ageing, including the aetiology of later life diseases. Being closer to the former, this book encompasses a range of issues beginning from conceptualization of the core subject to a number of issues with a bearing on social, economic and health aspects of ageing in India. Spreading over a total of 5 major sections and 14 subsections, the study begins with a discussion of theories and concepts of gerontology and moves to a set of major socio-economic and health ramifications of ageing. These discussions are further supplemented by a perspective on gender and cultural aspects and finally moved to several key issues linked with positive and active ageing.

This book is therefore a welcome addition and I commend both the editors for their attempts to come out with this timely publication. I must also admit that the book has considerable potentials and will definitely add to the existing literature and knowledge in the field of social gerontology.

**Moneer Alam**
Professor, Institute of Economic Growth (IEG), Delhi

# Preface and Acknowledgements

The pieces of evidence of having more older people than youngsters are becoming clear through demographic transition. Due to the advancements in health care and technology, the length of life has increased considerably. At present, the world has more people with extreme old age than ever before. Now, the question of sustainability with quality of life arises: Whether the more number of elderly will survive for longer period with good health, develop a sustained sense of quality of life with dignity, will have a social and productive engagement with a positive attitude, and many such queries need to be addressed with a great concern. There are enough reasons to be concerned with the contemporary unprecedented changes that include global transformation and rapid urbanization, followed by changing social structure. One worries whether the lives of the elderly would be associated with inadequate health care, followed by more illness, disability and dependency without care mechanisms. In a diverse population structure, ranging from developing to developed countries, this situation has become more complex. This book is a timely publication that has made an attempt to raise questions and reinstate the policy dialogues through conceptual and theoretical understanding supported by empirical evidences.

Population ageing is a matter of concern that requires continued efforts at all levels. Establishing a support mechanism to the family caregivers, building relevant infrastructure, institutions for old-age care, financial support to the deserving elderly, support for productive engagement, adequate budget allocation for a trouble-free life to the elderly, framing not just policies but also ensuring effective implementation for a quality and dignified life, and many such initiatives are the need of the hour. These efforts have to be made without delay, otherwise it can make the attempts more costly, less effective and results could be far reaching. The policies and implementations should be made pro-elderly that can address their diverse and context-specific needs.

The new demographic reality has to be confronted with a practical and feasible approach. We hope that this book would create responsiveness about an elderly friendly environment. Above all, the mindset of the people needs to be transformed with a very supportive and positive attitude. Practice, policy with effective implementation and relevant research on the issues concerning gerontology can help in bridging the knowledge base and practice.

The book has systematically illustrated 'Gerontology' in the perspectives of various disciplines including social work, sociology, anthropology, demography, law, political science, health studies, policy analysis and economics. It reflects the ideas, information and research literature on diverse ageing issues. The book provides a broad understanding of social gerontology, covering ageism, intergenerational solidarity, institutional mechanisms, gender, culture, care, welfare measures and theoretical as well as demographic context of the 'ageing' population. The book is thematically categorized into five broad sections. These sections are distinct as well as connected to the broader understanding of gerontology. There are total 14 chapters with an Introduction to the book. The introductory note has highlighted various ageing issues covered in this book. Section I, 'Understanding Gerontology', throws light upon various theories and concepts on Gerontology. It highlights that the future of ageing research needs greater attention to interdisciplinary theories. Section II, 'Social Security and Economic Issues', aims to focus on the social security issues, poverty in old age and rights of elderly. Section III, 'Health Issues: Dimensions and Strategies', depicts information on the socio-cultural perspectives of the health status of the elderly in India. It discusses the cross-cultural variation of health in diverse population groups. Section IV, 'Gender and Culture', deals with gender issues in ageing population, with a focus on policy perspectives. The section discusses the impact of gender inequalities with inadequate and partial policy responses towards ageing women in India. Section V, 'Positive Ageing: Outlook and Approaches', describes the concept of positive ageing with relevance of intergenerational solidarity, technological initiatives and welfare measures that go beyond violence among elderly. The book portrays an element of optimism and new outlook towards constructive ageing. Providing a comprehensive introduction, this book would be scholastic and a pleasant read for students, teachers, researchers, ageing professionals, policymakers and others associated with ageing issues.

Our deepest sense of gratitude and heartfelt thanks to all the authors who have shared their ideas, experiences and contributed in shaping the book in its present form. They cooperated and responded to the editorial queries at different points of time. Despite his demanding schedule, Professor Moneer Alam has written an inclusive and informative foreword for the book and he deserves a special mention. The experts and the anonymous reviewers have helped in giving productive comments in the manuscript and articles, helping in reinforcing the significance of the book. We express our gratitude to our Vice-Chairman, Professor Y.K. Alagh of SPIESR for his inspiration as a senior citizen.

We appreciate the invaluable cooperation of our family members who have been patient, accommodative and encouraging throughout this journey. We extend our deep sense of gratitude to Supriya Das, Elina Mazumdar and the entire SAGE team for their continued professional support throughout this effort. Our special appreciations are extended to all those who have directly and indirectly contributed in bringing out this book.

We dedicate this book to all the elderly across the globe, who have been great source of inspiration and motivation to complete this academic and useful endeavour. We will be grateful if our efforts can reach them.

**Tattwamasi Paltasingh and Renu Tyagi**

# Issues in Gerontology: An Introduction

*Tattwamasi Paltasingh and Renu Tyagi*

## Background

Gerontology, the study of ageing process, incorporates the social, psychological and biological variations with advancing age. It is a multi-disciplinary field and it examines the impact of ageing on both the individual and the society. Gerontology observes the physical and mental health and its effect on the elderly. The sociological aspects of ageing, such as social networking, retirement, loneliness, etc., and their impact on the elderly population are closely examined by gerontologists. Gerontology studies how different cultures respond and deal with their ageing populations. It is committed towards demystifying the myths and taboos associated with the ageing. The importance of psychosocial factors of ageing does not ignore the existence of illness, decline or impairment linked to biological ageing. With the contemporary unprecedented changes, including global transformation, urbanization and changing social structure, issues in gerontology have started gaining significant attention (Paltasingh and Tyagi, 2012). Therefore, the concept of gerontology needs to be understood from multiple perspectives. In this book, gerontology is explained from a broad spectrum. In India, the research in the field of gerontology is still in infancy, which requires rigorous academic intrusion.

The present book is an attempt towards an integrated understanding of gerontology from different perspectives, largely based on Indian context. More focus has been preoccupied with confronting ageing issues and related efforts towards positive ageing that has relevance in today's world. Awareness and understanding of the rights and welfare measure can empower the elderly population. A critical analysis of the existing measures has been discussed in the relevant section. Other important concerns include the bridging of inter-generation gaps, provision of adequate attention to health care, the gender-sensitive intervention in old age, exclusive policy initiatives for ageing women, tackling poverty issues for elderly engaged in unorganized sector, technology supports, strict measures against crime and mistreatment and relooking at family transitions with alternative care mechanism for the elderly. All these relevant themes have been adequately discussed in five different sections of the book, that is, (1) Understanding Gerontology; (2) Social Security and Economic Issues (3) Health Issues: Dimensions and Strategies (4) Gender and Culture and (5) Positive Ageing: Outlook and Approaches. There are total 14 chapters thematically arranged in these sections. There is an attempt to explain the connection of different dimensions of gerontology and ways to transform such linkages towards healthy and positive ageing.

# Understanding Gerontology

Gerontology can be viewed in terms of four distinct processes: chronological ageing, biological ageing, psychological ageing and social ageing. Chronological ageing is defined on the basis of the number of years a person survives from birth. Chronological age by itself, however, is never an accurate indicator of a person's biological, psychological or social age (Aiken, 1995). The biological ageing refers to the changes that reduce the physical health. Psychological ageing is determined by the changes that occur in sensory and perceptual processes, cognitive abilities, adaptive capacity and personality. Social ageing refers to an individual's changing roles and relationships with family, friends and society (Hooyman and Kiyak, 2011). Gerontology as a subject has evolved considerably since last three to four decades. However, in India, the studies on gerontology have gained importance since last one decade.

The introductory chapter highlights various ageing issues, considering the topics covered in this book. According to the United Nations, the world population would reach to 9.1 billion by 2050. In India, the number of people above 60 years was only 1.9 crores in 1947, went up to 10 crores (10% of the total population) by 2001 and is projected to be 15 crores by 2020 (Murty, 2008; Census of India, 2011). The forces of globalization, modernization, technological advancement, migration and the astonishing increase in the lateral transmission of knowledge are making changes in the lifestyles and cultural values, thereby making it difficult for the elderly population to adjust to the changing circumstances. Persistent social issues such as crime against the elderly, the gendered aspects of ageing, the politics of power relations between the generations, community care and related issues are matters of serious concern. There is a dearth of theoretical understanding of gerontology in India as well in the global context. Theoretical developments in gerontology have lagged well behind compared to other social science disciplines (Bengtson, Parrott and Burgess, 1997). Considering the lack of theoretical literature in gerontology, this section has made an attempt to identify the gap between the information on demography, empiricism and theories.

Theories of ageing are important to understand the complex social questions that intrude on who and what we are (Powell, 2009). **Chapter 1** in this section throws light upon various theories and concepts on gerontology. Authors have highlighted an absence of consensus for a definite path and an existence of a universal theory in gerontology. The chapter examines the evolution of the conceptual and theoretical perspective in this area. The authors discuss a range of explanations and theories on gerontology, incorporating a multidisciplinary perspective largely drawn from biology, psychology and sociology, feminism, postmodernism and political economy. The chapter also highlights how theoretical understanding can be supportive to understand the process of ageing and for framing the appropriate social policies for the benefit of the elderly. Gerontological research has been repeatedly found to be enriched with data and inadequate in theories (Riley and Riley 1994; Hendricks, 1995; Hendricks, Applebaum and Kunkel, 2010). The authors point out towards an excess of demographic information that has been narrowly defined and interpreted, ignoring many other important issues, especially the theoretical development to understand the complete ageing process. The authors suggest more exploratory and interdisciplinary approach to research on theoretical understanding of the ageing process. The future of ageing research strives for greater attention to theory, particularly interdisciplinary theories.

# Social Security and Economic Issues

Economic, health and social insecurities have become major areas of concern in India (World Bank, 2001; Alam, 2007). In developed countries, the elderly are largely under the social safety net; however, the incidence and magnitude of the social and economic insecurity are high in developing countries (Pandey and Misra, 2009; WSSR, 2011). In India, majority of the elderly depend on their sons or daughters as the reliable source of support in old age (Alam, 2007). The problems faced by the elderly generally upsurge due to inequality of opportunity for employment, inadequate income, lack of suitable social and health services, changing family structures and family relations, changes in inter-generational bonding and lack of productive engagement after retirement (Raikwar and Khan, 2012; Paltasingh and Tyagi, 2014). India, which used to have a strong system of joint family, has undergone changes due to industrialization, modernization, the changing attitude of younger people towards the elderly, steady migration of people towards large industrial complexes, cities and towns, and increasing number of working women (Patel, 2005; Asiya, 2010). The chapters in this section deal with social security issues for the elderly, tackling poverty in old age and rights of elderly in connection to socio-economic security.

**Chapter 2** discusses old age, vulnerability and growing insecurities being faced by the aged in Odisha, which is one of the poorest states of the country. The concentration of aged in terms of its share to the total population is significantly higher in Odisha as compared to other states in India. The chapter is largely based on the findings of two different macro surveys of National Sample Survey Organization (NSSO) (GOI, 1998; 2006). The author highlights the health risks being the biggest challenge for the elderly as well their families, causing them serious economic losses. The chapter examines the inadequacy of social assistance in the state. A critical evaluation of the National Social Assistance Programme (NSAP) and its partial implementation (Mahendra Dev, Subbarao, Galab and Ravi, 2007) all over the country has been adequately discussed. An urgent need for social insurance that can take care of the physical and emotional need, particularly health insurance for the destitute old people, has been recommended.

In India, one-third of the elderly persons live below the poverty line. However, in line with the Millennium Development Goals (MDG), reduction of chronic poverty in old age has never been a priority, either for the state or for the funding agencies and is left largely to public charity. **Chapter 3** discusses the ways and means of tackling poverty in old age. The author highlights that how the lower level of economic development in India, coupled with the absence of relevant policies, infrastructure and services, adds to an increasing number of ageing population, especially elderly women in poverty. Elderly women suffer more than elderly men for many such reasons. The author explains the inadequacy of the present poverty reduction measures for elderly population. The chapter reflects on non-contributory pension scheme as an effective means to tackle poverty in old age while addressing the related issues of social exclusion and isolation (NSAP, 2011). At present, the benefits of the scheme are available to a restricted category, that is, only to the people living below the poverty line. The chapter emphasizes on the economic issues related to elderly population, particularly with a focus on work, retirement and pension benefits. The author has suggested an inclusive approach that can involve elderly persons in preparation, revision, monitoring and evaluation of the old-age benefit schemes. In addition, an effective implementation of the National Policy for Senior Citizens (NPSC) is desirable.

**Chapter 4** explores the rights of the elderly and various socio-economic welfare measures contributing towards social security. It highlights some existing programmes and schemes for the senior citizens. A long and healthy life has been perceived as a challenge as well as a positive phenomenon. The author recognizes elderly as precious human resources and a reservoir of knowledge, wisdom and experience. In the backdrop of increasing longevity and share of the elderly, the author suggests adoption of strategies and approaches are at different levels of policymaking, planning and programming. The author also highlights the limited social security coverage in India with some discussion on specific regions. Ignorance about the existing welfare programmes and schemes among senior citizens, especially the social security measures, social security cell, TracFone service and economic security measures, such as old-age pension, need to be relooked. Awareness of rights regarding Maintenance and Welfare of Parents and Senior Citizens' Act, 2007 and the special tribunals to deal with disputes related to senior citizens is found to be poor among the Indian elderly. Author recommends an exclusive policy intervention for issues such as health, legal and socio-economic security. A critical evaluation of policies and programmes for the aged has been attempted in the chapter.

Author points out the various reasons for limited acceptance of old-age homes in India and the insignificant number of elderly beneficiaries as compared to the higher proportion of needy and disadvantaged elderly. More and more involvement and participation of the elderly in the socio-economic development process is suggested. There is a need for positive intervention by the non-governmental organizations (NGOs), community-based organizations (CBOs), trusts and charitable institutions to achieve the desired goals for welfare of the elderly.

# Health Issues: Dimensions and Strategies

'Health' refers to physical, mental and social well-being of an individual. The socio-economic problems of the elderly are intensified due to lack of social security and inadequate facilities for health care and rehabilitation. There is a need to pay attention to the health and socio-economic problems faced by the elderly in India. This can enable to develop some strategies for bringing an improvement in the quality of life of the elderly. Health should be seen as a positive resource for everyday living and not merely as an absence of disease (WHO, 2002). Health issues should be equally supported with relevant policies and programmes that promote mental health and social networking of the senior citizens. This section with four chapters aims to optimize the well-being of all senior citizens, including those who are frail, disabled and in need of care. A cultural variation in health issues is an important aspect that needs to be considered prior to formulating any policy or programme for the senior citizens. The quality of life related to health issues need to be understood in a better way. Socio-economic correlates towards health vulnerability of the elderly population and prospective approach towards healthy ageing have been emphasized in this section.

The state of physical health is defined in terms of the count of chronic diseases and impairments suffered by an elderly adult. **Chapter 5** discusses the social as well as cultural perspectives of the health status of the elderly in India. It is based on a countrywide representative sample collected as a part of the 60th round of the National Sample Survey (NSS). The authors highlight an association between ill health and the state of financial dependence while considering the gender differentials. The chapter points out an increased vulnerability of the widowed elderly as compared to their married counterparts. In addition, the authors have delineated the factors, including the socio-economic status, which play a significant role in determining the health of the elderly (Zimmer, 2008; Alam and Karan, 2011; Audinarayana, 2012). The authors underline the elderly as a distinct group than the rest of the population in various aspects, such as work participation rates, likelihood of being married, financial dependence, disease patterns and health care needs, etc. More attention towards the relevance of good quality of life among the elderly has been emphasized. Health being an important component of the quality of life needs to be addressed in a long-term policy perspective. The necessity and importance of the geriatric care in India have been covered in the chapter. Further, the quantum and the type of geriatric care required in country like India may differ from region to region, as the process of ageing is not uniform. The authors recommend the region-specific health policies in an economic context to mitigate the effect of financial constraints, widowhood, gender, caste and religion for better quality of life among the elderly.

Increasing life expectancy has resulted in a larger proportion of the population to be in the age range where chronic non-communicable diseases are the major cause of morbidity and mortality (WHO, 2002; Bhatt, Gadhvi, Sonaliya, Solanki and Nayak, 2011). **Chapter 6** in this book has discussed the cross-cultural variation of health in diverse population groups inhabiting in different regions of India, that is, Odisha, Uttarakhand, Manipur, Himachal Pradesh and Delhi. Distinct ageing effects on cardiovascular health have been observed, which were not only localized to urban population, but also apparent in traditional and transitional population as well (Mungreiphy and Kapoor, 2010; Kapoor, Dhall and Tyagi, 2010). The authors have focused on the heterogeneity among the elderly with regard to the economic and socio-cultural characteristics. The possible risk factors that predispose the elderly towards functional impairment have been discussed. Such studies support the need of comprehensive health trends before implementing any intervention programme for the elderly population. The authors recommend the lifestyle modifications and social networking to ensure healthy and graceful ageing with dignity.

Most of the countries, especially in Asian continent, are facing the dual challenges of a rapidly greying population and inadequate financial resources for its support. Age-related disability is a global and serious issue (Tas et al., 2007; Patel et al., 2011) that needs to be tackled with more preparation. **Chapter 7** highlights issues of disability and related morbidity among elderly. The proportion of ageing population with disabilities is increasing considerably, while its status and security are declining. The regional and gender variations in disability among the elderly have been cited with evidences from the NSSO. Various legal provisions and national policies, that is, National Policy on Disability and National Policy for Senior citizens (NPSC, 2011), have been discussed with a special focus on disabled elderly. The authors point out the ignorance of elderly population about the existing programmes and policy initiatives meant for it. There is a need to address the issues of ageing with an inclusive approach involving government, corporate sectors, civil societies and other stakeholders. The policymakers must recognize regional and gender variations to frame disabled-friendly policies. Right-based visions need to be adopted while addressing issues concerning the elderly. In view of the varied diseases and disabilities affecting the elderly as well as their lifestyle patterns, the social support in health services needs to be more equipped in terms of infrastructure and training for human resources. The chapter concludes with some policy recommendation, citing examples of some positive practices at both national and international fronts.

Involvement of the elderly in various activities carries significance, as it helps in transforming the socio-culturally defined negative images of old age. The continued participation of the elderly can be ensured with good health that contributes towards healthy ageing (WHO, 2012). **Chapter 8** discusses the prospective approach to healthy ageing that needs comprehensive, holistic services for short-term and long-term care. It may be a mix of public–private partnership that can include relevant stakeholders. The authors emphasize that facility for health care should be developed and located at the nearest point for the elderly to facilitate their rehabilitation, respite, long-term, palliative and terminal care. The families from the disadvantaged groups need to be encouraged with good incentives for the care of senior members. Health care requirements should be designed by targeting specific age groups of elderly. The health insurance companies need to bring a comprehensive plan for elderly care. Family education in the form of developing knowledge and skills, an integrated education model of elderly care, establishment of day care centres, etc., need scientific and academic discourses. The authors recommend appropriate policy initiatives to empower the elderly.

# Gender and Culture

Longevity does not imply higher status for women. Life expectancy has to be considered in conjunction with the quality of life. The demographic patterns of ageing reflect that the elderly woman is likely to be widowed or single and would be economically dependent. Women's overall lifetime labour force participation rate is lower than that of men, especially after marriage, and this trend is evidenced across the globe. In Asia, women are the predominant informal caregivers. Their economic contributions are unrecognized, unrewarded and largely neglected by the society. Many middle-aged women bear the liability of childcare, elderly care along with their professional careers. Gender relations structure the entire life cycle, from birth to old age, including access to resources and opportunities at every stage and are influenced by cultural factors. Elderly women and men in both developed and developing countries face difficulties in accessing adequate health care facilities as well as economic and social security. However, gender and age discriminations make the life of the elderly women more difficult, as their rights are often violated. Neglect, widowhood, divorce, lack of caregivers, post-menopausal worries and inadequate health care are some of the difficulties exclusively experienced by the elderly women. Their ownership of, or access to, land may be restricted due to discriminatory inheritance laws and practices, resulting in their increased financial dependence on the family or the state. The two-fold discrimination against elderly women based on gender and age stereotypes, combined with their greater vulnerability in the labour market, creates higher risks of poverty. All the chapters in this section have dealt with gender issues in ageing population with a focus on policy perspectives.

The population of elderly women is growing rapidly and they are largely affected by this trend. Despite the demographic trend favouring elderly women, they continue to ensure unequal and inadequate access to health, education, employment and resources across cultures (Hall and Havens, 2005). **Chapter 9** discusses the impact of gender inequalities throughout a woman's lifespan that becomes more evident during old age, and it also discusses the global population ageing and its feminization. The authors have discussed gender discrimination with a special focus on unequal education and limited employment opportunities, economic issues with unequal property rights, health care and increasing crime against elderly women. There are evidences that various positive contributions of women in their lifetime have not been given due attention. Policy initiatives with a focus on gender dimension covering the Convention on the Elimination of all Forms of Discrimination against Women (CEDAW) for elderly women, national policies on senior citizens and other interventions have been discussed. The inadequacy of government policies to address serious issues related to elderly women requires further discussions and analysis. The voice of elderly women needs to be incorporated in policy formulation, planning and implementation. The authors have highlighted more awareness generation about rights and available provisions that can empower the elderly women.

The commitments made by the first National Policy on Older Persons have paid an insufficient attention to the gender issues in the policy document (GoI, 2006). **Chapter 10** critiques the inadequate and partial policy responses in addressing concerns related to ageing women in India. The chapter focuses on important issues that need policy response and action to contribute significantly in improving the quality of life of elderly women in the country. The 21st century has placed greater emphasis on gender and human rights perspective in policymaking and action plans impacting the quality of life of elderly men and women. There is a need to include elderly persons and specifically ageing women in the development process. However, elderly women in India contribute and create opportunities for development. Longer and healthier lives of women in the country can be directed towards recreating valuable resources for socio-economic development. Author has highlighted the limited directions outlined in government and non-governmental institutions to facilitate areas of operation and action specifically for ageing women. The revised policy framework is expected to adopt a radical change of perspective with gender concerns. There is an urgent need for a gender-sensitive and inclusive policy for elderly women. In the Indian society, the glaring gender differentials serve to highlight the many points of interventions from a gender perspective that need to be taken up at the policy level. Heterogeneity of elderly men and women population must be recognized in policy, programmes and action plans for an effective outreach. There is a need to focus on the gender perspective at all levels, including planning, programming, budgeting, maintaining and evaluating a good policy document.

Ageing is commonly viewed as the physical changes in a biological sense. **Chapter 11** under this section interprets the cultural understandings of the old age with a focus on elderly women. The cross-cultural studies reveal that the process of ageing itself can be viewed in different ways in different socio-cultural contexts. Further, the perspectives on ageing can change with time, socio-economic conditions, occupation and education. The author has discussed such issues with examples from both developing and developed societies. This chapter largely discusses that how the growing-up process can be gendered and vary across cultures. It becomes apparent through different evidences that socio-cultural variables can influence the manner in which age and ageing are perceived (Lamb, 2002; Kampchen, 2012). The author explains that the ageing experience gets influenced and interpreted differently across culture, gender, class and geographical boundaries.

# Positive Ageing: Outlook and Approaches

The positive view about the way people age is not only a scientific concept but is also in the mindset of elderly people (Bowling, 2006). Positive ageing and the related terms, such as 'healthy ageing', 'successful ageing', 'productive ageing', 'ageing well', etc., highlight the non-traditional paradigm of human ageing. The paradigm shift suggests possible improvement in future despite increasing longevity. Positive ageing foresees a new outlook for gerontology, based on postponing functional declines in old age with a goal of decreasing cumulative lifetime morbidity and mortality (Fries, 2012). Positive ageing is described by a broad set of bio-psycho-social factors that emphasize a diversity of positive conditions all through the ageing process. Intergenerational solidarity, technological initiatives to support the elderly, better economic welfare measures and infusing positive ageing among elderly could support the elderly in many ways, and this has been the thrust of this section.

The wide gap in the 'ideology of living', feeling and thinking, particularly among the young and the elderly, is a matter of great concern (Khan, 2008). **Chapter 12** discusses some effective strategies for bridging inter-generational gap. A part of this chapter is based on the findings of an empirical study carried out to examine the existing pattern of interaction of children with their grandparents. Most of the children are found to be ignorant about the expectations of grandparents from them. However, the inter-generational interaction during this study has made majority of the children highly motivated and concerned about their grandparents. The author has made some critical analysis of the inter-generational gap and recommends replication of such studies for strengthening inter-generational bonding. It is suggested that the elderly also need to redefine their expectations in the context of the changing realities of life. The inter-generational relationship should be viewed from the perspective of children as well as the elderly. The chapter concludes with some suggested interventions such as an early sensitization of children for better bonding and the need for supporting the relationships among generations in families and societies.

Active ageing allows people to realize their potential and to participate in the society while providing them with adequate protection, security and care. The use of technology provides desirable support and assistance in everyday life to both the disabled and the ailing elderly. **Chapter 13** explains how technological advancement is contributing towards the support of the elderly and active ageing. Faced with gradual deterioration in their abilities, many elderly people wish to remain in their own home. For these individuals, use of assistive technology makes a difference that can help them in retaining their quality of life and self-respect. The chapter explains some of the new frontiers and suggests a roadmap in providing technology and need-based support for the care of the elderly. With the use of assistive devices, the elders can look forward to have a safe and secure living, both at home and the outdoors. Such devices reduce dependence on the caregivers and facilitate independent living for the elderly (Luciano et al., 2006). Assistive technologies can play a vital role in places such as community centres, old-age homes and day care centres. The authors recommend an association of elderly people for such technology interventions that could enrich their lives.

The elderly are confronting a number of challenges, including insufficient income, declining health, meagre social security, changing social roles, recognition and increasing crime against them. Disintegration of the traditional joint family system and increasing urbanization have added to the situation. **Chapter 14** highlights the possibilities and hopes in the process of ageing, emphasizing positive outlook and optimism. Various challenges confronted by the elderly population have been discussed under two broad categories, that is, 'socio-economic deprivation and disparities' and 'increasing mistreatment and crime against elderly'. Some safety initiatives and legal support for the elderly have also been discussed in the chapter. It also highlights the hopes and possibilities with a note of optimism that the elderly may envisage a peaceful and safe life without violence, crime and poverty. Inculcating the ideas of positive ageing can facilitate independence, security, participation, dignity and active engagement in life. The chapter makes an attempt to identify the strategies for healthy ageing, irrespective of the gender, class and cultural background. The chapter concludes with some relevant recommendations and suggestions that can promote the notion of 'ageing well'.

# Conclusion

In this book, through the contribution of experienced and eminent scholars, the concept and understanding of gerontology have been further explored. The growing incidence of crime against the elderly has become a major area of concern. There has been a special focus to discuss and analyse the evidence of violent activities against this greying population. Adequate health care, economic independence, social inclusion of elderly and protection against crime, etc., determine positive ageing to a great extent. Improvement in existing health infrastructure (Bhumika et al., 2011), involvement of elderly people in productive activities, adequate policy provisions and improved relationships within families (Holmes and Joseph, 2011) support positive ageing. There is a need for specific legislation on crime against elderly, their socio-economic deprivation and similar other serious issues. Education and public awareness campaigns informing people about elder abuse, their rights, gender-sensitive policy, welfare measures and transforming the stereotyped attitude and behaviour towards elderly are necessary.

The wisdom and the valuable contributions of the elderly should be recognized. Productive involvement can empower them and support quality ageing. The technology interventions for barrier-free movement at home and outside, accessible public transport, encouragement of healthy social relationships, new roles as volunteers and frequent intergenerational interaction support the physical and mental well-being of the elderly. Innovative scientific devices and services, such as senior citizens' cells and toll-free helpline number, availability of TracFone for the safety of the elderly, can enable them to lead a trouble-free life without fear. Throughout the text, a sensitive approach towards successful ageing has been reflected. However, an extensive research is needed to understand the factors contributing to the diversities involved in the ageing process. Researchers, academicians, policymakers as well as practitioners play a major role in framing policies and the effective implementation. It is time to understand gerontology with optimism, adopting an all-inclusive vision, and encourage quality life with dignity.

# References

Aiken, K.L. (1995). *Ageing: An introduction to gerontology.* USA: SAGE Publication Inc.

Alam, M. (2007). *Ageing in India: Socio-economic and health dimensions.* Delhi: Academic Foundation.

Alam, M. & Karan, A. (2011). *Elderly health in India: Dimension, differentials and determinants* (BKPAI Working Paper Series No. 3). New Delhi: United Nations Population Fund.

Asiya, N. (2010). Family in transition and challenges for elderly persons. *Indian Journal of Gerontology, 24*(4), 501–508.

Audinarayana, N. (2012). *Rural elderly in India.* Delhi: B. R. Publishing Corporation.

Bengtson, V.L., Parrott, T. & Burgess, E. (1997). Theory, explanation and a third generation of theoretical developments in social gerontology. *Journal of Gerontology, 52B*, S72–88.

Bhatt, R., Gadhvi, M.S., Sonaliya, K.N., Solanki, A. & Nayak, H. (2011). An epidemiological study of the morbidity pattern among the elderly population in Ahmedabad, Gujarat. *National Journal of Community Medicine, 2*(2), 233–236.

Bhumika N., Raj, P., Singh, Z., Jayanthi, V., Purty, A.J. & Senthilvel, V. (2011). Healthy ageing: Are we ready to meet the challenge? *Indian Journal of Medical Specialties, 3*(2), 130–137.

Bowling, A. (2006). Lay perceptions of successful ageing: findings from a national survey of middle aged and older adults in Britain. *European Journal of Ageing, 4*, 57–58.

Census of India. (2011). Government of India, Office of Registrar General, Delhi.

Fries, J.F. (2012). The theory and practice of active ageing. *Current Gerontology and Geriatrics Research.* Available at: http://dx.doi.org.

GoI. (1998). *The aged in India: A socio-economic profile: NSS 52nd Round (July 1995–June 1996)* (Report No.446). Delhi: National Sample Survey Organisation.

———. (2006). *Morbidity, health care and the condition of the aged. NSSO 60th Round (January –June 2004),* (Report No. 507). Delhi: National Sample Survey Organisation.

Hall, M. & Havens, B. (2005). *The effect of social isolation and loneliness on the health of older women.* Winnipeg: Prairie Women's Health Centre of Excellence.

Hendricks, J. (1995). Exchange theory in ageing. In G. Maddox (Ed.), *The encyclopedia of ageing* (2nd Ed.). New York: Springer.

Hendricks, J., Applebaum, R. & Kunkel, S. (2010). A world apart? Bridging the gap between theory and applied social gerontology. *The Gerontologist, 50*(3), 284–293.

Holmes, W.R. & Joseph, J. (2011). Social participation and healthy ageing: A neglected, significant protective factor for chronic non communicable conditions. *Globalization and Health, 7*,43.

Hooyman, N.R. & Kiyak, H.A. (2011). *Social gerontology: A multidisciplinary perspective* (9th Ed.). Boston: Pearson Education.

Kampchen, M. (2012, 29th July). The order of things. *The Sunday Statesman*, p. 6.

Kapoor, A.K., Dhall, M. & Tyagi, R. (2010). Nutritional status and ageing among Car Nicobarese and Nolia males of India. *The Open Anthropology Journal, 3*, 155–160.

Khan, A.M, (2008). Emerging challenges of ageing: role of civil society. In R.N. Kapoor & T.M. Dak (Eds.), *Population ageing and development in India*. Udaipur: Institute of Social Development.

Lamb, S. (2002). Love and ageing in Bengali families. In D. P. Mines & S. Lamb (Eds.), *Everyday life in South Asia* (pp. 56–68). Bloomington: Indiana University Press.

Luciano, G., Mariano, A., Giacinto, B., Malena, F., Francisco, I. & Lisa, P. (2006). Cognition, technology and games for the elderly: An introduction to elder games project. *PsychNology Journal, 4*(3), 285–308.

Mahendra Dev, S., Subbarao, K., Galab, S. & Ravi, C. (2007). Safety net programmes in India: Outreach and effectiveness. *Economic and Political Weekly, 42*(35), 3555–3565.

Mungreiphy, N.K. & Kapoor, S. (2010). Socioeconomic changes as covariates of overweight and obesity among Tangkhul Naga tribal women of Manipur, north-east India. *Journal of Bio-Social Sciences, 2*(3), 289–305.

Murty, S. (2008). *Female ageing population: Problems and prospects* (p. 7). Jaipur: RBSA Publications.

NPSC (National Policy on Senior Citizens). (2011). Ministry for Social Justice and Empowerment, Government of India. Available at: from socialjustice.nic.in.

NSAP (National Social Assistance Programme). (2011). Government of India. Available at: http//: www.nsap.nic.in.

Paltasingh, T. & Tyagi, R. (2012). Social security and policy on senior citizens: Evidences from Asian countries. *Ageing and Society: The Indian Journal of Gerontology, 12*, (1& 2), 1–19.

———. (2014). *Emerging issues in gerontology: Relevance and possibilities*. New Delhi: Bookwell.

Pandey, P.K. & Misra, P. (2009). Legal protection of elderly persons in India: An overview. *Vidhigya: The Journal of Legal Awareness, 4*(1), 49–53.

Patel, T. (2005). *The family in India: Structure and practice*. Delhi: SAGE Publications.

Patel. V., Chatterji, S., Chisholm, D., Ebrahim, S., Gopalakrishna, G., Mathers, C., et al. (2011). Chronic diseases and injuries in India. *Lancet, 377*,413–428.

Powell, J.L. (2009). The sociological construction of ageing: Lessons for theorising *International Journal of Sociology and Social Policy, 29*(1/2), 84–94.

Raikwar, M. & Khan, A.M. (2012). A comparative study of engagement of retired men and women. *Help Age India-Research and Development Journal, 18*(3), 19–31.

Riley, M.W. & Riley, J.W. (1994). Age integration and the lives of older people. *The Gerontologist, 34*, 110–115.

Tas, U., Verhagen, A.P., Bierma-Zeinstra, S.M.A., Hofman, A., Odding, E., Pols, H.A.P., et al. (2007). Incidence and risk factors of disability in the elderly: The Rotterdam Study. *Preventive Medicine, 44*, 272–278.

WHO Secretariat. (2002). Adapted from documents A55/17 and A55/17 Add.1. *55th World Health Assembly (13–18 May)*. Geneva: World Health Organization. Available at: http://www.who.int/gb/.

WHO, Regional Health Forum. (2012). *South East Asia Region*. Special issue on Ageing and Health. 16 (1).

World Bank. (2001). *India: The challenge of old age income security* (Report No. 22034). Finance and private sector development: South Asia region, Washington, DC: World Bank.

WSSR. (2011). *World Social Security Report 2010/11: Providing coverage in times of crisis and beyond*. Geneva: International Labour Office.

Zimmer, Z. (2008). Poverty, wealth inequality, and health among older adults in rural Cambodia. *Social Science and Medicine, 66*, 57–71.

# Section I

## Understanding Gerontology

# 1

# Theories and Concepts in Gerontology: Disciplines and Discourses

*Tattwamasi Paltasingh*

## Introduction

Population ageing is an outcome of increased life expectancy. Decline in infant mortality and advancement in medical technology, better nutrition, improved hygiene and better public health have extended the average lifespan (Gupta and Sankar, 2003; Beaglehole and Bonita, 2004). Ageing is interplay of both environmental and genetic factors; identifying and responding to these factors form greater understanding (Comfort, 1979). Theories of ageing help to recognize and understand the factors responsible for the age-associated changes. Theories related to ageing have been analysed by biologists, sociologists, psychologists, economists, feminists and others with their distinct viewpoints. The future of ageing research is expected to pay even greater attention to theory, especially with an interdisciplinary approach. An integrative bio-psycho-social approach to ageing is visualized for healthy ageing (Ryff and Singer, 2009). Such integrative analysis is expected to provide solutions to many complex issues that can further help in the productive and healthy lifestyle of the elderly in the future.

The purpose of this chapter is to examine the key ideas of theories on social gerontology in order to have a better understanding of the ageing process. The chapter discusses the ageing theories and relevant issues, with analysis and central themes from different disciplines. The different theoretical perspectives discussed in the chapter include a critical analysis of psychological, biological, social, political, feminist and economic theories. Each theory has been presented with its critique in the light of its inadequate focus on constructive ageing and the complexities involved in the process. The feminist theory has been discussed to elaborate gender-specific issues. While discussing different theories, the core attempt of the chapter remains integral in examining the ageing issues that can facilitate positive and active ageing. Despite discussion from different disciplines, the chapter has incorporated a special focus on social gerontology. Subsequent section of the chapter has made an attempt to identify the need for research on positive ageing and the role of key players among the academic fraternity who can influence the policies with effective implementation. The concluding section has summed up the issues discussed in each section in the light of promoting active and positive ageing.

## Ageing Theories: Disciplines and Dialogues

Understanding ageing has gained relevance and developed over the years. Rapid expansion of ageing research over the last several decades has made the theory more important. The theories help us to understand the ageing process better, and thus to improve longevity and quality of life. Theories of ageing are important to continue our quest for more answers, to the complex questions that intrudes on the individual's identity and the growing up process (Powell, 2009). There is a dearth of theories on social gerontology (Birren, 1999; Bengtson, Silverstein, Putney and Gans, 2009). A unified theory that includes the entire phenomenon associated with ageing is unrealistic. Age-related changes do not occur uniformly among the individuals, rather they are controlled by genetic, environmental and socio-cultural factors that add to the difficulty of finding a universal theory. Theories on ageing are touched upon by gerontologists from different schools of thought (Merker, Stolzing and Grune, 2001). Theoretical understanding has advanced over the years by analysing and critiquing from a specific perspective. This section is a reflection of such thoughts.

# Biological Theories

The early theories outlined are biological theories that attempt to explain the cause of the decline of the physical functions of the body. According to Shock (1997), biological theories can be categorized into three categories, that is, primary, secondary and tertiary ageing. Theories that place the emphasis on genetic or hereditary causes are primary ageing theories, such as programmed ageing, free radical and theory of errors, etc. Those that attribute ageing to pathological, degenerative causes and natural wear, due to the passage of time, are included as secondary ageing, such as wear and tear theory, crossed-linking theory, etc. Tertiary ageing postulates that the changes are due to the degeneration of some or of all the physiological systems or mechanisms, such as decreased immunological function, endocrine system transformation, etc. Many of the proposed theories interact with each other in manifold ways. Most popular biological theories include (1) the free radical theory given by Harman (2006) that identifies some reactive oxygen metabolites that cause cumulative damage with advancing age; (2) caloric restriction that explains delayed ageing; (3) somatic mutation arising from genetic damage; (4) hormonal theories proposing hormonal imbalance to cause rapid ageing and (5) immunological theories that attribute ageing to a weak immune system. The nature of biological changes that occur with ageing is distinctly elastic and can be reformed.

The critics have pointed out that biological theories do not take into account cohort or generational differences; only the programmed ageing theory addresses individual differences. None of the biological theories make any convincing arguments for the aetiology of ageing that can be attributed to any of them. Indeed, it seems that error and error accumulation theories are inaccurate, as these theories ignore the curative capacity of the organism. Free radical theory (Harman, 1956) and Pearl's theory of wear and tear have been widely supported with experimental evidences (Prinzinger, 2005). On the contrary, Orgel's theory of the catastrophic error, which was widely accepted in the 1960s, could not be confirmed by experimental research (Harley, Pollard, Chamberlain, Stanners and Goldstein, 1980). While these theories do not deny ageing, they are disempowering in approach. Despite several biological theories have been proposed for ageing, none of these appear to be fully agreeable (Davidovic et al., 2010).

## Psychological Theories

Psychological theories of ageing explain the numerous psychological changes in individuals in their middle and later years of the lifespan (Bengtson, Putney and Johnson, 2005). Self-concept is considered to be the organized, coherent and integrated pattern of self-perceptions that include self-esteem and self-image (Cavanaugh and Blanchard-Fields, 2002; Whitbourne, 2005). Lifespan theorists advocate the view that personality is determined by the interactions between an inner maturational plan and the external societal demands. The theory defines the concept of ageing as multidimensional, and these dimensions include the possibility of growth, recovery and learning of new skills at older ages (Baltes, Freund and Li, 2005). The lifespan development theory has given rise to an overall psychological theory of successful ageing (Baltes and Baltes, 1990) called Selective Optimisation with Compensation Theory (SOC). Theory on SOC explains how individuals can manage adaptive or successful (social, cognitive and physical) development in old age. As per the theory of cognitive plasticity, the development is assumed to be modifiable or plastic' during all phases of the lifespan, including old age (Willis, Schaie and Martin, 2009). Consideration of plasticity at the behavioural and socio-cultural level is central to this theory. Many of these theories of ageing are interlinked in the same complex way the bio-social and psychological changes occur in the body. The limitations in such theories have paved the way towards formulating and refining an understanding of social gerontology.

## Sociological Theories and Social Gerontology

Theoretical progress has been more challenging in social gerontology unlike the theory development in the biological and behaviour sciences. This could be partly attributed to complex and fluid nature of the social phenomena over the course of life. Ageing is the transformation of the human organism after the age of physical maturity, usually accompanied by changes in appearance, behaviour, knowledge, social status and roles. As people grow older, changes in their behaviour, social interactions and their activities are evident. The broad focus of sociological theories is on the changing roles and relationships and how they have an impact on the older individual's ability to adapt. The disengagement theory of ageing explains the age-related decline in social contact, psychological effect and bio-physiological decrements (Cumming and Henry, 1961). Some other theoretical perspectives are theory on age stratification (Riley, Johnson and Foner, 1972), competence theory (Kuypers and Bengtson, 1973), political economy of ageing (Estes, Swan and Gerard, 1982), exchange theory (Hendricks, 1995) and continuity theory (Atchley, 1999). In the ageing literature, these theories are considered to be the second-generation theories, originated during 1970s–mid-1980s. Many of these theories have been discussed and reinterpreted with minor differences and emerged as a third-generation theory with a multidisciplinary focus.

## Disengagement Theory

It is observed that as people age, they experience greater distance from the society and they develop new types of relationships with the society. Older people's desire to remain occupied and their involvement with activities are not taken into consideration. Imposed withdrawal from the society may be harmful to elders as well as the society in the same manner. With the changing social relationships, older people may have fewer and deeper social relationships. This theory is indifferent towards old age and related issues (Bond and Coleman, 1993) by understating the cultural and economic structures that can create the intentional consequences of withdrawal. Such withdrawal can pose threat to the promotion of a positive and involved lifestyle for older generation (Kastenbaum, 1993). The Gerotranscendence theory promoted by Tornstam (1989) is a modification of disengagement theory of normal ageing. Ideologically, it is assumed that the process towards gerotranscendence is lifelong, continuous and normal, but it can be obstructed at any point of time (Tornstam, 1989). Disengagement is considered to be one of the most controversial theories of ageing having no evidence to support, hence criticized by researchers. This theory does not explain the large number of older people who do not withdraw from the society. In some industrially developed countries, there is evidence of forced withdrawal on older people without considering their interests.

## Activity Theory

Activity theory was developed in 1953 by Havighurst and associates with an assumption that remaining active and engaged with the society are very important to ensure satisfaction in old age. The activity theory highlights a positive relationship between activity and life satisfaction (Sana and Sajatovic, 2008). Life task participation has been linked to greater life satisfaction and positive effect, lower levels of stress and less scores in depressive symptoms (Park, 2009). Activity theory is based on the notion that successful ageing is possible by maintaining the attitudes and activities of middle age. One of the empirical studies in the Indian context has identified that activities show protecting and benefiting effects on subjective well-being. However, the abilities with satisfaction to perform those activities are more important than the activities themselves (Sharma, 2013).

This theory has some elements of positive ageing, but it tends to deny ageing to a certain extent. Some elderly cannot maintain a middle-aged lifestyle due to functional limitations, lack of income or desire to do so. Some elders may insist on continuing activities in later life that pose a danger to themselves and others like driving or crossing the road with low vision or climbing with severely arthritic knees, etc. Activity theory is based on the assumption that successful ageing is due to maintaining the attitudes and activities of middle age. The critics of the activity theory state that it overlooks inequalities in health and income that hinder the ability of older people to engage in such activities. Also, some older adults do not desire to engage in new challenges (Priscilla, 2005). The activity theory reflects the functionalist perspective that the stability developed by an individual in middle age should be maintained in later years. The theory predicts that the role loss faced by older adults may substitute former roles with other alternatives. Though in recent years, the acceptance of the activity theory has diminished, it is still used as a standard to compare observed activity and life satisfaction patterns (Schulz, 2006).

## Continuity Theory

The activity theory relates that personality, preferences, activities and patterns of behaviour, including values, etc. are consistent throughout the lifespan. The continuity theory views life as a continuous process, and each stage in life helps to prepare for the next stage in a positive direction. However, individual's behaviour is complex and maintaining the consistency in each stage and given context could be unrealistic. The major criticism of the continuity theory is its definition of normal ageing (Quadagno, 2007). The theory distinguishes normal ageing from pathological ageing, neglecting the older adults with chronic illness. The feminist theories also attack the continuity theory for defining normal ageing around a male model (Quadagno, 2007). One weakness of the theory is that it fails to demonstrate how social institutions impact the individuals and the way they age.

## Exchange Theory

As per the exchange theory, positive relationships are considered where the benefits are more than the expense and the negative relationships involve more costs compared to the acquired benefits. However, such analysis fails to acknowledge that older people have knowledge and experience to offer to the younger generation (Bernheim, Shleifer and Summers, 1985; Bengtson, Parrott and Burgess, 1997). Involving costs can be viewed as reductions and narrow with negative implication to the individual relationship. Spending money, time and efforts into a relationship cannot have an exchange value in pure economic terms.

## Modernization Theory

Modernization theory can be more contextualized in developing countries where family has played pivotal role in extending support to the elderly (Bali, 2002; Patel, 2005). Due to modernization and industrialization, large-scale migration has taken place, deserting a large number of elderly. However, there is a dearth of theoretical analysis in the Indian context. Population figures and projections have no doubt generated huge information base on the elderly, but there is a dearth of theories that can explain diminishing support from the family and the community. Other theories of ageing are labelling and social stratification theories. Labelling theory views old age as a deviant condition. Older people become the victims of the stereotype and see themselves in a negative way. This creates the false impression that older people are a homogeneous group. The social stratification theory divides people according to age, and age is viewed as a way of explaining how people should behave or else the individuality of people is denied. In addition, equilibrium theory also explains gerontology. In India, the equilibrium stage can be categorized into three stages. The first one is the stage of equilibrium characterized by high birth rates (fertility) and high death rates (particularly infant mortality). In the second stage, birth rates remain high while mortality rates are on the decline. Finally, in response to a complex mixture of social, economic and environmental factors, both births (fertility) and death (mortality) rates decline and a state of equilibrium is reached (Sen, 1994).

## Social Theories: A Critical Analysis

Despite the immense contribution in understanding ageing process, theories often reflect culturally dominant views on what should be the appropriate way to analyse social phenomena. These have been developed adhering to the norms and values of the given context and time. Disengagement theory is inherently ageist and does not support successful ageing. Nevertheless, activity theory neglects some important issues, such as power, inequality and conflict between different age groups. Based on several assumptions, such as there is an abrupt beginning of old age, the ageing leaves people unaccompanied. People need to be encouraged to be active, involved and develop own-age friends. Projection of standards and expectations of middle age to older age puts the activity theory for further criticism. Both disengagement and activity theories imply how human behaviour should change instead of discussing how it keeps altering with age. Political economy and the exchange theories that put a high emphasis on productivity and economic activity make it difficult to value other forms of social exchange in terms of informal care, experience and wisdom, shared between the elderly and the society.

There have been general agreements that all theories of ageing should be considered helpful as long as they contribute to overcome problems and not just remain as self-fulfilling predictions. It can be said that different theories can be applied, depending on the situation and the individual. Theories of ageing can be used not just to develop policy and promote positive attitudes to ageing but also to help understand the ageing process itself. The broad sociological theories on ageing can have significant impact on research in these areas. However, these theories have not covered adequately the major components, such as ethnicity, gender, lifestyle, socio-economic issues, cross-cultural experiences and variations, etc. These theories are not substantiated with evidence-based data and supported by real situation. Because of the uncertain nature and lack of convincing support in each instance, further research and theory development are desirable. There is inadequate attention to the link between theory and applied research in social gerontology. It has been argued that this delinking weakens research and hinders the functions that theory can play to organize the accumulation of knowledge. It is important to address this challenge of missing link between theories and applications (Hendricks, Applebaum and Kunkel, 2010).

# Recent Development in Social Gerontology

The recent schools of thought emerged in social gerontology include critical gerontology and postmodern gerontology. Social gerontology emerged as a field of study attempt to respond to the social policy implications of demographic change (Vincent, 1996). Such disciplines were shaped by significant external forces. First, by state intervention to achieve specific outcomes in health and social policy and, second, by political and economic environments that viewed an ageing population as creating a 'social problem' for the society (Jones, 1993).

Phenomenology, a theoretical tradition in the social sciences, provides a foundation for several theoretical approaches in social gerontology, that is, feminist theories, critical theories and postmodernist perspectives. Phenomenology focuses on illuminating the human meanings of social life and emphasizes how individuals understand the means by which phenomena, originating in human consciousness, come to be experienced as features of the social world. An integrative theory of social gerontology can blend a macro-perspective, examining the social, economic, environmental, cultural and political contexts influencing human behaviour and health, with the micro-individual and family (Bengtson et al., 2009).

## Political Economy

The political economy theory explains how old age was socially constructed, adapting to the needs of the economy (Estes, 1979). This critical branch of Marxist gerontology originated as a direct response to the hegemonic power of structural functionalism. The focus of this theory is on interpreting the relationship between ageing and the economic structure. Older people are viewed as a burden on economies and consequent pressures on public expenditure are created (Phillipson, 1998). This theory puts a challenge for both the theoretical dominance of functionalist view and the bio-medical models of age and ageing. The important argument to be made is that inequalities in the distribution of resources should be understood in relation to the distribution of power within the society, rather than in terms of individual variation. Political economy considers older people as belonging to a homogenous group, unaffected by dominant structures in the society (Estes, 1979). However, many gerontologists do not accept the views of considering elderly as a homogeneous group, as they are affected by a distinct social situation coming from unique socio-cultural background. There is varied understanding of the issues pertaining to the aged, further relating these to polity, economy and the society. Ageing is shaped by socio-economic factors, and people experience ageing depending on the way the society values them. Capitalism may not be the sole responsible factor that creates marginalization among elderly population. In the Indian context, the capitalist ideology can also influence people from all age groups.

## Feminist Theories

There is a general agreement that women face—greater problems in old age than men. The demographic data indicate greater share of elderly women than their men counterparts in many countries. The issues of women's vulnerability and dependency through the life course have received significant attention in the recent decades. These issues can be examined through various feminist theories in different situations (Paltasingh and Lingam, 2014). Globalization has multi-dimensional impact that has been instrumental in the rise of neo-liberal, market-based policies. Such implications have reduced the protection of women in social policy and other relevant areas. The growing population of older women has raised distinct issues of caretaking whether they are serving as caretaker or as care recipients. They are doubly marginalized because of age and gender. Women are conveniently used as substitutes for others as caregivers as well as multiple role players. Progressive and transformative theories have been encouraged by legal theorists with a special focus on the gender concern.

There is a dearth of research on ageing, particularly from a theoretical perspective that addresses women's issues. Despite researchers have started showing interest in analysing gerontology theories to understand the ageing process, gender orientation remains in its infancy. There are attempts and isolated voices, encouraging scholars to promote ageism to a central issue with a thrust on women's concern (Troll, Israel and Israel, 1977). Most of the ageing theories are based on the structured assumption that older people are one homogenous category and do not generally address differences between people (Lynott and Lynott, 1996; Marshall, 1996; Ray, 1996). Despite the diversity and range of feminist perspectives, each theory has critiqued the male-centered view of conventional theorizing due to denial of women's importance in the ageing experience. Feminist theory in the field of ageing has drawn largely from socialist feminism that has critiqued the theory and research in ageing for ignoring the structure of gender relations in the historical context (Calasanti and Zajicek, 1993; Arber and Ginn, 1995). For instance, many studies conceptualize caregiver stress as a woman's responsibility and have oriented policies to promote support groups rather than bringing reforms and changes to facilitate elderly women (Abel and Nelson, 1990). Feminist theories propagate the views that gender-based inequities are created and can be changed positively to bring new possibilities for women. It involves both social critique as well as positive social change (Ray, 1996). A real and more difficult task is to change attitudes and the society, reshaping values and practice in favour of women (Patel, 2007). Structural factors influence women's socio-economic status, their health status and living arrangements. There may be different viewpoints within feminism, but the common agreement among the feminist criticism is that ageing theory and research ignore the structure of gender relations that is deep rooted in a patriarchal structure.

## Postmodern Gerontology

The postmodern gerontology originates from analysis of the discovery and elaboration of Alzheimer's disease in the USA (Gubrium, 1975). There has been a postmodern perspective of age and ageing identity. Postmodernism has been supported for better lifestyles and increased leisure opportunities for older people due to increasing use of bio-technologies (Blaikie, 1999; Powell and Biggs, 2002). Direct use of new technologies that modify the appearance or performance of an ageing identity is indicated in this theoretical discourse (Powell and Biggs, 2000). It is believed that the body can be re-coded due to availability of bio-medical and information technologies. Through the application of the advance technology, human body can be re-shaped, remade and empowered. Use of proper diet and exercise are the techniques in later adulthood, connected to the growth identities during late life (Powell and Biggs, 2000, 2002). However, postmodern gerontology has been criticized by other schools of thought in ageing. Too much importance on the use of technology in reversing the ageing process can be debated, as it alienates the importance of social interaction within the family and community. Another major issue is its limited application in understanding old age in the context of developed economy, ignoring the elderly in developing countries.

# Need for Theoretical Development

Mainstream gerontological research has paid insufficient attention to the degree to which age and ageing are socially constructed (Baars, 1991). Both age and ageing are currently in the process of transformation as a result of the set of social forces influenced by the processes of globalization. There is a dearth of critical analysis, and the attempts to understand the social processes involved in ageing and the life course have been affected consequently. It is time for the social gerontologists to work on the creation of alternative commencements and visions about the future of old age. The general inadequacies of theory building within gerontology have been reflected in the studies conducted across the globe and specially made prominent in European and North American studies of ageing (Birren, 1988;

Lynott and Lynott, 1996; Bengtson and Schaie, 1999). The existing theoretical approaches have been appropriately criticized for their lack of attention to the actual experience of ageing. By definition, such approaches give little attention to interpretive phenomena, such as the rich and complex fields of experience, consciousness and action (Gubrium, 1993). Both age and ageing are experiences that are loaded with meaning and can have powerful effects on health and physiology as well as the ageing process.

Theories of ageing cannot be analysed and understood with exclusive perspective that can bring misleading interpretation. Meaningful understanding of ageing requires multidisciplinary collaboration and efforts. Without this collaboration, ageing research would face the problem of methodological limitation. Given the heterogeneity of elderly population and the complexities involved in this issue, there is an urgent need for serious research. Besides, there is a need to promote gerontology more widely as a part of the curriculum in the social sciences and other disciplines. Academic workshops can be considered on ageing and older people, theories and perspectives on ageing. There is a unifying theme running through every attempt and that appears to be a concern to determine what constitutes positive ageing and how it can be promoted through shaping the theories in gerontology. There should be emphasis on encouraging positive attitudes towards the elderly and the process of ageing, which can be reflected in academic discourse. Older persons are a great social resource that is currently under-used and under-valued. Greater participation by elderly people in the community life should be promoted.

## Role of Academia

There is a need to develop a better theoretical understanding of ageing across the regions and culture. Consolidated efforts should be diverted to highlight the positive contribution of older people to the society and promote intergenerational solidarity. There is a need to develop a coherent strategy to combat negative attitudes, based on a theoretical framework that takes account of relevant theories of ageing and a sound understanding of how attitudes, values and stereotypes are formed. Ageing cannot be understood in isolation. There should be a multidisciplinary focus that can include philosophy, literature, psychology, sociology, medicine, health administration, psychiatry, education, social policy and the media as well as the views of a wide range of practitioners directly involved in promoting positive attitudes to ageing. The government and the academic institutions should make some serious attempts, keeping in mind the longitudinal and cross-sectional diagnosis of the issues concerned. All the disciplines should move away from the traditional methodology and should not overlook experimenting with the interdisciplinary and multidisciplinary approaches. Researchers, academicians, scientists, policymakers and administrators should seriously take it as a challenge to promote more research in this area, so that the results can be applied universally to understand the various dimensions and concepts of ageing and to evolve scientific and systematic solutions for them.

The fundamental structure-based difference across the life course is rarely mentioned and articulated. An adequate understanding of human ageing requires the contributions of all the approaches described above, despite their limitations. It requires recognition of the importance of cohort analysis based on cross-cultural and historical perspectives. Serious attention to the processes of meaningful construction and self-constitution at the microlevel with close interaction are needed. These assertions represent some of the key insights of critical theory—the other paradigmatic sources of critical gerontology, that can be built upon the contribution through serious efforts.

# Conclusion

Gerontology as a subject has evolved considerably since last three to four decades. Despite such development, one can notice imbalance between the accumulation of data and the development of the theory (Riley and Riley, 1994; Hendricks, 1995). More importance is given on the demographics of ageing rather than the core issues involved in this process. There was no dearth of data and statistics on the population in the past, having an impact on the present and the future. Interestingly, projected population figures are available for the coming decades. This interest in data generation, projecting the older population figures for the forthcoming years, certainly has positive impacts, as it can make the society and the state aware of the future concerns in accommodating a huge population of the elderly. On the contrary, the generated data are narrowly defined and interpreted, ignoring the other key issues. Theoretical development in this area is insufficient to understand such complex issues. Inadequate attention has been devoted to larger theoretical issues (Hagestad, 1990). To capture the complex empirical reality, lot more research on theories is required both at global level as well as in the Indian context.

Age is used politically and democratically as a principal force of social organization and social control. Age is also a feature of culture, carrying the force of meaning and power back into the minds and bodies of citizens. When such forces are recognized, it becomes clear that age-related outcomes are not mere consequences of the organismic ageing, but of complex interrelations that combine social, structural, cultural and interactional processes. The theories have been at the forefront of understanding old age. Taken together, these theoretical dimensions have been influential in providing social gerontology with a rich social dimension. Such social theories have been used also to analyse pressing social issues, such as elder abuse, the gendered nature of age, the politics of power relations between older people and the state/society and community care. Rapid expansion of ageing research over the last several decades has made the theory more important. However, there is a need for rigorous refinement of existing theories, without which understandings of ageing cannot be readily achieved. The theory-driven interdisciplinary investigations of ageing should be the wave of the future.

# References

Abel, E. & Nelson, M. (Eds). (1990). *Circles of care: Work and identity in women's lives.* Albany: State University of New York Press.

Arber, S. & Ginn, J. (Eds). (1995). *Connecting gender and ageing: A sociological approach.* Bristol, PA: Open University Press.

Atchley, R.C. (1999). *Continuity and adaptation in ageing.* Baltimore: The John Hopkins University Press.

Baars, J. (1991). The challenge of critical gerontology: The problem of social constitution. *Journal of Ageing Studies, 5,* 219–243.

Bali, A.P. (2002). *Care of the elderly in India: Changing configurations.* Shimla: Indian Institute of Advanced Study.

Baltes, P.B. & Baltes, M.M. (1990). Psychological perspectives on successful ageing: The model of selective optimization with compensation. In P.B. Baltes & M.M. Baltes (Eds), *Successful ageing: Perspectives from the behavioural sciences* (pp. 1–34). New York: Cambridge University Press.

Baltes, P.B., Freund, A.L. & Li, S. (2005).The psychological science of human ageing. *The Cambridge handbook of age and ageing* (pp. 47–71). Cambridge: Cambridge University Press.

Beaglehole, R. & Bonita, R. (2004). *Public health at the crossroads: Achievements and prospects* (pp. 15–46). London: Cambridge University Press.

Bengtson, V.L., Parrott, T. & Burgess, E. (1997). Theory, explanation and a third generation of theoretical developments in social gerontology. *Journal of Gerontology, 52B*, S72–88.

Bengtson, V.L., Putney, N.M. & Johnson, M. (2005). Are theories of ageing necessary? In M. Johnson, V.L. Bengtson, P. Coleman & T. Kirkwood (Eds), *The Cambridge handbook of age and ageing* (pp. 3–20). Cambridge: Cambridge University Press.

Bengtson, V.L. & Schaie, K.W. (Eds). (1999). *Handbook of theories of ageing.* New York: Springer Publishing.

Bengtson, V.L., Silverstein, M., Putney, N.M. & Gans, D. (Eds) (2009). Handbook of theories of ageing. New York: Springer Publishing Company.

Bernheim, B.D., Shleifer, A. & Summers, L.H. (1985). The strategic bequest motive. *Journal of Political Economy, 93*, 1045–1076.

Birren, J.E. (1988). A contribution to the theory of the psychology of ageing: A counterpart of development. In J.E. Birren & V.L. Bengtson (Eds), *Emergent theories of ageing* (pp. 153–174). New York: Springer Publishing.

————. (1999). Theories of ageing: A personal perspective. In V.L. Bengtson & K.W. Schaie, (Eds), *Handbook of theories of ageing* (pp. 459–471). New York: Springer.

Blaikie, A. (1999). *Ageing and popular culture.* Cambridge: OUP.

Bond, J. & Coleman, P. (1993). Ageing into the twenty-first century. In J. Bond, P. Coleman & S. Peace. (Eds), *Ageing in society: An introduction to social gerontology* (pp.333–350). London: SAGE.

Calasanti, T.M. & Zajicek, A.M. (Eds). (1993). A socialist-feminist approach to ageing: Embracing diversity [Special issue]. *Journal of Ageing Studies, 7*: 117–132.

Cavanaugh, J. & Blanchard-Fields, F. (Eds). (2002). *Adult development and ageing* (4th ed.). Belmont, CA: Wadsworth Thompson Learning.

Comfort, A. (1979). *The biology of senescence.* London: Churchill Livingstone.

Cumming, E. & Henry, W. (1961). *Growing old: The process of disengagement.* New York: Basic Books.

Davidovic, M., Sevo, G., Svorcan, P., Milosevic, D.P., Despotovic, N. & Erceg, P. (2010). Old age as a privilege of the "selfish ones". *Ageing and Disease. 1*,139–146.

Estes, C. (1979). *The ageing enterprise.* San Francisco: Jossey Bass.

Estes, C., Swan, J. & Gerard, L. (1982). Dominant and competing paradigms in gerontology: Towards a political economy of ageing. *Ageing and Society, 12*, 151–164.

Gubrium, J.F. (1975). *Living and dying at Murray Manor.* New York: St. Martins.

————. (1993). Voice and context in a new gerontology. In T.R. Cole, W.A. Achenbaum, P.L. Jakobi & R. Kastenbaum (Eds), *Voices and visions of ageing: Toward a critical gerontology.* New York: Springer.

Gupta, I. & Sankar, D. (2003). Health of the elderly in India: A multivariate analysis. *Jounal of Health and Population in Developing Countries, 24*, 1–11.

Hagestad, G.O. (1990). Social Perspectives on the Life Course. In R.H. Binstock & L.K. George (Eds), *Handbook of ageing and the social sciences* (3rd Ed.). San Diego, CA: Academic Press.

Harley, C.B., Pollard, J.W., Chamberlain, J.W., Stanners, C.P. & Goldstein, S. (1980). Protein synthetic errors do not increase during ageing of cultured human fibroblasts. *Proceedings of the National Academy of Sciences*, 77(4), 1885–1889.

Harman, D. (1956). Ageing: A theory based on free radical and radiation chemistry. *Journal of Gerontology*, 11, 298–300.

———. (2006). Free radical theory of ageing: An update. *Annual New York Academic Sciences*, 1067, 1–12.

Havighurst, R.J. (1973). Social roles, work, leisure and education. In C. Eisdorfer & M.P. Lawton (Eds), *The psychology of adult development and ageing* (pp. 598–618). Washington, DC: American Psychological Association.

Hendricks, J. (1995). Exchange theory in ageing. In G. Maddox (Ed.), *The encyclopedia of ageing* (2nd Ed.). New York: Springer.

Hendricks, J., Applebaum, R. & Kunkel, S. (2010). A world apart? Bridging the gap between theory and applied social gerontology. *The Gerontologist*, 50(3), 284–293.

Jones, C. (1993). *State social work and the working class*. London: Macmillan.

Kastenbaum, R. (1993). Encrusted elders. In T. Cole (Ed). *Voices and visions of ageing*. New York: Springer.

Kuypers, J.A. & Bengtson, V.L. (1973). Social breakdown and competence: A model of normal ageing. *Human Development*, 16, 181–201.

Lynott, R.J. & Lynott, P.P. (1996). Tracing the course of theoretical development in the sociology of ageing. *The Gerontologist*, 36, 749–760.

Marshall, V. (1996). The state of theory in ageing and the social sciences. In R.H. Binstock & L.K. George (Eds), *Handbook of ageing and the social sciences* (4th ed., pp. 12–30). San Diego, CA: Academic Press.

Merker, K., Stolzing, A. & Grune, T. (2001). Proteolysis, caloric restriction and ageing. *Mechanism of Ageing and Development*, 122, 595–615.

Paltasingh T. & Lingam, L. (2014). Production and 'reproduction' feminism: Ideas, perspectives and concepts. *Society and Management Review*, 3(1), 45–53.

Park, N.S. (2009). The relationship of social engagement to psychological well-being of older adults in assisted living facilities. *Journal of Applied Gerontology*, 28, 461–481.

Patel, T. (2005). *The family in India: Structure and practice*. Delhi: SAGE Publications.

———. (2007). *Sex-selective abortion in India: Gender, society, and new reproductive technologies*. New Delhi: SAGE Publications.

Phillipson, C. (1998). *Reconstructing old age*. London: SAGE Publications.

Powell, J.L. (2009). The sociological construction of ageing: lessons for theorising. *International Journal of Sociology and Social Policy*, 29(1/2), 84–94.

Powell, J.L. & Biggs, S. (2000). Managing old age: The disciplinary web of power, surveillance and normalisation. *Journal of Ageing and Identity*, 5(1), 3–13.

———. (2002). Bio-ethics and technologies of the self: Understanding ageing, *Journal of Medical Humanities*.

Prinzinger, R. (2005). Programmed ageing: The theory of maximal metabolic scope. *EMBO Reports*, 6 (S1), S14–S19.

Priscilla, E. (2005). *Gerontological nursing and healthy ageing* (p. 108). Mosby: Elsevier Health Sciences.

Quadagno, J. (2007). *Ageing and the life course: An introduction to social gerontology* (4th Ed.). New York: McGraw-Hill Humanities/Social Sciences/Languages.

Ray, R.E. (1996). A post-modern perspective on feminist gerontology. *The Gerontologist*, 36, 674–680.

Riley, M.W., Johnson, W. & Foner, A. (Eds). (1972). *Ageing and society: A sociology of age stratification* (Vol. 3). New York: Russell Sage Foundation.

Riley, M.W. & Riley, J.W. (1994). Age integration and the lives of older people. *The Gerontologist, 34,* 110–115.

Ryff, C.D. & Singer, B. (2009). Understanding healthy ageing: Key components and their integration. In V.L. Bengtson, M. Silverstein, N.M. Putney, & D. Gans (Eds), *Handbook of theories of ageing* (2nd Ed., pp. 117–44). New York: Springer.

Sana, L. & Sajatovic, M. (2008). *Encyclopaedia of ageing and public health* (pp. 79–81). Barcelona: Springer Science and Business Media.

Schulz, R. (2006). *The encyclopaedia of ageing: A-K* (pp. 9–13). New York: Springer Publishing Company.

Sen, K. (1994). *Ageing debates on demographic transition and social policy.* London: Zed Books Ltd.

Sharma, A. (2013). Challenging activity theory for subjective well-being. *Indian Journal of Applied Research, 3*(12), 516–520.

Shock, N.W. (1997). Biological theories of ageing. In J.E. Birren, K.W. Schaie (Eds), *Handbook of the psychology of ageing.* New York: Van Nostrand Reinhold.

Tornstam, L. (1989). Gero-transcendence: A reformulation of the disengagement theory. *Ageing Clinical and Experimental Research, 1,* 55–63.

Troll, L., Israel, J. & Israel, K. (1977). *Looking ahead: A woman's guide to the problems and joys of growing older.* Englewood Cliffs, NJ: Prentice-Hall.

Vincent, J. (1996). Who is afraid of an ageing population? *Critical Social Policy, 47* (16), 3–26.

Whitbourne, K.S. (2005). *Adult development and ageing: Bio-psycho-social perspectives* (2nd Ed.). Australia: John Wiley and Sons.

Willis, S.L., Schaie, K.W. & Martin, M. (2009). Cognitive plasticity. In V.L. Bengtson, M. Silverstein, N.M. Putney & D. Gans (Eds), *Handbook of theories of ageing* (2nd Ed., pp. 295–322). New York: Springer Publishing Company.

# Section II

## Social Security and Economic Issues

# 2

# Social Security for the Elderly: Issues and Evidences*

*Aswini Kumar Mishra*

## Introduction

India is currently home to about 1.21 billion people, the second most populous country in the world, accounting for 17 per cent of the world's population. India crossed the 1 billion mark in the year 2000, one year after the world's population crossed 6 billion thresholds. Demographers expect India's population to surpass the population of China, currently the most populous country in the world, by 2030. Population projections for India anticipate that the country's population will reach between 1.5 and 1.7 billion by 2050. However, the most important point to mention at this juncture is that the population of the elderly in India is growing rapidly, and there is an increase in the proportion of the aged vis-à-vis the young. About 70.3 million (6.7% of the total population) of India's population was above 60 years old in 2000, and as per the Census of India 2011, the figure is 103.84 million, thereby witnessing a decadal growth of 47.7 per cent as compared to an overall growth of 17.7 per cent of the total population. This figure is expected to be 323 million (19.1% of the total population) by 2050 (UN-DESA, 2011).

* The writer is grateful to PhD supervisor late Prof. Sakti Padhi for his valuable comments and suggestions for the earlier draft of this paper and dedicates this paper to him. The writer is also thankful to Dr (Ms) Tattwamasi Paltasingh for providing the inspiration and encouragement for preparing this paper. The usual disclaimer applies.

Ageing as an issue is not confined to a particular region or a country; however, it is of global concern and is a product of demographic transition. Globally, one out of every ten persons was aged 60 or more in the year 2000. By 2020, the ratio will be about one in eight. By 2050, the number of elders will exceed the number of younger persons for the first time in modern history. The reasons include improved life expectancy, public health programmes, medical advances, health services and improved lifestyle (Krishnaswamy et al., 2008). Speaking at a seminar hosted by HelpAge International and partners in Washington, DC during 2002, Professor Joseph Stiglitz, Nobel Prize winner and former Chief Economist of the World Bank, said: 'There is no subject of greater importance than the ageing of the population and the provisioning of the social protection for older people. It affects the very nature of our societies and concerns not only older people, but all sections of the population.'

Until a couple of decades ago, the issue of the elderly was not in the forefront of the development agenda in the country; but now, the gradual marginalization of the elderly in the decision-making process in an average family and the breakdown of the family as a traditional social unit that took care of the elderly, sick, widows and orphans have brought forth problems of the elderly in the society (Government of India, 2002).

Recent studies have found that industrialization, migration, urbanization and Westernization have severely affected value systems. The erstwhile joint family—the natural support system—has crumbled. The fast-changing pace of life has added to the woes of the elderly. The worries of the elderly are not only concentrated on the economic front, but on the social front as well (James, 1994; Irudaya, 2004; Alam and Karim, 2005). More importantly, issues relating to ageing population should be analysed from regional perspectives, as there are considerable socio-economic and cultural variations for dealing with this specific demographic age group.

Against this backdrop, this chapter discusses the situation of the elderly in Odisha that earns the dubious distinction as one of the poorest state in the country as per the latest Planning Commission's estimates for the year 2004–2005. Also, it is the only state in India, where the incidence of extreme poverty has increased in recent years. This chapter assesses some major dimensions of vulnerabilities, which have a strong bearing on their well-being, and urges the need for social security from rights perspective. The chapter analyses in brief the trends in ageing across major states in India with particular reference to Odisha. The next section looks at the situation of the elderly in Odisha by assessing three major dimensions of socio-economic insecurity, such as (1) poverty incidence, (2) living arrangements, (3) economic dependence and economic support providers based on the National Sample Survey Organization's (NSSO's) two different survey reports carried out during 1995–1996 (NSS 52nd round) and 2004 (NSS 60th round). The chapter further examines the provision of social security arrangements in terms of its coverage and adequacy meant for the utterly destitute in the state followed by a few concluding observations.

# Trends in Ageing and Poverty in Odisha—A Closer Scrutiny

The growth in numbers and proportions of older people is most rapid in 'developing' countries. In India, in the year 2011, over 103 million (103.84 million to be precise) were in the age group of 60-plus. This population is expected to go up to 173 million by the year 2026 and a whopping 324 million by the year 2050 (Census of India, 2001; HelpAge India, 2005). It means that 8.6 per cent of the total population in the year 2011 belonged to what is referred to as the older age group. However, there are wide interstate variations, as shown in Table 2.1. The proportion is expected to increase to 11 per cent by the year 2025 and ultimately to 31.9 per cent by the year 2100 (UN-DESA, 2011).

A closer scrutiny of aged population in Odisha reflects that both in absolute and relative terms, it is rising rapidly in the state. The number of elderly (those belonging to the age group 60 years and above) which were 22.81 lakh in 1991 grew to 30.39 lakh in 2001 and finally to 39.8 lakh in 2011 (Table 2.2). A majority of the elderly of the state (86%) live in rural areas. The concentration of aged in terms of its share to total population is 9.5 per cent in the state. In fact, this proportion is found to be the highest among what are metaphorically called BIMARUO states (namely, Bihar, Madhya Pradesh, Rajasthan, Uttar Pradesh and Odisha) in India. Moreover, the share is likely to increase in the

**Table 2.1**

*Persons aged 60 and above (Rural+Urban) (as per cent of total population)*

| Major states | Male | | | | Female | | | | Persons | | | |
|---|---|---|---|---|---|---|---|---|---|---|---|---|
| | *1981* | *1991* | *2001* | *2011* | *1981* | *1991* | *2001* | *2011* | *1981* | *1991* | *2001* | *2011* |
| Andhra Pradesh | 6.48 | 6.64 | 7.16 | 9.20 | 6.82 | 6.93 | 8.04 | 10.38 | 6.65 | 6.78 | 7.59 | 8.58 |
| Assam | — | 5.65 | 5.81 | 6.62 | — | 4.98 | 5.9 | 6.71 | — | 5.33 | 5.85 | 9.79 |
| Bihar | 6.77 | 6.53 | 6.49 | 7.43 | 6.83 | 5.97 | 6.38 | 7.25 | 6.8 | 6.26 | 6.44 | 7.34 |
| Gujarat | 5.52 | 5.96 | 6.17 | 7.13 | 5.16 | 6.84 | 7.7 | 8.78 | 5.33 | 6.39 | 6.91 | 7.92 |
| Haryana | 6.87 | 7.43 | 7 | 8.07 | 5.73 | 8.01 | 8.06 | 9.32 | 6.34 | 7.7 | 7.49 | 8.65 |
| Karnataka | 6.46 | 6.8 | 7.15 | 8.87 | 6.79 | 7.18 | 8.24 | 10.10 | 6.62 | 6.99 | 7.69 | 9.48 |
| Kerala | 7.15 | 8.33 | 9.59 | 11.75 | 7.84 | 9.29 | 11.31 | 13.29 | 7.5 | 8.82 | 10.48 | 12.55 |
| Madhya Pradesh | 6.09 | 6.51 | 6.64 | 7.33 | 6.83 | 6.77 | 7.65 | 8.42 | 6.45 | 6.63 | 7.13 | 7.86 |
| Maharashtra | 6.07 | 6.69 | 7.8 | 9.02 | 6.72 | 7.3 | 9.73 | 10.81 | 6.39 | 6.98 | 8.73 | 7.87 |
| **Odisha** | **6.13** | **7.18** | **8.05** | **9.40** | **6.66** | **7.23** | **8.47** | **9.59** | **6.39** | **7.2** | **8.26** | **9.49** |
| Punjab | 8.28 | 8.07 | 8.56 | 9.86 | 7.25 | 7.58 | 9.5 | 10.85 | 7.8 | 7.84 | 9 | 10.33 |
| Rajasthan | 5.78 | 6.08 | 6.22 | 6.84 | 6.29 | 6.52 | 7.31 | 8.12 | 6.03 | 6.29 | 6.74 | 7.46 |
| Tamil Nadu | 6.52 | 7.65 | 8.71 | 10.13 | 6.3 | 7.25 | 8.94 | 10.69 | 6.41 | 7.45 | 8.83 | 10.41 |
| Uttar Pradesh | 7.05 | 7.22 | 7.08 | 7.74 | 6.6 | 6.46 | 7.01 | 7.84 | 6.84 | 6.86 | 7.04 | 7.79 |
| West Bengal | 5.32 | 5.93 | 6.72 | 8.23 | 5.8 | 6.17 | 7.53 | 8.75 | 5.55 | 6.05 | 7.11 | 8.48 |
| **All India** | **6.4** | **6.69** | **7.1** | **8.20** | **6.58** | **6.71** | **7.83** | **8.98** | **6.49** | **6.7** | **7.45** | **8.58** |

*Source*: Census of India: 1981,1991, 2001 and 2011.

*Note*: (1) All India excludes Assam for 1981 and Jammu & Kashmir for 1991.

(2) Old-age dependency ratio is defined as the number of persons in the age group 60-plus per 100 persons in the age group 15–59 years.

(3) Bihar, Madhya Pradesh and Uttar Pradesh include the reorganized states of Jharkhand, Chhattisgarh and Uttaranchal, respectively.

**Table 2.2**

*Selected demographic characteristics of elderly in Odisha by age and sex (1991–2011)*

| Distribution of aged by place of residence and different age category | Number (in lakh) | | | | | | | | |
| --- | --- | --- | --- | --- | --- | --- | --- | --- | --- |
| | 1991 | | | 2001 | | | 2011 | | |
| | Males | Females | Persons | Males | Females | Persons | Males | Females | Persons |
| Rural | 10.4 | 10.24 | 20.64 | 13.22 | 13.62 | 26.84 | 17.14 | 17.25 | 34.40 |
| Urban | 1.13 | 1.04 | 2.17 | 1.81 | 1.74 | 3.55 | 2.80 | 2.65 | 5.45 |
| Total(60+)-Old | 11.53 | 11.28 | 22.81 | 15.03 | 15.36 | 30.39 | 19.94 | 19.90 | 39.84 |
| out of which | | | | | | | | | |
| Total(70+)(Old-Old) | 4.25 | 4.14 | 8.4 | 5.96 | 5.71 | 11.67 | 7.69 | 7.62 | 15.31 |
| Total(80+)(Oldest Old) | 1.24 | 1.09 | 2.34 | 1.55 | 1.38 | 2.93 | 2.05 | 1.93 | 3.98 |

| | Proportion of elderly to the total population (in %) | | | | | | | | |
| --- | --- | --- | --- | --- | --- | --- | --- | --- | --- |
| | 1991 | | | 2001 | | | 2011 | | |
| | Males | Females | Persons | Males | Females | Persons | Males | Females | Persons |
| Rural | 7.54 | 7.51 | 7.53 | 8.4 | 8.77 | 8.58 | 9.75 | 9.93 | 9.84 |
| Urban | 4.98 | 5.29 | 5.12 | 6.2 | 6.68 | 6.43 | 7.72 | 7.84 | 7.78 |
| **Total(60+)-Old** | **7.18** | **7.23** | **7.2** | **8.05** | **8.47** | **8.26** | **9.40** | **9.59** | **9.49** |
| out of which | | | | | | | | | |
| Total(70+)(Old-Old) | 5.23 | 2.65 | 1.34 | 3.19 | 3.15 | 3.17 | 3.62 | 3.67 | 3.65 |
| Total(80+)(Oldest Old) | 0.77 | 0.7 | 0.74 | 0.83 | 0.76 | 0.8 | 0.97 | 0.93 | 0.95 |

(Table 2.2 Continued)

(Table 2.2 Continued)

| | Percentage distribution of elderly by region, age and sex | | | | | | | | |
| | 1991 | | | 2001 | | | 2011 | | |
| | Males | Females | Persons | Males | Females | Persons | Males | Females | Persons |
|---|---|---|---|---|---|---|---|---|---|
| Rural | 90.2 | 90.78 | 90.49 | 87.98 | 88.67 | 88.33 | 85.96 | 86.70 | 86.33 |
| Urban | 9.8 | 9.22 | 9.51 | 12.02 | 11.33 | 11.67 | 14.04 | 13.30 | 13.67 |
| Total(60+)-Old | 100.00 | 100.00 | 100.00 | 100.00 | 100.00 | 100.00 | 100.00 | 100.00 | 100.00 |
| out of which | | | | | | | | | |
| Total(70+)(Old-Old) | 36.86 | 36.7 | 36.83 | 39.65 | 37.16 | 38.39 | 38.55 | 38.29 | 38.42 |
| Total(80+)(Oldest Old) | 10.75 | 9.66 | 10.26 | 10.31 | 9 | 9.65 | 10.27 | 9.70 | 9.99 |

Source: Census of India—Odisha: 1991, 2001 and 2011.

coming years and is attributed to the demographic transition. As per the population projections, the number of elderly in Odisha is likely to be around 62.69 lakh in 2026, that is, an increase of more than two times in a span of 25 years, and the share of the elderly is expected to be 13.8 per cent of the total population (Census of India, 2001).

An important way of looking at the burden of the elderly for any society is the *old-age dependency ratio*. The old-age dependency ratio (defined as the number of persons in the age group 60 years and above per 100 persons in the age group 15–59 years) is a useful, notional indicator of the extent of economic support to be provided by the working age group to the dependent elderly. The old-age dependency ratio has increased from 12.74 per cent in 1991 to 15.45 per cent in 2011, being somewhat higher for females than for the males. The ratio is found to be the fourth highest in the case of Odisha, among the major states in the country, following Kerala, Punjab and Maharashtra (Table 2.3). As per the population projections, the ratio would be around 21.2 per cent in 2026 (ibid.). Any increase in the old-age dependency ratio implies that an increasing number of the elderly, generally with altered physiological, psychological or sometimes even professional capabilities and with reduced work participation rates, have to depend more and more on the population in the working age group for support. This could have serious implications for the well-being of the elderly at household level (Government of India, 2002).

# Selected Dimensions of Socio-Economic Insecurity among the Elderly in Odisha

## Poverty Incidence of Households Having Older Persons

The elderly in a poverty-ridden state like Odisha are most vulnerable and in this context, the issue of social security assumes greater significance. To understand the nuances, an examination of some demographic and socio-economic indicators of older persons—in terms of their living arrangement, the extent of economic independence, economic service providers and health condition—is required. At the outset, it needs

**Table 2-3**

*Old-age dependency ratio–(Rural+Urban) combined (in %)*

| Major states | Male | | | | Female | | | | Persons | | | |
|---|---|---|---|---|---|---|---|---|---|---|---|---|
| | 1981 | 1991 | 2001 | 2011 | 1981 | 1991 | 2001 | 2011 | 1981 | 1991 | 2001 | 2011 |
| Andhra Pradesh | 8.36 | 11.67 | 11.88 | 14.50 | 12.5 | 12.14 | 13.36 | 16.31 | 10.05 | 11.9 | 12.61 | 15.40 |
| Assam | — | 10.34 | 10.18 | 10.94 | — | 9.31 | 10.51 | 11.11 | — | 9.85 | 10.34 | 11.02 |
| Bihar* | 13.27 | 12.68 | 12.58 | 13.98 | 14.83 | 11.4 | 12.22 | 13.62 | 13.99 | 12.06 | 12.41 | 13.81 |
| Gujarat | 10 | 10.32 | 10.23 | 11.32 | 11.61 | 11.96 | 12.83 | 14.01 | 10.78 | 11.11 | 11.47 | 12.61 |
| Haryana | 13.3 | 13.91 | 12.42 | 13.18 | 11 | 15.25 | 14.36 | 15.06 | 12.22 | 14.53 | 13.31 | 14.07 |
| Karnataka | 11.87 | 11.96 | 11.78 | 13.76 | 12.79 | 12.82 | 13.74 | 15.79 | 12.32 | 12.38 | 12.74 | 14.76 |
| Kerala | 12.59 | 13.72 | 15.24 | 18.58 | 13.49 | 15.07 | 17.73 | 20.60 | 13.05 | 14.41 | 16.53 | 19.64 |
| Madhya Pradesh* | 11.54 | 12.11 | 12.09 | 12.36 | 13.19 | 12.7 | 14.13 | 14.38 | 12.33 | 12.4 | 13.07 | 13.34 |
| Maharashtra | 10.88 | 11.66 | 13.03 | 14.20 | 12.35 | 12.88 | 16.73 | 17.24 | 11.58 | 12.25 | 14.78 | 15.66 |
| Odisha | 11.25 | 12.67 | 13.8 | 15.35 | 12.47 | 12.81 | 14.48 | 15.54 | 11.85 | 12.74 | 14.14 | 15.45 |
| Punjab | 15.05 | 14.22 | 14.53 | 15.56 | 13.07 | 13.23 | 15.88 | 16.78 | 14.12 | 13.76 | 15.16 | 16.14 |
| Rajasthan | 11.14 | 11.55 | 11.74 | 11.90 | 12.33 | 12.4 | 13.86 | 14.10 | 11.71 | 11.95 | 12.76 | 12.96 |
| Tamil Nadu | 11.18 | 12.55 | 13.78 | 15.46 | 10.72 | 11.71 | 13.93 | 16.12 | 10.95 | 12.13 | 13.85 | 15.79 |
| Uttar Pradesh* | 13.8 | 13.89 | 13.69 | 13.90 | 12.72 | 12.35 | 13.45 | 13.92 | 13.29 | 13.17 | 13.58 | 13.91 |
| West Bengal | 9.36 | 10.29 | 11.15 | 12.73 | 10.71 | 11.06 | 12.82 | 13.69 | 9.99 | 10.65 | 11.95 | 13.19 |
| All India | 11.84 | 12.16 | 12.45 | 13.60 | 12.24 | 12.23 | 13.77 | 14.89 | 12.04 | 12.19 | 13.08 | 14.23 |

*Source:* Census of India—1981, 1991, 2001 and 2011.

*Note:* (1) All India excludes Assam for 1981 and Jammu & Kashmir for 1991.

(2) Old-age dependency ratio is defined as the number of persons in the age group 60-plus per 100 persons in the age group 15–59.

(3) Asterisk sign denotes the undivided status of the state.

to be mentioned here that barring very few studies (Panda, 1997), no such systematic attempts have been made so far in order to assess the growing insecurities being faced by the aged in Odisha. However, NSSO's two different round surveys (NSSO 52nd round, NSSO 60th round) give valuable information about the nature and dimensions of socio-economic conditions of the elderly in the state. The results of these two surveys in addition to that of the results of the two Censuses (Census, 1991; Census, 2001) have been used in subsequent analysis and, wherever possible, inferences have been drawn to assess the changes over this period.

It is worth mentioning that the poverty incidence, which was 65.29 per cent in 1983, declined significantly to 48.56 per cent in 1993–1994 and further marginally to 46.4 per cent in 2004–2005 (which is found to be 1.7 times higher than that of all-India figure). Moreover, the absolute number of poor persons is found to be increasing at a significant rate of 1.5 lakh persons per annum between 1993–1994 and 2004–2005, and as of now, 178.5 lakh people are below the poverty line in the state. Moreover, a recent study shows that in all the states except Odisha, the incidence of extreme poverty or hard core poor in total population has declined between 1993–1994 and 2004–2005 (Mahendra Dev and Ravi, 2007).[1] Here, a cursory attempt has been made to estimate the incidence of poverty as well as the profiles of poor households having aged persons on the basis of 60th round NSS unit level data for the state and the result is shown in Table 2.4. A perusal of data from the table brings out the following facts:

- 46 per cent of households having older persons live below the poverty line and another 19 per cent just marginally over it, and large disparities in terms of the incidence of poverty are found between rural and urban areas in Odisha.
- About one-fifth of the households having older persons are found to be in the grip of perennial poverty (i.e., very poor) and the incidence of extreme poverty as a sub-set of very poor was within a narrow range of 3–4 per cent in rural and urban areas.
- Though the gap in poverty incidence of households having older persons between rural and urban areas is large enough, but the distribution of these households in terms of moderately poor and very poor is found to be more or less the same in these areas.

**Table 2.4**

*Profiles of households having aged persons in Odisha*

| | Proportion of households (HHs) having aged persons (%) | | | Distribution of poverty incidence (%) | | |
|---|---|---|---|---|---|---|
| | Total | Rural | Urban | Total | Rural | Urban |
| Marginally above poverty line | 18.86 | 20.68 | 11.88 | — | — | — |
| Below poverty line | 45.54 | 48.91 | 32.57 | — | — | — |
| Moderately poor | 25.73 | 27.53 | 18.77 | 56.5 | 56.3 | 57.65 |
| Very poor | 19.81 | 21.38 | 13.79 | 43.5 | 43.7 | 42.35 |
| Extremely poor | 3.63 | 3.88 | 2.68 | — | — | — |

*Source:* Computed from NSS 60th round (January–June 2004) Household data CD.

*Note:* (1) Marginally above poverty line HHs are those whose per capita consumption lies between 100 per cent and 125 per cent state-specific poverty line.

(2) Moderately poor HHs are those whose per capita consumption lies between 75 per cent and 100 per cent state-specific poverty line.

(3) Very poor HHs are those whose per capita consumption is less than 75 per cent of the state-specific poverty line.

(4) Extremely poor HHs are those whose per capita consumption is below 50 per cent from state-specific line.

(5) Here, in case of Odisha, the state-specific official poverty line was ₹325.79 and ₹528.49, respectively, for rural and urban areas in 2004–2005.

(6) The definition of moderately poor, very poor and extremely poor is based on Radhakrishna, Rao, Ravi and Reddy (2004).

(7) From the above definition of moderately poor and very poor, the distyribution of poverty sums up to 100.

Therefore, what is found from the recent data that on the one hand, the magnitude of poorer people is relatively high compounded by an increase in the incidence of extremely poor and on the other, the share of elderly population is increasing at a steady rate. So, it suggests that a large number of older people in the state are either poor or at serious risk of poverty and extreme poverty. Chronic Poverty Research Centre identifies a large segment of unemployable (like the old and the handicapped, the widows and the orphans)—owing to life cycle contingencies or exigencies—to fall into the category of being chronically poor in any society. The study shows that households with older people are poorer, almost without exception, in comparison to those households without them (Schwartz, 2003). The next section addresses some basic issues pertaining to older people in Odisha.

## Living Arrangement

The term 'living arrangement' is used to refer to one's household structure (Palloni, 2001). Irudaya, Mishra and Sharma (1995) explain living arrangements in terms of the type of family in which the elderly live, the headship they enjoy, the place they stay in and the people they stay with. Two rounds of surveys of NSSO give information on living arrangements of the elderly. The 2004 results for Odisha show that about 50 per cent of the aged were living with their spouses and other members, and another 30 per cent were living without their spouses but with their children, while about 3 per cent were living with other relations and non-relations. Nevertheless, about 12 per cent were living with their spouses only, while about 3 per cent were still living alone. Moreover, the living arrangement of the aged has changed to some extent over time since 1995–1996. A perusal of data between these two survey periods (1995–1996 and 2004) reveals the following (Table 2.5):

- The proportion of the aged who lived with their spouses only had gone up significantly from 8 to 12 per cent in urban areas and remained the same in rural areas.
- The proportion of the aged who lived with their children only had, however, gone down from an already low of 31 per cent to 26 per cent in urban areas. On the contrary, the proportion of the aged who lived with other relations and non-relations had gone up from 3 per cent to 5 per cent in urban areas. This probably reflects the further weakening of the extended family system in the state as evidenced in other part of the country.

## Economic Independence

The living arrangement depicts how the physical well-being of the aged is taken care of in the family in our society. Similarly, the economic independence reveals the associated problem of day-to-day maintenance of livelihood of the elderly. The distribution of aged persons by state of economic independence for the state as per NSSO survey (NSS 60th round for the year 2004) shows that as high as 70 per cent of the aged had to depend on others for their day-to-day maintenance. The

**Table 2.5**

Per 1,000 distribution of elderly by type of living arrangement in Odisha and India

| Area | Living alone | | Living with | | Without spouse but with | | | | Total | Aged persons Estd (00) |
|---|---|---|---|---|---|---|---|---|---|---|
| | As an inmate of old-age home | Not as an inmate of old-age home | Spouse only | Spouse and other members | Children | Other relations | Non relations | Not recorded | | |
| **1995–1996** | | | | | | | | | | |
| | | | | | **Person** | | | | | |
| Rural Odisha | 9 | 34 | 117 | 518 | 287 | 20 | 6 | 9 | 1,000 | 16,430 |
| Urban Odisha | 14 | 18 | 80 | 527 | 310 | 29 | 3 | 19 | 1,000 | 2,094 |
| Combined | 10 | 32 | 113 | 519 | 290 | 21 | 6 | 10 | 1,000 | 18,524 |
| India | 9 | 35 | 101 | 464 | 335 | 44 | 4 | 9 | 1,000 | 463,661 |
| **2004** | | | | | | | | | | |
| | | | | | **Person** | | | | | |
| Rural Odisha | 2 | 32 | 119 | 492 | 301 | 21 | 4 | 28 | 1,000 | 25,527 |
| Urban Odisha | 3 | 20 | 120 | 536 | 263 | 19 | 5 | 33 | 1,000 | 2,729 |
| Combined | 2 | 31 | 119 | 496 | 298 | 21 | 4 | 28 | 1,000 | 28,256 |
| India | 5 | 47 | 120 | 448 | 321 | 39 | 5 | 17 | 1,000 | 663,779 |

*Source:* GoI. (1998). Report No.446—The Aged in India: A Socio-Economic Profile. NSS Fifty-Second Round (July 1995 – June 1996), NSSO. ———. (2006), Report No. 507-Morbidity, Health Care and the Condition of the Aged. NSS 60th Round (January–June 2004), NSSO.

*Note:* Table generated from the raw data from the GoI (1998, 2006 Reports).
The combined value represents the weighted average of rural and urban figures.

**Table 2.6**

*Per 1,000 distribution of aged persons and number of aged persons by state of economic independence in Odisha, India*

| | State of economic independence | | | | | Aged persons |
|---|---|---|---|---|---|---|
| | *Not dependent on others* | *Partially dependent on others* | *Fully dependent on others* | *Not recorded* | *Total* | *Estd (00)* |
| **1995–1996** | | | **Person** | | | |
| Rural Odisha | 287 | 180 | 513 | 21 | 1,000 | 16,430 |
| Urban Odisha | 251 | 185 | 503 | 60 | 1,000 | 2,094 |
| Combined | 283 | 181 | 512 | 25 | 1,000 | 18,524 |
| India | 303 | 158 | 516 | 23 | 1,000 | 463,661 |
| **2004** | | | **Person** | | | |
| Rural Odisha | 270 | 167 | 538 | 25 | 1,000 | 25,527 |
| Urban Odisha | 311 | 129 | 535 | 24 | 1,000 | 2,729 |
| Combined | 274 | 163 | 538 | 25 | 1,000 | 28,256 |
| India | 335 | 133 | 518 | 14 | 1,000 | 663,779 |

*Note:* Table generated from the raw data from the source same as Table 5.
The combined value represents the weighted average of rural and urban figures.

estimated number of aged dependent was found to be around 20 lakh in the state. Compared to 1995–1996, the results of the NSS for the year 2004 indicate the following (Table 2.6):

- The incidence of economic independence has decreased among the elderly in rural areas.
- The proportion of the aged who had to depend on others (for their day-to-day maintenance) fully has increased both in rural and urban areas.

  The economic condition of elderly females has deteriorated both in rural and urban areas.

## Economic Support Providers

As has been observed above, a large proportion of the elderly are economically dependent on others for their livelihood. It is, therefore, pertinent to know the persons who are providing economic support

**Table 2.7**

*Per 1,000 distribution of economically dependent aged persons by category of persons supporting the aged persons in Odisha, India*

|  | Spouse | Own children | Grand children | Others | Not recorded | Total | Estd (00) |
|---|---|---|---|---|---|---|---|
| **1995–1996** | | | | **Person** | | | |
| Rural Odisha | 108 | 806 | 35 | 36 | 15 | 1,000 | 11,379 |
| Urban Odisha | 120 | 799 | 52 | 18 | 11 | 1,000 | 1,442 |
| Combined | 109 | 805 | 37 | 34 | 15 | 18,524 | 12,821 |
| India | 141 | 710 | 51 | 67 | 31 | 1000 | 312,353 |
| **2004** | | | | **Person** | | | |
| Rural Odisha | 144 | 763 | 36 | 57 | 0 | 1,000 | 18,007 |
| Urban Odisha | 110 | 801 | 25 | 64 | 0 | 1,000 | 1,813 |
| Combined | 140 | 767 | 35 | 57 | 0 | 1,000 | 19,820 |
| India | 132 | 779 | 27 | 62 | 0 | 1,000 | 431,892 |

*Note:* Table generated from the raw data from the source same as Table 5.
The combined value represents the weighted average of rural and urban figures.

to the elderly. Such information was collected in the rounds of two NSSO surveys mentioned above. It is seen from 2004 NSS data that of the economically dependent aged, a majority (767 per thousand or about 76%) had to depend on their children and a sizable proportion (14%) on their spouses for economic support. Their grandchildren supported only 4 per cent and the rest (6%) had to depend on 'others', including non-relations. Between the years 1995–1996 and 2004, the distribution of the aged who were economically dependent changed in respect of the category of persons supporting them for their livelihood. During the inter-survey period, these are the major findings (Table 2.7):

- The proportion of those depending on their spouse and on 'others', including non-relations, has increased (from 11% and 3.6% in 1995–1996 to 14% and 5.7% in 2004 on their spouse and on 'others', respectively) significantly in rural areas.

  The proportion of those depending on their spouse decreased marginally in the urban areas (from 12% to 11%). Nevertheless, the proportion of those depending on 'others', including non-relations, has increased significantly in the urban areas as compared to rural areas (from 18 per thousand or 1.8% in 1995–1996 to 64 per thousand or 6.4% in 2004).

Again this segment of population faces multiple medical and psychological problems. There is an emerging need to pay greater attention to ageing-related issues and to promote holistic policies and programmes for dealing with the ageing society (Government of India, 2011). The elderly, especially those who are weak and/or dependent, can suffer physical, emotional and financial abuse within their families and caregivers, and thus require physical, mental and emotional care and support. Particularly, abuse and violence against older women in Indian homes have been largely hidden and widely denied by communities due to the fear that an admission of its incidence will be an assault on the integrity of the family (Bagga and Sakurkar, 2011). A study by Panigrahi (2010) in Odisha found that about 25 per cent of the respondents preferred co-residence (that is with their spouse and children) for physical needs and emotional support. One more striking feature of his findings was that a higher proportion of males (30.8%) than females (16.8%) had reported the need for physical care and emotional support as the reason for preferring a particular living arrangement.

# Protective Social Security Arrangements for the Elderly in Odisha

From the above analysis, one may infer that the elderly in Odisha have a high degree of economic dependence (which is more—both in terms of extent and in terms of nature—in the case of females). This obviously is a major challenge for any civil society, for a section of the society whose contribution in the past could make the 'forgotten poor', like the 'invisible poor' women working at home-based activities, providing critical economic support to the family, besides their unpaid household work. Nevertheless, all the state governments and UTs have their own schemes of social assistance programmes. By the end of the Seventh Plan (1985–1990), all the states and UTs had old-age pension schemes; however, the extent of coverage was dependent on the resources of the state. Basically two social pension schemes, namely, National Old Age Pension Scheme (NOAPS)[2] and State Old Age Pension Scheme (SOAPS)[3] are in operation in the state. Over a decade till 2005–2006, the amount of assistance was set at a very low of ₹100 per month per beneficiary under these two schemes. Government of India [GoI] had been providing ₹75 per month and the state government ₹25 per month to each beneficiary under the NOAPS. This means that in terms of the grant amount, it was one-third of the government-estimated subsistence income for the state (since in case of Odisha, the state-specific official poverty line was ₹325.79 and ₹528.49 for rural and urban areas, respectively in 2004–2005). Now, the amount of assistance under these two schemes is ₹200 per month per beneficiary, which is even well below the state-specific official poverty line.

The Finance Minister of India in his Budget Speech for the year 2006–2007 urged the state governments to make an equal contribution from their resources so that a destitute pensioner would get at least ₹400 per month. As per the reports received, the states of Tamil Nadu, Uttarakhand, West Bengal, Rajasthan, NCT of Delhi, UT of Andaman and Nicobar Islands and Pondicherry have already started disbursing ₹400 per month or above for pensioners under NOAPS. However, it has not yet been revised in Odisha. More importantly, recent studies show that the criteria of destitute cannot be defined clearly and that the establishment of the destitution of beneficiary is difficult and ultimately it leads to the problems of identification and targeting (Mahendra Dev, Subbara, Galab and Ravi, 2007; Mishra, 2010).

# Concluding Observations

To conclude, this chapter has shown the extent of socio-economic vulnerabilities being faced by the elderly in the state and also has made an assessment of coverage under ongoing social security schemes for these destitute people. The Report of the Working Group on Social Protection Policy—National Social Assistance Programme and Associated Programmes, GoI (NSAPAP, 2006) observes that 'The NSAP was intended to be a significant step towards fulfilment of the *Directive Principles* in Article 41 of the Constitution' and has recommended for universalization of social assistance for persons who have little or no income, being unable to work, because of age, health or other reasons as a major form of comprehensive social security. It is high time to implement recommendations put forth by the Working Group with commitment without any delay from a human rights perspective. In fact, following the recommendations of the working group, the central government has revamped the existing NOAPS for wider coverage which henceforth is termed as Indira Gandhi National Old Age Pension Scheme (IGNOAPS) and the scheme supports to provide a ₹400 monthly pension [50:50 basis by the centre and states, but not yet been done in Odisha] to people over 65 years and living below the poverty line. It is found that either the coverage and quantum of benefits under ongoing social security schemes are very low or these are not reaching the intended beneficiaries. At the same, there is an urgent need for social insurance, particularly in the form of health insurance, for the destitute old people, as health risks being faced by them not only make them vulnerable but also their families by involving serious economic damages (Mishra, 2009). This also needs government intervention, since private provider cannot venture into this sector due to the risk of bankruptcy. Adding to this, older persons should have access to social services, including 'universal and equal access to healthcare services', and such facilities will not only cure them physically, but will also ensure their mental well-being.

# Endnotes

1.  Mahendra Dev and Ravi (2007) estimated it in terms of all those persons whose per capita expenditure is less than 75 per cent of the state-specific poverty line based on the NSS data. Their study shows that Odisha is the only state in India where the incidence of extreme poor has increased (from 23 per cent in 1993–1994 to 28 per cent in 2004–2005, which is found to be two and half times higher than that of all-India figure and that its relative share in poverty incidence has increased from 48% to 54% during these two periods).
2.  National Old Age pension (NOAP) scheme is the first component of 100 per cent Government of India-assisted programme, namely, National Social Assistance programme being implemented in the state since 15 August 1995. Under this scheme, destitute elderly of 65 years of age and above having no regular means of assistance are being paid with monthly pension at the rate of ₹200 per month from 1 April 2006. For implementation of the scheme, funds are being released by Government of India (GoI) in the form of Additional Central Assistance to be routed through the state plan budget. This NOAP scheme has been relaunched as Indira Gandhi National Old Age Pension Scheme (IGNOAPS) by the GoI w.e.f. 19 November 2007 where in the criteria for selection beneficiaries have been modified. As per the revised criteria, all persons 65 years or above and who are below the poverty line as per BPL survey of 2002 will be covered under IGNOAPS as against the earlier criteria of destitute persons under NOAP. The total beneficiaries under these schemes are 11, 93,176 for 2010–2011.
3.  The State Old Age Pension (SOAP) scheme was being implemented in the state w.e.f. 01.04.1975. Destitute elderly of 60 years of age and above, elderly with visible signs

of deformity and widows irrespective of their age were the beneficiaries. The annual income of all the above categories was ₹3,200 or less. Later on, the state government has introduced 'Madhu Babu Pension Yojana (MBPY)' by merging two pension schemes 'Old Age Pension Rules, 1989' and 'Disability Pension Rules,1985' which came into effect from 1 January 2008. The total beneficiaries under these schemes are 14, 08,400 for 2010–2011.

# References

Alam, M. & Karim, M. (2005, 18–23 July). *Beyond the current demographic scenario: Changing age composition, ageing and growing insecurities for the aged in India and Pakistan.* Paper presented at the 25th IUSSP International Population Conference, France.

Bagga, A. & Sakurkar, A. (2011). Violence in the lives of older women: It's impact on their mental health. *Helpage India-Research and Development Journal, 17*(3), 7–19.

Census of India. (1991). New Delhi: Office of the Registrar General & Census Commissioner, India.

——— (2001). Population Projections for India and States 2001–2026 (Rev. December 2006). New Delhi: Office of Registrar General & Census Commissioner, India.

Government of India. (2002). *National human development report 2001.* New Delhi: Planning Commission.

———. (2011). *Situation analysis of the elderly in India* New Delhi: Central Statistical Office, Ministry of Statistics and Programme Implementation,.

HelpAge India. (2005). Ageing and poverty vis-à-vis social security. *Research and Development Journal, 11*(2), 5–12.

Irudaya, R.S. (2004). *Chronic poverty among Indian elderly* (CPRC-IIPA Working Paper 17). New Delhi: CPRC-IIPA.

Irudaya, R.S., Mishra, U.S. & Sharma, P.S. (1995). Living arrangements among the Indian elderly. *Hong Kong Journal of Gerontology, 9*(2), 20–28.

James, K.S. (1994). Indian elderly: Asset or liability? *Economic and Political Weekly, 29*(36), 2335.

Krishnaswamy, B., Than Sein, U., Munodawafa, D., Varghese, C., Venkataraman K. & Leslie, A. (2008). Ageing in India. *Ageing International, 32* (4), 258–268.

Mahendra Dev, S. & Ravi, C. (2007). Poverty and inequality: All-India and states, 1983–2005. *Economic and Political Weekly, 42*(6), 509–521.

Mahendra Dev, S., Subbarao, K., Galab, S. & Ravi, C. (2007). Safety net programmes in India: Outreach and effectiveness. *Economic and Political Weekly, 42*(35), 3555–3565.

Mishra, A.K. (2009). Poverty, vulnerability, and social security of elderly in Odisha. *Helpage India-Research and Development Journal, 15*(1), 19–24.

Mishra, A. (2010). *State, economic reform and social security: Micro-level experiences in India.* Starbuccken: VDM.

NSAPAP. (2006). *Report of the working group on social protection policy—National Social Assistance Programme and Associated Programmes.* New Delhi: Ministry of Rural Development, Government of India.

NSSO 52nd Round, GoI. (1998). *The aged in India: A socio-economic profile* (Report No.446). *National Sample Survey,* 52nd Round (July 1995 – June 1996). New Delhi: Department of Statistics, Ministry of Planning and Programme Implementation.

NSSO 60th Round, GoI, (2004). *Morbidity, health care and the condition of the aged* (Report No. 507). National Sample Survey 60th round (January–June 2004). New Delhi: Department of Statistics, Ministry of Planning and Programme Implementation.

Palloni, A. (2001). *Living arrangements of older persons United Nations Population Bulletin* (Special Issue Nos. 42/43). New York: Department of Economic and Social Affairs, Population Division.

Panda, P. (1997). *Living arrangements of the elderly in rural Odisha* (Working paper No. 277). Thiruvananthapuram: Centre for Development Studies.

Panigrahi, A.K. (2010). *Living arrangement preferences of the elderly in Orissa, India* (Working Paper No 240). Bangalore: The Institute for Social and Economic Change (ISEC),.

Schwartz, A. (2003). *Old age security and social pensions.* Washington DC: World Bank.

UN-DESA. (2011). World Population Prospects: The 2010 Revision. Population Division of the Department of Economic and Social Affairs of the United Nations Secretariat. Available at: http://esa.un.org/unpd/wpp/index.htm.

# 3

# Tackling Poverty in Old Age

*Anupama Datta*

## Introduction

The growth in numbers and proportions of older people is most rapid in 'developing' countries. In India, currently 90 million people are estimated to be in the age group of 60-plus. This population is expected to go up to 324 million by the year 2050. In other words, the proportion of older persons is expected to increase from less than 10 per cent to 21 per cent by the year 2050. The general level of economic development in the developing countries, including India, is low, and this coupled with the absence of relevant policies, infrastructure and services and inadequate targeting would result in increasing numbers of people ageing in poverty. The worst affected are those who face chronic poverty in old age. In India, according to the National Policy on Older Persons, one-third of the older persons live below the poverty line (BPL). However, in line with the Millennium Development Goals (MDGs), reduction of chronic poverty in old age has never been a priority, either for the state or for the aid agencies and is left largely to public charity. This segment of the population is growing exponentially, and the efforts to tackle the issues concerning population ageing are at best sporadic and inconsistent.

There are three key features of chronic poverty in old age: reduced capacity to work to earn, ageing and consequent inability to earn and lack of social security. Majority of poor people depend exclusively on their ability to do physical labour, as most of them are unskilled and illiterate. The work opportunities reduce progressively as they age. As they belong to very poor families, the traditional support of the adult children is also not possible in these cases. Moreover, in rural areas, the young adults migrate in search of jobs, leaving the older parents to fend for themselves. Most of these people also find themselves excluded from the formal structures of support, such as the old-age pension, anti-poverty programmes, etc., because most of the anti-poverty programmes are targeted at people in the age group of 15–59 years, including the recent employment guarantee initiatives.

According to the National Sample Survey Organization, 60th Round report, in India, 52 per cent older persons were fully dependent on others and 33.5 per cent were not dependent on others (NSS, 2006). This should be read with the data according to which 84 per cent people work in the informal sector and another 8 per cent work as informal workers in the formal sector, but there is no system for social security in old age for these people. This datum has two related policy implications for social security in old age. First, for the fully dependent older persons, who may not be able to work, there is a need for meaningful non-contributory pension system that covers their basic cost of living. It could be calculated either on the basis of the poverty line or on the basis of minimum wages. The amount per month would range between ₹1,000 and ₹2,000. The second and equally, if not more, challenging option is to provide relevant opportunities for employment to those who have the capacity and willingness to work, so that they are not dependent on anybody. These opportunities, unfortunately, are ever shrinking for the older persons and there is no effort to retain or retrain workers. Even for those who are not dependent, there is no guarantee that with advancing age they will continue to enjoy economic security. So, there is need to focus on their needs as well. For ensuring the well-being of this burgeoning segment of the population and also for reducing the burden of ageing on the society, earnest efforts should be made.

Government has a scheme for the non-contributory pensions for older persons in India, which has been improved from time to time, and the most recent development has been the recommendations of the Task Force on National Social Assistance Programme (NSAP) on the amount of pension, inclusion criteria, expansion of scope and strengthening the implementation and monitoring processes that are timely and relevant (NSAP, 2013). However, there has been virtually no attempt in the direction of providing opportunities for gainful employment in old age, except for some nascent beginning in the National Rural Livelihood

Mission. This chapter focuses on the non-contributory pensions for those who require immediate and urgent attention, that is, chronic poor and the vulnerable segments of the ageing population.

Older women suffer more than older men in case of economic security for many reasons, most important being greater longevity and higher probability of widowhood, inequitable social conditions and extreme dependence on male relatives. In 2002, sex ratio in the older age group was 91:100, which decreased to 81:100 in the age group of 80 years and above (UN, 2006). In the year 2000, the percentage of currently married men in the age group of 60-plus was 75 as compared to 42 for older women. In the same year, 59 per cent men as compared to 18 per cent women were in the labour force (UN, 2006). Social Security is particularly important to women. Longevity of women is more than that of men; they marry men who are normally older than them. Besides, most of them have no employment or interrupted employment path. Even in developed countries, elderly unmarried women—including widows—get 51 per cent of their total income from social security. Unmarried elderly men get 39 per cent, while elderly married couples get 36 per cent of their income from social security. For 25 per cent of unmarried women, social security is their only source of income, compared to 9 per cent of married couples and 20 per cent of unmarried men. Without social security benefits, elderly poverty rate among women would have been 52.2 per cent and among widows, it would have been 60.6 per cent (NECIWG, 1998).

A review of the actions of government, civil society and international agencies to address old-age poverty indicates that ageing is still not on the agenda. Current poverty reduction measures and proposals have not sufficiently acknowledged the intergenerational dimension of poverty, nor has attention been paid to older people's own survival strategies. Though the Constitution under Article 41 has directed that the State shall, within the limits of its economic capacity and development, make effective provision for securing the right of public assistance in cases of old age. There are other provisions, too, which direct the state to improve the quality of life of its citizens. Right to equality has been guaranteed by the Constitution as a Fundamental Right. These provisions apply equally to older persons. Social security has been made the concurrent responsibility of the central and state governments. In this context, it is also important to know the National Policy Statement given in the National Policy for Older Persons (NPOP) that indicates the principles underlying the policy, the directions, the needs that will be addressed and the relative roles of all stakeholders and action in the direction of a humane age-integrated society. The chapter reflects some important dimensions on tackling poverty in old age.

# National Policy Statement

The National Policy seeks to assure older persons that their concerns are national concerns and they will not live unprotected, ignored or marginalized. The goal of the National Policy is the well-being of older persons. It aims to strengthen their legitimate place in the society and helps them to live the last phase of their life with purpose, dignity and peace. The policy visualizes that the state will extend support for financial security, health care, shelter, welfare and other needs of older persons, provide protection against abuse and exploitation, make available opportunities for development of the potential of older persons, seek their participation and provide services so that they can improve the quality of their lives. The policy is based on some broad principles. It recognizes the need for affirmative action in favour of the elderly. It has to be ensured that the rights of older persons are not violated and they get opportunities and equitable share in development benefits; different sectors of development, programmes and administrative actions will reflect sensitivity in older persons living in rural areas. Providing special attention to older females will be necessary, so that they do not become victims of triple neglect and discrimination on account of gender, widowhood and age.

The policy views the life cycle as a continuum, of which post-60 phase of life is an integral part. It does not view age 60 as the cut-off point for beginning a life of dependency. It considers 60-plus as a phase when the individual should have the choices and the opportunities to lead an active, creative, productive and satisfying life. An important thrust therefore should be given for an active and productive involvement of older persons and not just their care. The policy values an age-integrated society. It will endeavour to strengthen integration between generations, facilitate two-way flow and interactions and strengthen bonds between the young and the old. It believes in the development of a social support system, informal as well as formal, so that the capacity of families to take care of older persons is strengthened and they can continue to live in their family. The policy recognizes that older persons, too, are a resource. They render useful services in the family and outside. They are not just consumers of goods and services, but also their producers. Opportunities and facilities need to be provided, so that they can continue to contribute more effectively to the family, the community and the society. The policy recognizes that larger budgetary allocations from the state will be needed and the rural and urban poor will be given special attention. However, it is neither feasible nor desirable for the state alone to attain the objectives of the National Policy. Individuals, families, communities and institutions of civil society have to join hands as partners.

The policy emphasizes the need for expansion of social and community services for older persons, particularly women, and enhances their accessibility and use by removing socio-cultural, economic and physical barriers and making the services client oriented and user friendly. Special efforts will be made to ensure that rural areas, where more than three-fourths of the older population lives, are adequately covered. The statement shows a progressive perspective, as older persons are considered productive members of the society with a right to live with dignity. The government should facilitate the process so that older persons get opportunities for a fulfilling life in the last phase. It also acknowledges the role of family in taking care of older persons and the responsibility of the government in encouraging the family to do so. Allocation of adequate budgetary resources to fulfil the promises and provision of special attention to vulnerable segments, such as women and rural population, is also mentioned.

The NPOP has delineated principal areas of intervention and action strategies, and under that the first is 'Financial Security'. This section of the policy document acknowledges that two-thirds of the older persons in the country have weak economic condition. It further states that for elderly persons under BPL, old-age pensions provide some succour. The coverage under the old-age pension scheme for poor persons will be significantly expanded with the ultimate objective of covering all older persons under BPL. Simultaneously, it will be necessary to prevent delays and check abuses in the matters of selection and disbursement. The rate of monthly pension will need to be revised at intervals, so that inflation does not deflate its real purchasing power. Simultaneously, the public distribution system will reach out to cover all 60-plus persons under BPL,

# Challenges of Universal Social Security in India

The third and most direct form of social security available to the poor consists of social assistance schemes. The most important of them are old-age pensions for the 'destitute' poor. The first state to introduce old-age pensions in India was Uttar Pradesh in 1957. In subsequent decades, almost all the states in India have introduced old-age pension schemes for the poor above the age of 60 or 65 years. In addition to general old-age pension schemes, many states have more liberal schemes for agricultural labourers who are likely to be the poorest among the elderly. Pensions have also been provided to widows and to the physically handicapped in the form of survivor, disability and employment injury benefits to families or victims involved in specified high-hazard occupations, such as fishing, construction work, tree tapping, well digging, pesticide spraying, tractor driving, loading and so on.

There is a wide variation in the coverage, benefits and eligibility conditions among the states and also in implementation efficiency, take-up and levels of budgetary expenditures (Sankaran, 1993). However, two states in India—Kerala and Tamil Nadu—have demonstrated the potential of such schemes. The Kerala pension scheme has been estimated to cover almost the entire target group of the elderly poor, and some form of social assistance is available to half the workers in the unorganized sector. A detailed evaluation suggests that about a third of the elderly poor were covered by old-age pensions in Tamil Nadu in 1990 (Guhan, 1992). In both states, pensions are likely to meet 50 per cent or more of subsistence requirements. A very high proportion of beneficiaries, nearly 60 per cent, are women. The introduction of the NSAP in the year 1995–1996 was a pioneering move towards the evolution of minimum standards in the matter of social assistance for the poor. National Old Age Pensions was one of the components of the NSAP. The NSAP is certainly a breakthrough in the hitherto neglected area of social assistance for the poor and meets an important gap in the portfolio of direct anti-poverty programmes. The states of Tamil Nadu and Andhra Pradesh have implemented the schemes in most districts.

The factors that have contributed to the massive and multi-tiered exclusion in social security can be located at many levels. As our review of policy formulations in successive plan documents has shown, attention has been almost exclusively concentrated on social security for workers in the organized sector, with only some fleeting and feeble references to the social security needs of unorganized workers, the unemployed and the unemployable among the poor. The adoption of formal social security has been historically induced through models transplanted from industrial countries (especially Britain because of the colonial connection) rather than in the responses to needs and circumstances relevant to India. Since adopted, the formal model has struck roots.

The principal beneficiaries—public employees and organized workers—have exerted pressure to ensure that over time priority is given to the vertical extension (enlargement of coverage and benefits in the formal system) rather than to the horizontal extension in favour of the large unprotected mass of the population. Public employees, who are in the enviable position of both improving and administering entitlements to themselves, have no problems with effective access, while industrial workers are subject to various bureaucratic constraints, as discussed earlier, in realizing the benefits due to them in a timely and adequate manner.

The counterpart to the concentration in the organized sector is the policy blindness to the social security needs of the massively excluded segments. The underlying perception has been that, given the very large proportion and numbers of the poor in India, it would not be feasible to think of protection against contingent poverty unless and until the level of chronic poverty becomes reduced in the process of normal growth. This might be possible by promoting appropriate schemes that can afford some relief for the contingencies involved. In this view, given the massive needs, budgetary constraints in meeting them will be overwhelming; or, in the alternative, they would enable only an insignificant part of needs to be met. Thus, callousness, a superficial exaggeration of financial constraints, and an all-or-nothing approach to social security for the poor have all combined to contribute to the colossal nature and magnitude of exclusion.

The need for social assistance is acknowledged in the Constitution, and state governments introduced schemes as early as 1957 to provide non-contributory pension. The central government announced an all-encompassing social security scheme (NSAP) in the year 1995.

However, a large proportion of the Indian population, consisting of workers in the unorganized sector, the unemployed and the unemployable, is still excluded from the benefits of social security. The social security system appropriate to Indian conditions will have to be a wide one, including promotional, ameliorative and protective measures. It cannot be confined to the narrower domain of 'formal' social security, as understood and institutionalized in the advanced industrial countries. The reasons are mainly threefold. First, formal social security is addressed for relieving prolonged or temporary loss of earnings on account of contingencies, such as unemployment, sickness and disability, maternity, employment injury, old-age widowhood and large family sizes. In economies where primary incomes are generally adequate to ensure a reasonable standard of living, the loss of income arising from such contingencies has been viewed as the predominant cause of poverty (Beveridge, 1942). Accordingly, formal social security has been focused on reducing the downward variability of incomes rather than being concerned with upgrading their level. In contrast, in developing countries such as India, where poverty is massive, widespread and persistent, social security, if it is to be meaningful, needs to be aimed both at improving incomes and standards of living for the poor and reducing their vulnerability to deprivation whether caused by chronic poverty or temporary adversity.

Second, credit and private insurance markets are underdeveloped in developing countries, necessitating a large role for social insurance and social assistance. The scope for social insurance based on payroll deductions or taxes on regular incomes is limited because the labour market is characterized by high proportions of those who are self-employed or are casual workers with unstable and irregular employment while inadequate tax resources. Third, there is a whole set of administrative problems involved in delivering social security of the formal type in societies where the needy population is predominantly rural, widely scattered and occupationally diverse with a high degree of irregular employment and fluctuating earnings. In such a situation, the needs assessment, selection of eligible beneficiaries and effective delivery of benefits pose a serious challenge for governance.

The characteristics of the Indian labour market besides financial and administrative constraints would make it impossible for the formal social security model to be extended to them. However, a sizeable dent on exclusion can be made through a combination of promotional measures, the insurance market and social assistance. With the introduction of the National Social Assistance Scheme (NSAP) 1995, a beginning has been made in the extension of social security to the poor, the unorganized sector and rural areas. In the coming years, these schemes will need to be effectively implemented. It will also be necessary, and should be feasible, to extend and enlarge social assistance benefits. The central government expanded the coverage and increased the amount under Indira Gandhi National Old Age Pension Scheme (IGNOAPS) where it contributes ₹200 per month per person for older persons from BPL family. The state government is also expected to contribute a matching grant. Therefore, the amount given to older people covered under the scheme varies from ₹1,000 to ₹2,000, depending on the state contribution. There are challenges of selection, coverage and delivery that need to be addressed.

## Non-contributory Pension in India

According to Census figures, the proportion of older people in the population in India was 5.3 per cent in 1961 and is expected to reach 9.9 per cent in 2021. There is a transformation occurring in households in India, where the traditional extended family make-up of households is moving to a nuclear one. There is also a trend of migration from rural to urban areas, leaving many older people without familial support in rural areas. In addition, according to a World Bank estimate, the number of people under BPL ($1.25/day) increased from 421 million in 1981 to 456 million in 2005. However, given the growing population, the share of the population in poverty fell from 60 per cent to 42 per cent. Almost half of India's poor and one-third of India's population are concentrated in the three states of Uttar Pradesh, Bihar and Madhya Pradesh (Global Poverty Estimates, 2005). The weakening family and social support system and the growing numbers of older people resulted in the Government of India playing a bigger role in providing a social safety net for destitute older people.

The National Old Age Pension Scheme (NOAPS) is a means-tested scheme, meaning that it specifically targets older people in poverty. The scheme was a centrally sponsored programme, where 100 per cent of the assistance was extended to the states/union territories to make allocations based on the guidelines and conditions set forth by the central government. Under the NOAPS guidelines, assistance will be provided for fulfilment of the following criteria: (1) The age of the applicant (male or female) should be 65 years or more and (2) the applicant must be a destitute in the sense of having little or no regular means of subsistence from his/her own sources of income or through financial support from family members or other sources. The amount of the old-age pension in 1995 was ₹75 per month per beneficiary. In the year 2002–2003, it was transferred to state plan, and funds are now being released as additional central assistance by Ministry of Finance to state finance departments.

Changes to the NOAPS occurred in November 2007. At that time, the government renamed the pension programme as 'Indira Gandhi National Old Age Pension Scheme'. The pension amount was raised to ₹200 per month per beneficiary, and the state governments were allowed to contribute over and above this amount. In addition, eligibility under this scheme was now based on older people aged 65 and above who are under BPL ($1.25/day). Following the institution of the pension programme, the government introduced a food security scheme, called Annapurna, in April 2000. This scheme provides food security to older persons who, though eligible, have remained uncovered under NOAPS. Under the Annapurna scheme, 10 kg of food grains are provided to the beneficiary every month at no cost. In the fiscal year 2005–2006, the NOAPS and Annapurna covered approximately 8.84 million older persons in the country and the government released a budget of $266.5 million for both of these programmes. The estimated number of beneficiaries for the subsequent year (FY 2006–2007) increased to 10.17 million, and the government's budget also increased to $456 million. In the year 2010–2011, 17 million people were covered under IGNOAPS at the cost of ₹54.8 million (NSAP, 2011). The government is contented by achieving its financial and physical targets; but, it is important to go beyond and understand the significance of the pension to the lives of older persons and their families. Besides, it is pertinent to understand the dynamics of the implementation process at micro-level so as to find solutions that are not purely administrative, but also empowering for the older persons by way of including them in the identification and monitoring process, so that these schemes proceed in the direction of rights of older persons to make them live with dignity.

# Effects of Old-age Pension on the Lives of Poor Older Persons

A research study was undertaken by HelpAge India in collaboration with HelpAge International in the year 2008. It is aimed to find out the extent to which non-contributory pension programmes reduce poverty among beneficiary households, facilitate household investment, reduce inequality and support capabilities. This would be an appropriate and effective means available to the government to fulfil its promise for life with dignity in old age. The available evidence from various studies in developed and developing countries suggests that non-contributory pension programmes reduce poverty among older people and their households, enable investment in human and physical capital within beneficiary households, strengthen intergenerational solidarity and transfers, insure poorer rural communities against the adverse effects of agricultural reform and encourage local economic activity (Barrientos, 2006).

## Purpose and Methodology

This participatory study was undertaken to gain insight into the economic and social impacts of pension among older people through the collection of their perceptions and opinions, as well as perceptions of community stakeholders. It was also undertaken to assess whether the monitoring by older people's groups contributes in making the pension scheme more effective and efficient in the view of the stakeholders. To explore these two issues, a participatory study was undertaken in two districts: Unnao district of Uttar Pradesh and Mandla district of Madhya Pradesh. Both of these districts were under the Poorest Areas Civil Society (PACS) programme initiated by HelpAge India, supporting older people's groups in advocating for their rights and entitlements. Under this programme, the older people's groups (*Vridh Sanghs*) were formed at village level, and the friends of older people (*Vridh Mitra*) were trained to develop awareness among older people, as well as state and non-state actors, on issues concerning older people. Within each district, two villages were selected for gathering information. In Unnao district, the villages were SaraiMalkadim and Nindemau, and in Mandla district, the villages were Munu and Pipariya.

The study tools were both individual interviews and focus group discussions. In Mandla district, 20 individual interviews were held in each village with beneficiaries and non-beneficiaries. In Unnao district, four individual interviews were held in each village on similar lines. This was followed by group discussions with beneficiaries in each district. The socio-economic profile of the participants remained the same. Each group had about 10–12 elderly members. Two individual interviews were also held with the local community leader and one government official in each district.

## General Characteristics of the Respondents

All the respondents were in the age group of 60–85 years and had been receiving pension for the last 1–2 years. Most of the respondents were economically inactive; some were working intermittently in the village. Most of them had worked as agriculture wage labourers during their productive years, although some had very small agricultural plots, which in old age were either sold off to meet some emergency/social obligation or divided amongst their sons. The older people respondents were all destitute. Those living with family had income of not more than ₹1,000 per month. The average size of families in most cases was not less than six members. In Mandla district, all the respondents lived alone or with a spouse. They did not have any source of family income. They were completely dependent on the social pension for meeting basic needs. In many cases, they also reported taking loans to fulfil their basic needs. In Unnao district, some of the older people respondents were living with other family members. In the case of extended family living arrangements, the proportion of social pension ranged from 30 to 40 per cent of the total monthly family income (See Tables 3.1 and 3.2 for details).

### Quality of Life

Many respondents felt that the past was better than the existing situation as they were able to work and sustain themselves. According to some women, life was more comfortable when the husband was alive. When their husbands died, they claimed they were thrown out of the house by the sons and the land was divided amongst the sons.

**Table 3.1**

*Sample profile in Unnao district, Uttar Pradesh*

| Detail | Male N = 4 | Female N = 4 |
|---|---|---|
| Age (Years) | | |
| 60–69 | 2 | 2 |
| 70–79 | 1 | 1 |
| 80–89 | 1 | 1 |
| 90–100 | — | — |
| Economic status | | |
| Active | — | 1 |
| Not active | 4 | 3 |
| Marital status | | |
| Currently married | 2 | — |
| Widow/Widower | 2 | 4 |
| Living arrangement | | |
| Alone | 1 | 1 |
| With spouse | 2 | – |
| With family | 1 | 3 |

All the respondents had no income except the social pension.

An increase in the cost of living was also a major cause of concern for older persons. Most of them expressed inability to work due to failing health. But, some did continue to work in the village intermittently for wages and some were paid in kind. Their daily routine was mainly to do household work, some did manage the cattle and some took care of the grandchildren.

> *My quality of life has deteriorated as I do not get a pension or have regular work.*—Chamu Gaud (78-year-old male, and a non-beneficiary)
>
> *We use this amount (pension) with the amount that my son earns to run the household.*—BabuLal (83-year-old male)

The same sentiment was echoed in the focus group discussions as well. The older persons felt that the life in the past was better than the present and cited inability to work, failing health and neglect by younger people as reasons for their current predicament.

**Table 3.2**

*Sample profile of Mandla district, Madhya Pradesh*

| Details | Male N = 7 | Female N = 13 |
|---|---|---|
| Age (Years) | | |
| 60–69 | 1 | 4 |
| 70–79 | 5 | 9 |
| 80–89 | 1 | — |
| 90–100 | — | — |
| Economic status | | |
| Active | — | 1 |
| Not active | 7 | 12 |
| Marital status | | |
| Currently married | 3 | — |
| Widow/Widower | 4 | 13 |
| Living arrangement | | |
| Alone | 3 | 13 |
| With spouse | 3 | — |
| With family | 1 | — |

*The condition of the families in the village is such that nobody wants to take care of the older person. The condition is worse if the children have migrated in search of employment and the spouse is dead.*—Ganga Ram Sahu (69-year-old male)

## Use of the Pension

In Mandla district, the respondents spent approximately three-fourths of the monthly social pension on household expenditures (food and personal supplies) and one-third on health-related expenditures (health care services and medicine). All of the older persons interviewed were living alone, as it was a district with very high rate of out-migration of adults in search of wage employment and most women were widowed. Almost all the respondents had no family support or regular income of their own. So, the pension was of critical significance for them. Some of them borrowed money in advance to cover expenditures for current needs.

In Unnao district, the respondents spent two-thirds of the pension on health-related expenditures and about one-third on household expenditures (food and personal supplies). Some respondents did spend small amounts on their grandchildren as well. Many of the respondents, particularly the women from upper caste, were found to be completely dependent on the family because of cultural taboo on working of women from upper caste. The spending patterns varied depending on whether the respondent was living with the family. For those living with extended family, the pension money was coupled with the general income of the family to spend on the needs of the household. The proportion of health-related expenditures was higher in Mandla district, largely due to the extended family living arrangement. Some older persons reported spending about 5 per cent of the pension money on the education of their grandchildren and some also reported saving a portion of the pension amount for an emergency.

## Impact of the Pension

Respondents in Unnao district reported getting subsidized food grains, sugar and kerosene oil from the ration shops. Some also benefited from the Indira Awas Scheme that provided financial support to build low-cost housing. But in Mandla district, nobody received any other support except the pension amount. So, the respondents in Mandla district indicated unanimously that life had improved after the receipt of the pension. Although, they also indicated that the amount has been just enough to cover the subsistence expenses for themselves (a single person). Those living with spouse found it difficult to even meet their subsistence needs.

*Earlier I had to work to make ends meet, but after I started receiving the pension I have mental peace. Earlier I was always worried about finding wage employment.*—Ramkali (70-year-old female)

Most of the respondents reported having a poor health condition. The common ailments were deteriorating eyesight, persistent cough and joint problems. Some did mention the usefulness of pension to enable them to access basic/primary health care facilities, but some were of the view that the amount was not enough to get an effective treatment.

The respondents acknowledged the usefulness of the pension in improving their quality of life, such as maintaining their social status in the family (where applicable), ensuring dignity, lessening dependence, dealing with destitution and at times enabling them to support other family members. They indicated that the usefulness of the pension, however, was limited due to increasing cost of living and absence of any other support system.

*It has improved relations with the family as I am now able to contribute.*—Shyam Kumari (80-year-old female)

*Family members give some attention to older persons who receive the pension, though the amount is very small.*—Muliya Bai (62-year-old female).

### Impact on Lifestyle and Poverty

According to older people, community leaders and government officials, the social pension schemes provide a secure means of monthly income for older people, especially the poor and the weak. The amount, though small, proves useful for the elderly from both the districts, as it means less dependence on the family, greater dignity and confidence. It relieves them of the daily worries in old age and the need to work to arrange for daily food and necessities. In Madhya Pradesh, the socio-economic and cultural systems were such that most of the older people lived alone, hence the pension was considered extremely useful to them. Some of them also had the flexibility to work in the village in order to get payment in kind. In Uttar Pradesh, those who lived with families were able to contribute to the family, especially in cases of emergency or urgent need.

The pension plays a very important role of poverty reduction among older people in the four villages in this study. Many of the respondents reported that they would be in desperate conditions without the pension, as they would be dependent entirely on family and community for basic needs or simply going without these basic needs in the absence of the pension. Other respondents noted that the pension had improved their quality of life through greater independence in their decisions, improved status in the family and greater self-confidence.

## Status of Monitoring Groups

In Mandla district, it was found that the monitoring groups were very active during the PACS programme. Each Vridh Sangh had 20–25 members who met monthly. But, after the completion of the programme, people had noticed some inactivity and lack of interest by the members. Efforts had been made to reactivate these forums and to hold meetings at least once in two to three month period; nevertheless, some groups remained strong and were active in getting pensions for older persons. In Pipariya village, 9 applications were submitted through the groups and in Munu village, 19 new cases were taken up and accepted by the local authority. The Vridh Sangh now focuses mainly on the pension scheme, which is the dominant topic at monthly meetings.

## Need for Monitoring Groups

The participants of the focus group discussions were critical of the village administration (*Panchayat)* and its role in getting pension or other benefits for them. According to them, many deserving people could not get their names included in the official list of the BPL families in the village. The village head person (*Sarpanch*) was also criticized for not taking up matters concerning the older people in the village with any sense of urgency or priority.

*The Panchayat does not benefit older persons. The secretary of Panchayat overlooks our demand for employment. He always says that the work available is not suitable for older people.*—BilkobaiSahu (78-year-old female)

Community stakeholders also noted that the groups supported the overall pension process by providing important information to prospective beneficiaries.

*There are many problems at the level of implementation. Very few people get the pension benefit in the village. The relevant information does not percolate down to the village level.*—Former village head person (*Sarpanch*) in Pipariya

## Role of Monitoring Groups

The participants of the focus group discussions were generally appreciative of the role played by the Vridh Sangh in creating awareness about the benefits under the pension scheme and efforts made to get many older persons included in the list of beneficiaries. The participants in Unnao district also recognized the role played by the Vridh Sangh in building their capacity to interact with the district administration.

*Yes, it is good to form groups of older persons in the villages. But, the groups should be based on equality and members should be helpful.*—Fundu Das (75-year-old male)

*Now, we are no longer scared to approach the Block Development Officer or even the District Magistrate to talk with them. We put forth our problem in a united way. Now we are so confident that we can also talk to the Prime Minister!*—Shiv Charan (66-year-old male)

Those respondents who were members of the monitoring groups highlighted the contribution of the groups in facilitating the application procedure, the increased number of approvals and the availability of relevant information on the schemes and benefits. The majority were of the view that the groups could play a very constructive role in voicing the concerns of older persons at all levels. There was no variation in opinion between the two districts in terms of the role of the monitoring groups.

*Yes, the association provides timely information on the pension procedures and benefits, and also helps older people deal with the difficulties they face from time to time.*—Jagdish Ram (62-year-old male)

*I did not face any difficulty. The group helped in the application process and also in getting the benefit.*—Gyarasi Patel (78-year-old female)

## Importance of Monitoring Groups

Under the PACS programme, HelpAge India worked in Unnao and Mandla districts from the year 2005 to 2007 for advocacy of rights of older persons. Under this project, associations of older persons called Vridh Sanghs were formed at the village level and Vridh Mitra were trained to develop awareness among older persons and state and non-state actors on issues concerning older persons. The monitoring groups (Vridha Sanghs) were of recent origin in both the districts. The groups have not gained momentum to work for all the issues concerning ageing and older people's rights and entitlements in the villages. Most of them have confined their work in facilitating the pension application process.

The groups appeared to be more active and useful in Unnao district than in Mandla district, where older people complained of inactivity. Almost all older people were of the view that groups had the potential to play useful role in creating awareness and in advocating for the rights and entitlements of older people. Many of them suggested improvements, including frequent meetings, involvement of all older people in the village and facilitating travel to the block office or district headquarter's office. Monitoring groups, when active, are effective in ensuring awareness of the pension application process and support to older people in applying to the district administration. Their effectiveness, however, will vary according to the administrative capacity of the district and the number of applicants. Where there is weak administration and a large number of applicants, the monitoring groups can play a useful role in supporting the administration. Where strong administration already exists, the monitoring groups will play a less important role in awareness raising and facilitating the application process.

# Conclusion

Non-contributory pension is an effective means to tackle poverty in old age and also address related issues of social exclusion and isolation. Regular monthly income, even if meagre, goes a long way in ensuring some basic amenities for older persons in poverty-stricken families and could be a way of ensuring the dignity of the older person, in not so poor families, by allowing them to contribute to the general expenditure of the household. At the moment, the benefits of the scheme are available only to the people under BPL and until the social assistance schemes for older persons are not made universal. It is also important that the older people themselves be empowered to monitor and evaluate the efficiency of the schemes meant for providing such relief. Without control from the civil society, the scheme is likely to be ineffective and may go wrong on inclusion and exclusion, thereby diluting the objective of such a scheme. Moreover, the effort of the scheme should not only be limited to providing basic subsistence allowance to the older persons, but also giving them opportunities for participation in the process. This is one of the basic principles of the UN and also reflected in the National Policy. As stated earlier, the National Policy on Older Persons is not only limited to welfare provisions for economic well-being of older persons, it recognizes them as equal partners in the society. There, in implementing the policy, government should take steps to develop mechanisms for involvement of older persons from preparation, revision to monitoring and evaluation of the old-age benefit schemes. With the development of panchayat and municipal bodies as true representatives of the people, it should not be very difficult to do so.

# References

Barrientos, A. (2006). Cash transfers for older people reduce poverty and inequality. *Draft Background Paper-WDR 2006: Equity and Development*. Manchester: IDPM, University of Manchester.

Beveridge, W. (1942). *Social security concept given in the famous Beveridge Report for Post War welfare state*. Available at http://en.wikipedia.org/wiki/William_Beveridge.

Global Poverty Estimates. (2005). *World Poverty Estimates*. Available at: http://www.worldbank.org.in.

Guhan, S. (1992). Social security in India: Looking one step ahead. In B. Harris, S. Guhan & R.H. Cassen (Eds), *Poverty in India: Research and policy*. Oxford: Oxford University Press.

NECIWG (National Economic Council Interagency Working Group). (1998). *Women and Retirement Security. Report prepared on Social Security*. National Economic Council Interagency Working Group.

NSAP (National Social Assistance Programme). (2011). *Annual reports 2005–06, 2006–07 and 2010–11*. New Delhi: Government of India. Available at: http//: www.nsap.nic.in.

———. (2013). *Proposal for Comprehensive National Social Assistance Programme: Report of the Task Force Ministry of Rural Development*. New Delhi: Government of India.

NSS. (2006). *Morbidity, health care and condition of the aged*. NSS 60th Round National Sample Survey Organisation. New Delhi: Ministry of Statistics and Programme Implementation; Government of India.

Sankaran, T.R. (1993). *Report of working group on social security*. Available at: http://planningcommission.nic.in/aboutus/committee/wrkgrp11/wg11_rpsoc.pdf.

UN. (2006). *UN Population Division: Department of Economic Affairs. population/publications/ageing/graph.pdf* Retrieved from *http://www.un.org/esa/*

# 4

# The Rights of the Elderly and Socio-economic Security

*J. John Kattakayam*

## Introduction

A human being's life is normally divided into five main stages—infancy, childhood, adolescence, adulthood and old age. In each of these stages, an individual finds himself/herself in different situations and faces different problems. In old age, the physical strength deteriorates, mental stability diminishes, flow of money decreases and negligence from the younger generation increases. Ageing is a universal, biological fact and a natural process. The perception of age is one that is socially constructed. Isolation, exclusion and marginalization of older persons are the consequences of age discrimination. It not only undermines the status of older persons in society, but also threatens the overall development of a society. Since the traditional norms and values of the Indian society laid stress on respect and care for the aged, the aged member of the family were normally taken care of in the family itself. In recent times, the rapid socio-economic transformation has affected every aspect of traditional Indian society. Industrialization with resultant urbanization and migration of population has paved the way to settle more elderly people in old-age homes, thus departing from the joint family set-up. Technological advancement, impact of mass media and the higher degree of mobility have influenced long-established lifestyles, conventional value systems and customary place of aged and women in the society. Thus, the society is witnessing a gradual but definite withering of the joint family system, as a result of which a section of the family, primarily the elderly, is exposed to somewhat emotional neglect and a lack of physical support. In the realm of values, today's family is moving towards materialism, individualism and liberalism.

The aged population constitutes a precious reservoir of human resources gifted with the knowledge of myriad dimensions, varied experiences and deep insights. The proportion of older people in India is growing faster than any other population group. Certain strategies and approaches at different levels of policymaking, planning and programming will have to be adopted. It will help in harnessing this vast human resource for promoting their involvement and participation in socio-economic development process on a much larger scale. Social security coverage varies significantly at global level. In India, to protect and promote the elderly, social security measures are implemented and fundamental rights of elderly people have been framed. In spite of the media revolution, the majority of the elderly are yet to realize their rights and are unaware of policies and programmes. In this chapter, special policies to deal with the most disadvantaged segment of society, the elderly, are discussed and highlighted with a positive note.

# Elderly Persons in Transition

The cherished values such as respect for age, concern for elderly persons, devotion to one's duty, cooperation are now replaced by competition, neglect of the elderly and material disharmony, etc. Problems such as child neglect, behaviour problems in children, indiscipline among the youth, alcoholism and drug addiction are on the increase today, and there are indications that the family is not able to handle the changes in a desirable manner. Improvements in health care, nutritious food and socio-economic status have led to the demographic transition and increased life expectancy of the people. The number of aged persons as a proportion of the total population has increased all over the world. The rate is more in developed countries as compared with developing countries. The increasing proportion of ageing people is accompanied by a falling proportion of young persons. Presently, India has the second largest aged population in the world. India is also one of the youngest countries in the world. By 2020, the average age of an Indian will be

29 years, compared to 37 for China and 48 for Japan. But, India faces serious socio-economic challenges due to the consequent increasing aged population. Globally, the population of older persons is growing at a rate of 2.6 per cent per year, faster than the population as a whole, which is increasing at 1.2 per cent annually. Developing countries will become old before they become rich, while industrialized countries became rich before they grew old (United Nations, 2009). Elderly population has grown at a relatively much faster rate than the general population, particularly since 1951, and is likely to grow relatively faster since 2001 (Table 4.1). The decadal per cent increase in the elderly population in the period 2001–2011 is likely to be more than double the rate of increase of the general population (Census of India, 2011). The growth rate of elderly population by sex reveals a greater increase in elderly females since 1991 and it is expected to be greater further. This progressive advantage in favour of women in elderly population is primarily due to the increasingly lower mortality rates of women at middle-to-late ages compared with men. A relatively higher increase in per cent of females to males in elderly population is observed in the last four decades.

**Table 4.1**

*General population and population aged 60 years and over by sex in India*

| Period | % decadal variation of general population | | | % decadal variation of population aged 60 and over | | |
|---|---|---|---|---|---|---|
| | *Males* | *Females* | *Total* | *Males* | *Females* | *Total* |
| 1901–1911 | 6.29 | 5.41 | 5.75 | 12.4 | 6.6 | 9.2 |
| 1911–1921 | 0.13 | –0.75 | –0.31 | 4.9 | 0.2 | 2.4 |
| 1921–1931 | 11.19 | 10.6 | 11 | 7.1 | 3.7 | 5.4 |
| 1931–1941 | 14.52 | 13.92 | 14.22 | 28 | 25.9 | 27 |
| 1941–1951 | 13.34 | 13.49 | 13.31 | 8.8 | 8.7 | 8.7 |
| 1951–1961 | 21.97 | 21.29 | 21.64 | 27.8 | 24.3 | 26 |
| 1961–1971 | 25.52 | 24.03 | 24.8 | 36.6 | 28 | 32.2 |
| 1971–1981 | 24.77 | 25.25 | 24.86 | 33.3 | 35.8 | 34.5 |
| 1981–1991 | 24.31 | 23.35 | 23.87 | 30.2 | 26.4 | 28.4 |
| 1991–2001 | 19.25 | 20.3 | 21.54. | 23.7 | 26.5 | 25 |
| 2001–2011 | 15.84 | 17.1 | 17.64 | 34.9 | 36.9 | 35.9 |

*Source:* Census of India 2011.

The nuclear family system is dominating over the joint family system and the size of the family has reduced from many members to only the parents and children. The young are able to adjust to the fast-paced life and move on perfectly with it, but it is the old who are rocked due to the sudden shift from a traditional to a modern society. The old people have not only been thrown out of the mainstream, but are left with no resources and are seen as a burden by the young. Globalization and industrialization have led many young people to migrate to cities or overseas, leaving behind the old who are helpless in their homes. Thus, elderly populations are considered as a burden on the economic resources that can affect the younger generation maintaining their desired standard of living. The elderly in urban areas face fear, neglect, isolation and economic insecurity. Out of about 81 million senior citizens in India, 28 per cent elderly who live in the urban set-ups are confronted with such challenges (Menon, 2009). Their vulnerability makes them soft targets for crime. The elderly used to be more secure in the joint family system; however, this is diminishing due to the breakdown of the joint families into nuclear families. Empirically, it has been proved that despite nuclearization of families and the changing attitude and outlook of the younger generation, no institution or agency is still considered important other than the family by the old people whether residing in nuclear or joint family system. Care of the aged is perceived as the responsibility of family members (Asiya, 2010).

Presently, India faces serious socio-economic challenges due to the successively increasing aged population. This necessitates elderly specific health management to address the age-linked health problems. The government has allocated funds to provide the elderly access to the health system, socio-economic security, institutional care and homes for the destitute. In western and industrially advanced countries, pension schemes and social security system of the governments cover the economic needs of the old. However, in India, the situation is quite different. Nearly 90 per cent of the total workforce in India is employed in the informal sector. Thus, social security offered by pension schemes is available to only 10 per cent of the working population retiring from the organized sector (WSSR, 2011). Many of the older persons who do not have any social security, such as pension, have to depend on the earning of their children for their sustenance and medical expenses. It then becomes unimaginable to think of the condition of illiterate and poverty-stricken older persons. To highlight the value of elderly persons, the UN General Assembly has declared 1 October of every year as the International Day of Older Persons.

# Legal Rights and Constitutional Provisions for the Elderly

India is a land where age and wisdom are traditionally respected. Elderly people, in developing and developed countries, have complex problems in every walk of life. The existing legal provisions are not adequate to protect and promote the basic and fundamental rights of elderly people (Pandey and Misra, 2009). Once a senior citizen loses his or her possessions, he or she becomes an unwanted entity and a burden for his or her children. Over the years, the Indian government has taken several initiatives to grapple with the issue of social security for the masses. Worldwide concern for the quality of life of older people has resulted in several initiatives. The First World Assembly on Ageing in Vienna in 1982 acted as the first tangible outline to guide the policies and programmes related to older people. India, along with many other signatory countries, adopted the United Nations First International Plan of Action on Ageing. The plan emphasized the establishment of national machineries to address the humanitarian and developmental needs of older people appropriate in each culture (Prakash, 2007). The UN General Assembly on 16 December 1991 adopted 18 principles that are organized into five clusters—independence, participation, care, self-fulfilment and dignity of the older persons. The Second World Assembly on Ageing held in Madrid, (Spain) in April 2002 resulted in the adoption of a new International Plan of Action. This was the first international agreement to recognize the potential of older people to contribute towards the development of their societies and to commit governments to include ageing in all social and economic development policies.

In India, to protect elderly citizens, constitutional and legal provisions were enacted. To protect and promote the elderly, the basic and fundamental rights of elderly people were framed. For instance, elderly people should not be thought of as useless to society simply because some of them may need more care than the average person. Some of the basic fundamental rights of the elderly are: right to security, right to health care, right to an adequate standard of living, right to non-discrimination, right to participation and right to be free from torture or cruel, inhuman or degrading treatment. The principles provide a broad framework for action on ageing. Some of the principles are: (1) Older persons should have the opportunity to work and determine when to leave the workforce; (2) Older persons should remain integrated in society and participate actively in the formulation of policies that affect their well-being; (3) Older persons should have access to health care to help them maintain the optimum level of physical, mental and emotional well-being; (4) Older people should be able to pursue opportunities for the full development of their potential and have access to educational, cultural, spiritual and recreational resources of society; (5) Older persons should be able to live in dignity and security and should be free from mistreatment, mental and physical abuse (Age Concern and BIHR, 2009).

In the Constitution of India, Entry 24 in List III of Schedule VII deals with the 'Welfare of Labour' including the old-age pension, working conditions, provident funds (PFs), liability for workmen's compensation, invalidity and maternity benefits, etc. Article 41 of the Directive Principles of State Policy has specially focused on the old-age social security. Item No. 9 of the State List and items 20, 23 and 24 of the Concurrent List relate to old-age pension, social security, social insurance, economic and social planning. As per Article 41, each state within the limits of its economic capacity and development has to make effective provision for securing old-age people. Legal protection under personal laws has recognized the maintenance of parents as the moral duty. However, the position and extent of such liability vary from community to community. The statutory provision for maintenance of parents under the Hindu personal law is contained in Section 20 of the Hindu Adoption and Maintenance Act, 1956. This Act is the first personal law statute in India, which imposes an obligation on the children to maintain their parents who are financially unable to maintain themselves. Children have a duty to maintain their aged parents even under the Muslim law. The parents have a right of maintenance from their children and grandchildren who have the means, even if they are able to earn their livelihood. The Christians and Parsis have no personal laws providing for maintenance for the parents. Parents who wish to seek maintenance have to apply under the provisions of the Criminal Procedure Code. The provision for maintenance of parents was introduced for the first time in 1973, thereby inserting in Section 125, the Code of Criminal Procedure. It is a secular law that governs persons belonging to all religions and communities. Daughters, including married daughters, also have a duty to maintain their parents.

# Welfare Measures and Initiatives

The government of India has approved the National Policy for Older Persons (NPOPs) on 13 January 1999 in order to accelerate welfare measures and empower the elderly in various ways. There has been reportedly little progress in setting up a separate Bureau of Older Persons or an autonomous National Association of Older Persons, as laid down in the policy. The Ministry of Social Justice and Empowerment could not follow its mandate to make a detailed review of the progress made in the implementation of the policy after every three years. The Maintenance and Welfare of Parents and Senior Citizens Act, 2007 was enacted on 31 December 2007, which makes it a legal obligation for children and heirs to provide maintenance to senior citizens. The Act, 2007 has several financial implications for elderly parents; however, critics have pointed out that it can never be a substitute for the care given by an affectionate family member (Nayar, 2006).

## Social Security Measures

Social security refers to the action programmes of a government, intended to promote the welfare of the population through assistance, guaranteeing access to sufficient resources for food and shelter, and to promote health and well-being for the population at large and potentially vulnerable segments, such as children, the elderly, the sick and the unemployed. In India, majority of people earn barely enough to survive during their productive years and are not able to save anything for old age. The rapid population ageing has brought social change and economic transformation. In view of this, a holistic approach to population ageing has taken social, economic and cultural changes into consideration that are needed to effectively solve the emerging problems of the elderly. Based on the existing diversities in the ageing process, it may be stated that there is a need to pay greater attention to the increasing awareness on ageing issues, its socio-economic effects and to promote the development of policies and programmes for dealing with an ageing society. Decentralization and equal distribution of the social security should be the agenda of the coming plan periods for elderly population (Mishra, 2011).

## Senior Citizen Associations

A senior citizen association (SCA) is a community-based group of senior citizens, working together to improve the condition of older people and the community they live in. SCAs are enormous resource groups that can immensely benefit society. They are effective mechanisms through which older people can prepare for and respond to disasters within their communities. Senior citizens through their experience and familiarity with their communities are well placed to identify the needs and vulnerabilities of their families and neighbours, including the most vulnerable older people. They can play an important role in disaster preparedness planning. Participation in SCAs has increased confidence amongst older people, particularly older women. Involving older people in the planning processes would result in an inclusion of older people in emergency responses, thus mainstreaming ageing in disaster risk reduction plans and activities.

In India, SCAs are doing remarkable work, not only for the benefit of the older persons themselves but also for the society at large. Senior Citizens Forum, Bhopal, has successfully organized organ and body donation camps and is instrumental in setting up organ banks so that the donated organs become available to the needy in proper condition and without delay. Senior Citizens Forum in Faridabad, Haryana, contributed its efforts significantly in getting established the first ISO 9001 police station in the state. The Kerala Social Security Mission had started a toll-free helpline for senior citizens and their relatives to call in times of distress. The mission currently operates mobile clinics, attached to local body offices, for aged persons in all districts (Kurian, 2009). The Kerala Senior Citizens' Forum helps to develop social contact, share friendship and fellowship, exchange ideas and wealth of experience and expertise and minimize the severity of solitude and feelings of being neglected in the twilight years of the life.

## Health Care to the Elderly

Increasing life expectancy has added to the concerns surrounding the older population in Southeast Asia. Nearly 8 per cent of the Southeast Asian population, including India's, is above the age of 60 years (IANS, 2012). Anxiety, social security and loneliness are some problems that are increasingly affecting the elderly. Other than this, non-communicable diseases, such as cancer, diabetes and heart diseases, characterize old age in India. The National Programme for Healthcare for the Elderly (NPHCE) was introduced in the year 2010 by the Ministry of Health, with an aim to set up geriatric care centres across the country. Many of the government and public hospitals have started memory clinics and mental health programmes to facilitate proper diagnosis of dementia to enable slowing down the process and preparing the caregivers and families to manage Alzheimer's and Dementia. The National Institute of Social Defence (NISD) under the Ministry of Social Justice and Empowerment has initiated training of caregivers and functionaries as a special initiative during the Alzheimer's centenary year in 2006. Geriatric units at community, primary health centres and development of manpower (trained caregivers) are some of the highlights of the plan. This envisages training of human resource in areas such as specialization in geriatrics in medical courses, special courses on geriatric care in nursing training, training of social workers, especially for geriatric care and professional caregivers. Such trained hands will focus on dedicated health care for the elderly. Integrating psychological and social problems with non-communicable diseases of the older people will help in giving focused care services. Sri Lanka has established a National Charter for Senior Citizens and National Policy for Senior Citizens. Some of its key interventions are the Elders Maintenance Board, Care Givers programme and Elders Identity Card. Using the identity card, an elderly person in Sri Lanka can receive priority services from an array of government facilities, including government hospitals and transportation (Sri Lanka, 2002). In India, the Mediclaim policy, introduced in 1986, has remained limited to middle class, the urban tax payer segment of the population due to its high premiums. Health policy for long-term care in India has not yet been given due attention. Inadequate support systems for the care of older people would lead to a rapid increase of formal care provided by institutions, such as nursing homes, old-age homes, etc. At present, there are no social schemes or central government mechanisms for funding of health care for the ageing population. The health care of elderly population relies on the private sector, voluntary organizations and indigenous programmes. There is a need for an innovative and cost-effective health security measures for senior citizens (Aasha and Andrew, 2005).

## Social Security Cell

As per the Maintenance and Welfare of Parents and Senior Citizens Act, 2007, registration of the elderly at respective police stations is a must. A separate wing called the Social Security Cell (SSC) is mandated to be set up in every police station for the elderly. A helpline to call the police station has also been set up under the Act. It is mandatory for police officers to gather information of senior citizens living in the jurisdiction of respective police stations. Each police station sends one personnel, dressed in plain clothes, to make door-to-door visits to collect information. Personal details are ascertained, including whether they stay alone or with family, their age and where were they working. However, only people who are too old to move and who live alone have registered, whereas those who live with families do not feel the need. For instance, in Mumbai, only 3,500 elderly people are registered. The reason may be fear of misuse of the information. Apparent lack of faith in the police and lack of knowledge about the law are the two major reasons for a sparse number of senior citizens getting registered with the SSC.

## TracFone Service for the Elderly

With the meagre earnings, the elderly ignore a lot of crucial expenses, such as a cell phone that is now a vital gadget and plays a big role in the life of an individual. Since the elderly spend a lot of time at home alone, there is a necessity to have a phone for emergency purposes. The government is sponsoring free cell phones to the elderly. TracFone for the elderly is one of these programmes that are giving free cell phones to senior citizens who meet some necessary conditions. Each of the phones given to senior citizens allows them 60 free minutes of talk time on a monthly basis. In case they need more time than the allocated time, then they have to purchase prepaid minutes. The Bharat Sanchar Nigam Limited (BSNL), as part of its corporate social responsibility and

Rural Telephony project, has given free mobiles phones and SIM cards to 1,000 people belonging to below poverty line (BPL) families in two districts. Jhansi was among the two districts that were chosen for the pilot phase, the second one being Jaipur. BSNL, along with the District Rural Development Authority, distributed a prepaid lifetime SIM card with an initial talk value of about ₹100 and long battery mobile phone handsets to selected 1,000 poor people from these districts. BSNL has introduced a new 2G Special Prepaid plan for Senior Citizens (60 years and above) of the Kerala telecom circle.

## Economic Security Measures

Among the problems of the elderly in our society, economic problems occupy an important position. Mass poverty is the Indian reality and the vast majority of the families have income far below a level that would ensure a reasonable standard of living. The Ministry of Social Justice and Empowerment, Government of India (1999), in its document on the NPOPs, has specified the figure of 33 per cent of the general population below the poverty line, with one-third of the population in 60-plus age group (23 million) also being below that level. Today, people live longer and into much advanced age (say 75 years and over), so they might need more intensive and long-term care, and this in turn may increase financial stress in the family. Inadequate income is a major problem of the elderly in India (Siva Raju, 2002). The most vulnerable are those who do not own productive assets, have little or no savings or income from investments made earlier, have no pension or retirement benefits, and are not taken care of by their children or they live in families that have low and uncertain incomes and a large number of dependents. The pension is provided to the organized sector employees and is considered to be fulfilling the requirement of the largest segment of old-age security. Among pension schemes that are contributory in nature are the employees' state insurance scheme (ESIS), PF and deposit-linked insurance scheme, etc. The organized sectors constitute only 4 per cent of the workers in the country out of which the women account for just 15 per cent (Gopal, 2006). There is an inadequate focus on the gender implications of NPOPs, despite of the evidence that older women suffer

**Table 4.2**

*Financial outlay under NSAP*

| Year | Amount released in crores (₹) |
|---|---|
| 2005–2006 | 1190.00 |
| 2006–2007 | 2489.61 |
| 2007–2008 | 2889.73 |
| 2008–2009 | 4500.00 |
| 2009–2010 | 5155.60 |
| 2010–2011 | 5162.00 |
| 2011–2012 | 6658.00 |

*Source:* MRD (2012). Annual Report, Government of India.

greater vulnerability (Sujaya, 1999). There is no specific reference to women's situation under the sections on health care, nutrition, shelter and education in the policy (Paltasingh and Tyagi, 2012).

A massive programme has been charted to address the needs of the country's elderly. The National Policy for Social Assistance was set up in 1995 for the poor and it aims at ensuring minimum national standard for social assistance in addition to the benefits that states are currently providing or might provide in future. National Social Assistance Programme (NSAP) at present comprises of Indira Gandhi National Old Age Pension Scheme (IGNOAPS), Indira Gandhi National Widow Pension Scheme (IGNWPS), Indira Gandhi National Disability Pension Scheme (IGNDPS), National Family Benefit Scheme (NFBS) and Annapurna. The NSAP is a social assistance programme for the poor households and represents a significant step towards the fulfilment of the Directive Principles enshrined in Articles 41 and 42 of the Constitution of India, recognizing the concurrent responsibility of the central and state governments in the matter. The financial support under this programme has been shown in Table 4.2.

## National Old Age Pension Scheme

Countries where social security is more developed usually have a number of different pension schemes, either covering certain groups of the population or with various specific objectives (WSSR, 2011).

In India, old-age pensions have been introduced by state governments mostly for the destitute and infirm. For example, the government of Uttar Pradesh in 1957 became the first to introduce an old-age pension scheme. Since then, similar schemes have been introduced by other state governments. All state governments and union territories have their own schemes for old-age pension, and the criterion of eligibility and the quantum of pension amount vary among these states. The average old-age pension that is nearly ₹150 per month is below the average per capita income per Indian. The percentage of the elderly who benefited from the old-age pension scheme varies across states, with the minimum of 0.3 per cent to 68 per cent. The existing system of pensions that leaves more than 88 per cent of Indian workforce uncovered is unlikely to act as a social security umbrella for the ageing Indians. At present, 50 per cent of the older persons under BPL are covered under the National Old Age Pension Scheme (NOAPS). This scheme has been renamed as Indira Gandhi National Old Age Pension Scheme (IGNOPS) and was formally launched on 19 November 2007. Pension under IGNOAPS is granted to a person who is 60 years or above and belongs to a household below the poverty line. At present, old-age beneficiaries are getting between ₹200 and ₹1,000, depending on the state contribution.

## National Family Benefit Scheme

NFBS is implemented by the Ministry of Rural Development, government of India. It was transferred to the state sector scheme after 2002–2003. Prior to 2002–2003, the scheme was a central sector scheme of the government of India from August 1995. Under this scheme, social assistance benefits are given to the BPL families in case of the death of their primary breadwinner. The bereaved family gets a lump sum amount of ₹10,000. Until 2011–2012, over 36.57 lakh families have benefited under the NFBS since its inception in 1995. The proposed increase is about 37 per cent (from ₹6,158 crore in 2011–2012 to ₹8,447 crore in 2012–2013). The budget for the grant given on the death of the primary breadwinner of a BPL family in the age group 18–64 years has been proposed to be doubled from ₹10,000 to ₹20,000 under the NFBS (PIB, 2013).

## Annapurna Scheme

The Ministry of Rural Development has launched this scheme in 2000–2001. Indigent senior citizens of 65 years of age or above who are eligible for National Old Age Pension, but are not getting the pension, are covered in this scheme. Ten kilograms of rice or wheat per person per month are supplied free of cost under the scheme for the needy elderly. An amount of US$56 million was incurred and over 43.03 lakh elderly were covered in the 10th plan (2002–2007) in this scheme. From 2002–2003, it has been transferred to state plan along with the NSAP. The implementation of the scheme at the state level rests with the respective states/union territories.

It is understood from Table 4.3 that since the inception of Annapurna Scheme, in all the years, the allocation of food grains has increased year after year, whereas a lower amount of food grains was allotted for the year 2011–2012. The Planning Commission in consultation with the Ministry of Rural Development transferred the centrally sponsored schemes NSAP and Annapurna to the state plans for the year 2002–2003. Funds for these schemes are released as

**Table 4.3**

*Allocation of food grains (figures in 1,000 tons) under Annapurna Scheme in India*

| Year | Rice | Wheat | Total |
|------|------|-------|-------|
| 2001–2002 | 39 | 23 | 62 |
| 2002–2003 | 54 | 24 | 78 |
| 2003–2004 | 56 | 67 | 23 |
| 2004 2005 | 90 | 77 | 67 |
| 2005–2006 | 90 | 77 | 67 |
| 2005–2006 | 90 | 77 | 67 |
| 2007–2008 | 92 | 77 | 69 |
| 2008–2009 | 92 | 77 | 69 |
| 2009–2010 | 61 | 34 | 95 |
| 2010–2011 | 81 | 34 | 115 |
| 2011–2012 | 50 | 24 | 74 |

*Source:* Ministry of Consumer Affairs, Food and Public Distribution, Govt of India.

**Table 4.4**

Beneficiaries covered under National Social Assistance Programme

| Year | No. of beneficiaries covered NOAPS/IGNOAPS | NFBS | Annapurna |
|------|------|------|------|
| 2002–2003 | 7,471,509 | 85,209 | 796,682 |
| 2003–2004 | 6,534,000 | 209,456 | 958,669 |
| 2004–2005 | 8,079,386 | 261,981 | 850,768 |
| 2005–2006 | 8,002,561 | 272,828 | 857,079 |
| 2006–2007 | 8,645,371 | 171,232 | 750,319 |
| 2007–2008 | 11,514,026 | 334,168 | 1,076,210 |
| 2008–2009 | 15,483,836 | 395,460 | 883,232 |
| 2009–2010 | 16,333,578 | 343,726 | 1,015,655 |
| 2010–2011 | 16,929,408 | 228,380 | 963,689 |
| 2011–2012 | 19,029,604 | 360,585 | 769,045 |

Source: MRD. (2012). Annual Report, Government of India.
NOAPS – National Old Age Pension Scheme
IGNOAPS – Indira Gandhi National Old Age Pension Scheme
NFBS – National Family Benefit Scheme

additional central assistance. Table 4.4 depicts the number of elderly benefited under NOAPS, NFBS and Annapurna Scheme in India in the past 10 years.

## Integrated Programme for Older Persons

This programme includes some scheme for the elderly welfare. For instance, this scheme provides financial assistance to non-governmental organizations (NGOs) to establish and manage old-age homes, day care centres, mobile medicare units and to provide non-institutional services to older persons. The scheme also works towards other needs of older persons, such as reinforcing and strengthening the family, generation of awareness on related issues and facilitating productive ageing. Such endeavours of the state governments, if implemented effectively, would no doubt help elderly persons to lead a respectable life. The programme aims at enabling senior citizens to assume an active role in maintaining and improving their own health, besides encouraging others to do the same. The facilities, such as old-age homes and caregiving facilities, to senior citizens are mainly centred in the urban areas. However, in rural societies, the older men/women are largely deprived of such facilities.

Longevity is a most challenging, positive, demographic phenomenon of this era. More than at any other time in history, the world's population is living longer. Increase in life expectancy involves many other associated changes. Many of today's grandparents are mobile and active, which is a positive sign of progress and a reason to rejoice. Among the other developing countries, India is moving ahead to safeguard and protect the best interest of older persons through central legislation. Such provisions are ensured through care and protection of older persons within the family and early settlement of maintenance claims through a tribunal. The Indian government has also assured that efforts to prevent destitution would be made by having enough institutional facilities and provisions of old-age homes, covering all the districts to ensure facility to accommodate 150 needy elderly in each of them. The Department of Pensions has set up a pension portal to enable senior citizens to get information regarding the status of their application, the amount of pension, documents required, if any, etc. The department has also provided additional pension as per the recommendation of the Sixth Pay Commission (20% for 80+, 30% for 85+, 40% for 90+, 50% for 95+ and 100% for 100+). The Ministry of Health and Family Welfare stipulates (1) separate queues for older persons in government hospitals; (2) geriatric clinic in several government hospitals and (3) implemented NPHCE from 2010–11. 'Agewell Foundation' has been set up to seek the opinion of the aged on measures to make life easier for them, quicker settlement of pension, PF, gratuity, etc. in order to save the superannuated persons from any hardships. According to Sections 88-B, 88-D and 88-DDB of Income Tax Act, there are discounts on tax for elderly persons. New provisions have been introduced so that the public distribution system would reach out to cover all senior citizens living below the poverty line. Taxation policies are reflecting sensitivity to the financial problems of senior citizens that accelerate due to very high costs of medical and nursing care, transportation and support services needed at homes. Schematic and non-schematic items proposed for the 12th Plan includes revision of the scheme of Integrated Programme for Older Persons (IPOP) and strengthening of the NISD, setting up National Centre of Excellence to look into Dementia-related ailments, setting up National Helpline for Older Persons, protection of life and property and sensitization about the needs and rights of the elderly. World Health Organization has warned India that it is witnessing a greying population and it will face serious problems in tackling Dementia-related ailments (Sinha, 2012). The government of India has begun to realize the extent of the situation and the need to establish dementia-sensitive services. In the next few years, the establishment of the National Institute of Ageing, special provisions for people with dementia in the National Policy for Older People and the National Mental Health Programme are expected to address the problem in a better way. Government should include awareness generation and provision of basic facilities for the older people, especially among the rural elderly. The national policies need to be implemented with more seriousness. The ageing issues should be mainstreamed into national development frameworks and poverty reduction strategies. More databases are urgently needed to support policy formulation and effective implementation of existing programmes.

# Suggestions and Conclusion

Various social security measures can be suggested and implemented by the Indian Government. These include the provision of setting up a pension fund for ensuring security for the persons working in the unorganized sector; construction of old-age homes and day care centres for every three to four districts; establishment of resource centres and re-employment bureaus for elderly people; concessional rail/air fares for travel within and between cities; enacting legislation for ensuring compulsory geriatric care in all the public hospitals; sensitizing school children to live and work with the elderly; more round-the-clock helplines to discourage social exclusion of the older persons; National Council for Older Person, providing several insurance schemes for the benefit of aged persons, that is, Jeevan Dhara Yojana, Jeevan AkshayYojana, Senior Citizen Unit Yojana, Medical Insurance Yojana by the Life Insurance Corporation of India (LIC); allocating 10 per cent of the houses constructed under government schemes for the rural elderly; provision of separate queues for older persons in all government hospitals and geriatric clinic; new policy provisions for the public distribution system to reach out to cover all senior citizens living below the poverty line and offering loans at reasonable rates of interest to senior citizens to start small businesses and to support with microfinance for senior citizens through suitable guidelines issued by the Reserve Bank of India. The need of the hour is to spread awareness and timely supply of proper information on social security schemes and the rights of the elderly. There is little awareness of senior rights despite five years having gone by since the Maintenance and Welfare of Parents and Senior Citizens' Act, 2007, was implemented. It is also two years since special tribunals were set up to deal with disputes related to senior citizens. Helplines should be initiated and all major services need to be made available to them under one roof, so they need not to run from pillar to post.

Old-age homes are not the best or the only solution for the problem of indigent elderly because till date, old-age homes are not as culturally acceptable in India as it is in the West. The beneficiaries among the older persons of various schemes and programmes initiated by the government are very insignificant when compared to the enormous size and growth rate of this population. Elderly people need to have some level of awareness, willingness and support to access help and utilize existing programmes. The NGOs have a role to play in creating awareness among people. SCAs have to be formed actively and should function aggressively so that they can help people who would like to approach tribunals for redressal. The elderly have to be motivated to register under the SSC, wherever they have been set up. The NGOs can build small enterprises for the elderly, thereby keeping them occupied and helping them earn a living. Smaller libraries can be started in the neighbourhoods for them to have a place to read and enjoy their retired lives, as senior citizens are the pillars of our society. To place in context the public spending in the country without prejudicing any other cause, when millions of dollars are spent in restoring heritage buildings, archaeological expeditions and museums, why cannot we work with more zeal to protect the elderly, as their knowledge and wisdom is a treasure for us and our country.

# References

Aasha, K.M. & Andrew, S. (Eds). (2005). *Chronic poverty and development policy in India.* New Delhi: SAGE Publications.

Age Concern & BIHR. (2009). *Older people and human rights—Research and mapping report.* Joint Report of Age Concern England and British Institute of Human Rights

Asiya, N. (2010). Family in transition and challenges for elderly persons. *Indian Journal of Gerontology, 24*(4), 501–508

Census of India. (2011). Provisional Tables. New Delhi: Office of Registrar General and Census Commissioner, Ministry of Home Affairs.

Gopal, M. (2006). Gender, ageing and social security. *Economic and Political Weekly, 41*(42), 4477–4486.

IANS. (2012). World Health Day: Sedentary lifestyles affecting health of India's elderly. Available at: *http://indiatoday.intoday.in/story/world-health-day*.

Indira, J.P. (2007). Maintenance and welfare of parents and senior citizens bill, 2007: Some reflections. *Helpage India–Research and Development Journal, 13*(3), 5–9.

Kurian, S. (2009, September 25). *Tribunals to aid helpless parents.* Available at: http://www.hindu.com.

Menon, A.R. (2009, August). Soft targets. *Harmony,* 22–29.

Mishra, S.V. (2011). The elderly dependents in India: A critical review. *The Indian Journal of Spatial Science, 2*(2). Retrieved from http://www.indiansss.org/pdf/pdfset-5/issueset-7/Art_013.pdf

MRD. (2012). *Annual report.* New Delhi: Ministry of Rural Development, Government of India.

Nayar, P.K.B. (2006). Older Persons Maintenance, Care and Protection. Bill 2005—A critical review. *Helpage India—Research and Development Journal, 12*(11), 5–13.

Paltasingh T. & Tyagi R. (2012). Demographic transition and population ageing: Building an inclusive culture. *Social Change, 42*(3), 391–409.

Pandey, P.K. & Misra, P. (2009). Legal protection of elderly persons in India: An overview. *Vidhigya: The Journal of Legal Awareness, 4*(1): 49–53.

Prakash, I.J. (2007). Psychological issues in ageism and its prevention. *Indian Journal of Gerontology, 21*(2): 206–215.

Press Information Bureau—PIB. (2013). Government of India. Available at: http://pib.nic.in/newsite/erelease.aspx?relid=81066.

Sinha, K. (2012, April 12). Dementia cases worldwide will triple by 2050: WHO. *TNN.*

Siva Raju, S. (2002). Meeting the needs of the poor and excluded in India, situation and voices, the older poor and excluded in South Africa and India, UNFPA. *Population and Development Strategies, 2*: 93–110.

Sri Lanka. (2002). Sri Lanka: Statement at the Second World Assembly on Ageing.

Sujaya, C.P. (1999). Some comments on national policy on older persons. *Economic and Political Weekly, 34*(4): 72–74.

United Nations. (2009, December). *World population ageing* (Working Paper No. ESA/P/WP/212). New York: Department of Economic and Social Affairs Population Division.

WSSR. (2011). *World social security report 2010/11: Providing coverage in times of crisis and beyond.* Geneva: International Labour Office.

# Section III

# Health Issues: Dimensions and Strategies

# 5

# Social Context and the Health Status of Older Adults in India

*Sanjeev Bakshi and Prasanta Pathak*

## Introduction

Enhanced life expectancies are one of the characteristic features of an ageing population, resulting in a steadily increasing number and proportion of older adults in the population. However, this process poses a challenge to the quality of life (Walker and Mollenkopf, 2007) in the years that are added to the latter domain of lifespan. Health, an indispensable integrant of the quality of life, is no exception. The state of physical health is defined in terms of the count of chronic diseases and the count of impairments suffered by an older adult. A conceptual framework consisting of the socio–economic and cultural factors, that are relevant to the life of older adults, is proposed to model the association between the physical health and the socio–economic and cultural factors. An inclusive definition of health is given by the World Health Organization (WHO) as 'a state of complete physical, mental, and social well-being and not merely the absence of diseases and infirmities' (WHO, 1978). Thus, morbidity, disability, self-rated health and mental health may be regarded as different aspects of health (Deeg, 2007). Morbidities, both chronic and acute, and impairments, that lead to various kinds of disabilities, may be classified among the physical aspects of the health. The life expectancy at birth is a measure of the overall health conditions in a population. For that reason, it is considered as one of the indicators of human development (UNDP, 2012). The disease-free life expectancy and the disability-free life expectancy are other measures of health conditions in a population that are relevant in the context of ageing. The higher the value of these measures of health, the healthier is the population. However, these measures are aggregate measures, defined at a macro level. For an individual, the state of being disease free and impairment free is indispensable for achieving sound physical health.

The importance of sound health cannot be denied, as it is pivotal for all day-to-day activities. The process of ageing of populations is concerned with the perspective of the state of health (Lloyd-Sherlock, 2000) of the older adults. As this segment of the population starts occupying more and more demographic space, the issues related to older adults occupy prominence among the issues concerning a society. India has an ageing population and the state of health of the older adult demands due attention. In the year 1901, the life expectancy at birth was 22.5 years for males and 23.3 years for females. Estimates from the 2011 census, for the same, are 67.3 years for males and 69.6 years for females for the period 2011–2015 (Registrar General and Census Commissioner, India, 2011). Citing from earlier studies (Sharma and Agarwal, 1996; Satyanarayana and Medappa, 1997), Prakash (2003) has pointed that 'the progress India has made in extending the lifespan of its citizens has not been carried over to provide a healthy and disability-free old age.' In a study based on the National Sample Survey data, Alam and Karan (2011) emphasize that the proportion of older adults living in pain and without access to health facilities is growing in India. In addition to this, the older adults in India carry 'double disease burden' of degenerative and infectious diseases (Kumar, 2003).

Although biological processes are responsible for the state of health, nevertheless, the pathways to ill health can be traced to socio-economic factors (Link and Phelan, 1995). This means that health is associated with the socio-economic environment. This association has been investigated in various cultural settings across the globe. Studies conducted for the non-older adult populations (Kadushin, 1964; Antonovsky, 1967; Kitagawa and Hauser, 1973; Fox, 1989; Mackenbach et al., 1997) affirm this association. Affirmation of such an association for the older adults can be seen in various studies conducted in China, South East Asia and the developed world (Backlund, Sorlie and Johnson, 1996; Smith and Kington, 1997; Berkman and Gurland, 1998; Cambois, Robine and Hayward, 2001; Zimmer and Amornsirisomboon, 2001; Grundy and Sloggett, 2002; Huisman, Kunst and Mackenbach, 2003;

Zimmer, Martin and Li, 2003; Zimmer and House, 2003; von dem, Olaf, Cockerham and Siegrist, 2003; Hayward and Gorman, 2004; Kaneda, Zimmer and Tang, 2004; Zimmer, Chayovan, Lin and Natividad, 2004; Zimmer and Kwomg, 2004; Beydoun and Poplin, 2005; Matthews, Smith, Hamock, Jagger and Spiers, 2005; Matthews, Jogger and Harcock, 2006; Zimmer, 2008).

Studies from India, conducted in the districts of the state of Tamilnadu (Audinarayana, 2005; Audinarayana, 2012), the metropolitan cities, namely, Mumbai (Siva Raju, 2002; Chattopadhyay and Roy, 2005) and New Delhi (Alam, 2006), also point to the interplay of socio-economic environment and health. Similar results for the self-perceived health have been reported in the studies conducted by Sudha, Suchindran, Mutran, Irudaya Rajan and Sarma (2006) and Husain and Ghosh (2010). Prakash (2003) has given an exhaustive account of various studies conducted in India in the context of morbidity and disability among older adults. Still, the extent of this interplay is to be investigated on a countrywide scale, especially for the chronic diseases and impairments. This chapter is an attempt to investigate this interplay for the Indian socio-economic environment and health of older adults. The socio-economic environment of older adults is comprised of various factors relevant to the life of older adults. For example, these factors may include the marital status, the living arrangements and the financial dependency, to name a few. Further, one needs to distinguish between the economic status of the household an older adult belongs to and financial dependence of an older adult. This distinction has rarely been made in the literature. This chapter incorporates these aspects into the proposed model for health.

## Conceptual Framework

As mentioned earlier, for an individual, the state of being disease free and impairment free defines good physical health. Thus, the number of acute and chronic morbidities suffered by an individual and the number of impairments suffered by an individual can serve as indicators of the physical aspects of health; in this chapter, these are visualized as the burden of diseases and the burden of impairments, respectively. The socio-economic and cultural factors can be viewed as various kinds of exposures that older adults get subjected to during their lifetime. Moreover, the population of older adults is heterogeneous with respect to the socio-economic and cultural aspects. The differentials in the socio-economic and cultural aspects may correspond to the differentials in the health of older adults. However, if such an association is confirmed, it may be possible to control and ameliorate some of these factors that shape the health at older ages. This, in effect, may ensure sound health and thus healthy ageing.

The conceptual framework used in this chapter rests partly on the framework outlined in the final report of the WHO Commission on the Social Determinants of Health (WHO, 2007; Kelly et al., 2009). In brief, the framework consists of three levels of factors that influence health and health differentials in a society. These three levels are, namely, the socio-economic and political context (policies at the national and international level), structural determinants of health inequities (income, education, occupation, social class, race/ethnicity and sex) and the intermediary determinants of health (material, psychosocial, behavioural and biological, health system, etc.). These variables operate at the micro/individual level, the semi-macro/household level and macro level. This chapter shall study the association between health and structural determinants of health only, as the information on intermediary variables is not available and the effect of socio-economic and political environment will be similar for all the older adults in a country.

The variables, namely, income, education, occupation, social class, race/ethnicity and sex describe the socio-economic position of an individual. The variables, social class and race/ethnicity, which form a part of the WHO framework, are not included, as they are not relevant to the Indian older adult population. However, this chapter adds marital status, age, living arrangements, caste and religion to the list of structural determinants, as they are relevant in the social context of the older adults in India. The variables used in this chapter are discussed in the next section.

# Data and Methods

This chapter is based on a countrywide representative sample of 29,420 older adults, which was collected as a part of the 60th round of the National Sample Survey. The 60th round of the National Sample

Survey, conducted during 2004, provides rich information on diseases, impairments, self-rated health and health-seeking behaviour of older adults (National Sample Survey Organisation, 2006). All the persons aged 60 years or more constitute the population of older adults. The data provide information on 38 diseases, namely, diarrhoea/dysentery, diabetes mellitus, gastritis/gastric or peptic ulcer, under-nutrition, worm infestation, anaemia, amoebiosis, sexually transmitted diseases, hepatitis/jaundice, malaria, heart disease, eruptive, hypertension, mumps, respiratory diseases, diphtheria, tuberculosis, whooping cough, bronchial asthma, fever of unknown origin, disorders of joints and bones, tetanus, diseases of kidney/urinary system, filariasis/elephantiasis, prostatic disorders, gynaecological disorders, neurological disorders, psychiatric disorders, conjunctivitis, diseases of mouth/teeth/gum, glaucoma, accidents/injuries/burns/fractures/poisoning, cataract, cancer and other tumours, diseases of skin, other diagnosed ailments, goitre and other undiagnosed ailments. Information on sensory impairments, namely, locomotor, visual including blindness (excluding cataract), speech and hearing are also provided. It also provides rich details pertaining to the socio-economic and cultural aspects of the older adults. For the purpose of this chapter, all the observations are weighted to make them representative of the older adult population.

As mentioned earlier, the burden of diseases and the burden of impairments for older adults are respectively defined as the count of chronic diseases and the count of impairments reported by an older adult. These definitions are based on the assumption that all the chronic diseases/impairments considered in the chapter are equally harmful as far as maintenance of sound health is concerned. Thus, a count of '$n$' chronic diseases/impairments means a state of severity '$n$', irrespective of the nature and type of chronic diseases/impairments. Further, to keep the things simple, it is assumed that all the diseases/impairments occur independently of each other. Thus, the difference in severity for the counts '$n$' and '$n+1$' is same as the difference in severity of the counts '$n+1$' and '$n+2$'. Further, appearance of a chronic disease/impairment in an older adult is a random event that takes place in response to various socio-economic and cultural exposures. Thus, the count of diseases and the count of impairments are random variables. The conditional distribution of the count of chronic diseases/impairments conditioned on the age has been verified to follow a Poisson probability model for the given data. For this reason, this chapter proposes Poisson regression model for modelling association of the count of chronic diseases and impairments with the socio-economic and cultural factors. As indicated earlier, the age, gender, marital status, financial dependence, level of education, the living arrangements, household economic condition, place of residence, caste and the religion form the set of independent variable in the above-mentioned regression models.

Economic well-being of a household is reflected in the per capita monthly expenditure (PCME) of the household. The quintiles for the PCME are used to group the households into five economic strata to be called as first, second, third, fourth and fifth quintiles in the order of ascending economic affluence. These quintiles are formed separately for the rural and the urban areas, as the distribution patterns of expenditure are different in the two places of residence. The health of older adults in the fifth quintile shall be considered as a reference for comparing the health status in the rest of the quintiles. Irrespective of the state of economic affluence of a household, the older adult residing in the household may be dependent financially on others for his/her day to day needs. Therefore, the financial condition of an older adult may be classified into one of the three states, namely, dependent, partially dependent or independent. Out of these three states of financial dependence, the latter one makes an older adult least constrained with respect to financial resources. Thus, health in this state may serve as a reference for comparing the health in the rest of the states.

Health-seeking behaviour of an older adult is guided by his/her level of awareness regarding health. It is opined that the more the level of education, the more is the awareness regarding health. Therefore, education is included as an explanatory variable. The variable is categorical here with three categories, namely, 'illiterate', 'literate but below 10 years of schooling' and '10 or more years of education.' The last category may serve as a reference to compare the health status in the other two categories. The risk of losing a spouse looms large at the older ages. In the Indian society, remarriage/marriage at older ages is rare. Therefore, being widowed can be seen as the future transition state of the married older adults. Further, a small number of older adults never got married or are divorced or got separated from their spouse due to some reason. In this chapter, the marital status of this minority shall be called 'others'. The other two categories of marital status are 'currently married' and 'widowed'. Losing spouse may push an older adult into social neglect. This may affect his/her overall health. Therefore, in this chapter, the interest lies in comparing the health of the widowed with reference to the health of currently married older adults.

Another important aspect of the socio-economic life of older adults is their living arrangements. Living arrangements indicate how older adults live surrounded by other household members in the shared living space. There are basically two types of living arrangements, namely, alone and co-residence. Staying alone or with spouse only is called 'alone', otherwise it is called 'co-residence'. The cultural factors relevant to the Indian scenario are the caste and the religion. Castes are social groups classified as the scheduled castes (SCs), the scheduled tribes (STs) and the rest of the population to be called as the general castes. Due to the socially disadvantageous position of SCs and STs, this chapter intends to compare the health status of older adults belonging to these categories with respect to the health status of those belonging to the category 'general castes'. The religious categories considered in this chapter are Christians, Muslims (the major minority religious groups in India) and the rest of the religious group that serve as a reference. It is of prime importance to study the effect of increasing age on the health of older adults. Hence, this chapter includes age along with the socio-economic and cultural factors as an explanatory variable.

Two Poisson regression models are compared for each of the aspects of physical health, namely, the burden of chronic diseases and the burden of impairments. Model-I includes only the age as a covariate, while Model-II includes the socio-economic and cultural factors along with the age as covariates. The latter model is of prime interest for this chapter. Model-I serves as a comparison to assess the gain in the predictive power of the Model-II. To assess the fit of the models, the chi-square test is applied and deviance $R^2$ is calculated. The analyses were carried out with the help of the SPSS software.

# Findings

This chapter is based on a nationally representative sample of 29,102 older adults. Out of these, 77 per cent of the respondents reside in rural areas. The sex ratio is 985.40. The mean age of older adults is 67.07 years. More than 66 per cent of older adults are illiterate. 61.3 per cent are reported to be married and 83.4 per cent are co-residents. Only 33.7 per cent are financially independent. Characteristics of the sample by gender are shown in Table 5.1. An overview of the dependence of the burden of chronic diseases and the burden of impairments on age

**Table 5.1**

*Characteristics of the sample by gender (expressed as a percentage of the total frequency)*

| Sample size | Older males | Older females |
|---|---|---|
|  | 14,918 | 14,178 |
| *Marital status* |  |  |
| Never married/divorced/separated | 0.7 | 0.8 |
| Widowed | 17.7 | 59.2 |
| Currently married | 81.6 | 40.8 |
| *Financial dependence* |  |  |
| dependent | 32 | 74.2 |
| Partially dependent | 15.5 | 11.8 |
| Independent | 52.5 | 14 |
| *Level of education* |  |  |
| illiterate | 50.4 | 81.3 |
| Less than 10 years of schooling | 35.9 | 15.5 |
| 10 or more years of education | 13.8 | 3.2 |
| *Living arrangements* |  |  |
| Alone | 16.9 | 15.3 |
| Co-residence | 83.1 | 84.7 |
| *Place of residence* |  |  |
| Rural | 76.5 | 75.1 |
| Urban | 23.3 | 24.9 |
| *Caste* |  |  |
| Scheduled tribes | 6.6 | 6.2 |
| Scheduled caste | 17.5 | 17.1 |
| General castes | 75.9 | 76.7 |
| *Religion* |  |  |
| Christianity | 2.5 | 2.8 |
| Islam | 9.5 | 9.3 |
| Rest | 88 | 87.9 |

is shown in Figures 5.1 and 5.2, respectively. Both the indicators of ill health show a rise with increasing age.

Similar results in different categories of the independent variables are shown in Figures 5.3 and 5.4. The burden of chronic diseases

**Figure 5.1**

*Average number of chronic diseases among older adults in India by age*

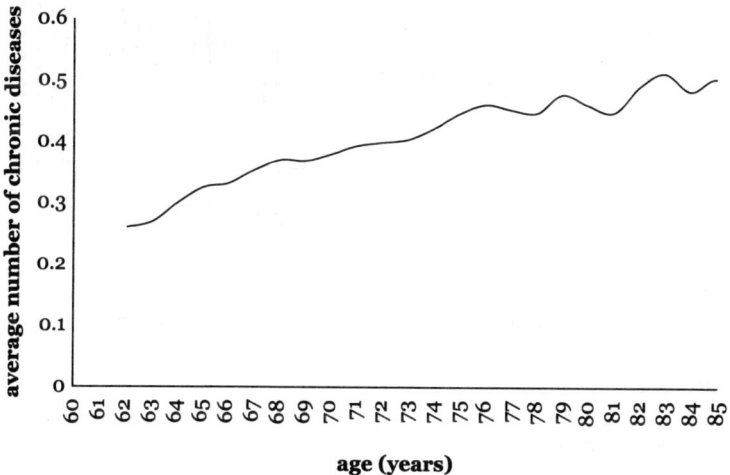

**Figure 5.2**

*Average number of impairments among older adults in India by age*

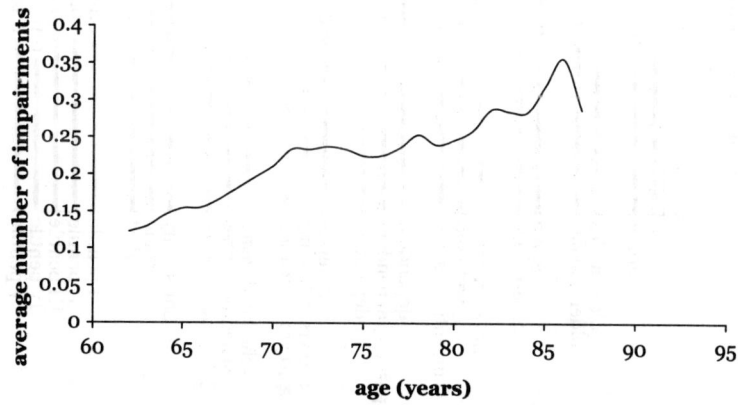

**Figure 5.3**

*Average number of chronic diseases reported by the older adults for various socio-economic and cultural characteristics*

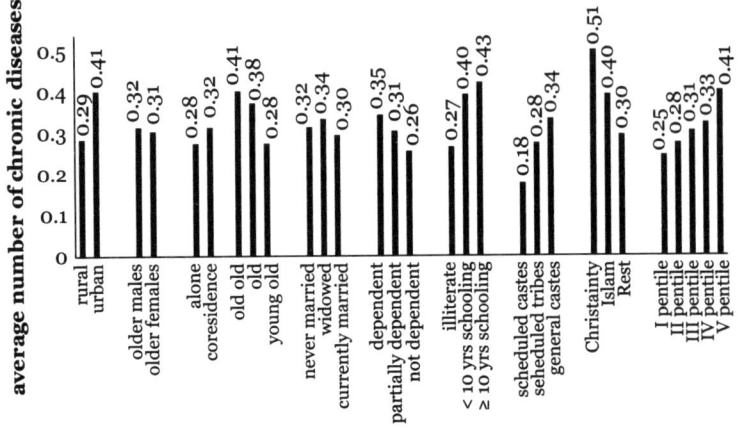

**Figure 5.4**

*Average number of impairments reported by the older adults for various socio-economic and cultural characteristics*

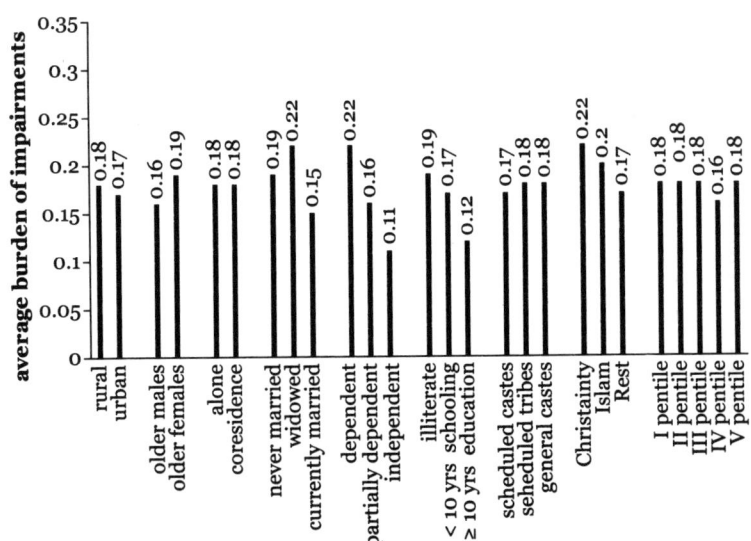

show highest prevalence rates for the urban, the older males, the co-resident, the widowed, the financially dependent, those having more than 10 years of education, the general castes, those belonging to the religious group Christians and those belonging to the most affluent households. Similarly, the burden of chronic impairments shows the highest prevalence rates for the rural, the older females, the widowed, the financially dependent, the illiterates and those belonging to the religious group Christians.

The Poisson regression model incorporates all these factors simultaneously. The effect of each of the significant socio-economic and cultural factors on the expected count of chronic diseases/impairments (called the expected count hereafter) for older adults is discussed below, while controlling for the rest of the regressors.

## Burden of Chronic Diseases

The expected count increases by 2 per cent per year with an increase in the age of older adults. With an expected count 9 per cent more, the older males are found to be more prone to chronic diseases when compared to the older females. Similarly, the widowed have an expected count 8 per cent more than the currently married ones. The financial situation also takes a toll on the health of older adults. It is evident from Table 5.2 that the dependent and the partially dependent older adults report 50 per cent and 29 per cent more chronic diseases when compared to the financially independent older adults.

The illiterates have 31 per cent lesser expected count when compared to the older adults having 10 or more years of education. The older adults living 'alone' have 7 per cent lesser expected count when compared to older adults living in 'co-residence' kind of living arrangements. As one moves from the highest stratum of economic affluence to the strata of lower economic affluence in the descending order, the expected count falls by 36 per cent, 27 per cent, 20 per cent and 15 per cent. The older adults residing in rural areas are less prone to chronic diseases, as their expected count is 21 per cent lower than the older adults residing in the urban areas. The differentials in health are also reflected in cultural factors, namely, caste and religion. The expected count for the older adults belonging to the scheduled tribes is 28 per cent lesser than that of the older adults belonging to

**Table 5.2**

*Parameter estimates for Poisson Regression of the burden of chronic diseases for the older adults in India*

| Variables | Model-I Effect (b) (p-value) | $e^b$ | 95% C.I. for $e^b$ | Model-II Effect (b) (p-value) | $e^b$ | 95% C.I. for $e^b$ |
|---|---|---|---|---|---|---|
| Intercept | −3.17(0.00) | 0.04 | (0.03, 0.05) | −2.27 (0.00) | 0.1 | (0.08, 0.13) |
| Age | 0.03(0.00) | 1.03 | (1.03, 1.03) | 0.02(0.00) | 1.02 | (1.02,1.02) |
| *Gender* | | | | | | |
| Male | | | | 0.09(0.00) | 1.09 | (1.04, 1.15) |
| Female® | | | | | | |
| *Marital status* | | | | | | |
| Never married/ divorced/separated | | | | 0.02(0.90) | 1.02 | (0.80, 1.30) |
| Widowed | | | | 0.08(0.00) | 1.08 | (1.03, 1.14) |
| Currently married® | | | | | | |
| *Financial dependence* | | | | | | |
| Dependent | | | | 0.41(0.00) | 1.5 | (1.42, 1.59) |
| Partially dependent | | | | 0.25(0.00) | 1.29 | (1.20, 1.38) |
| Independent® | | | | | | |
| *Level of education* | | | | | | |
| Illiterate | | | | −0.37(0.00) | 0.69 | (0.64,0.76) |
| Less than 10 years of schooling | | | | −0.05(0.20) | 0.95 | (0.88,1.03) |
| 10 or more years of education® | | | | | | |
| *Living arrangements* | | | | | | |
| Alone | | | | −0.08(0.02) | 0.93 | (0.87,0.99) |
| Co-residence® | | | | | | |
| *Household economic condition* | | | | | | |
| first quintile | | | | −0.44(0.00) | 0.64 | (0.60,0.69) |
| Second quintile | | | | −0.31(0.00) | 0.73 | (0.68,0.78) |
| Third quintile | | | | −0.23(0.00) | 0.8 | (0.75,0.85) |
| Fourth quintile | | | | −0.16(0.00) | 0.85 | (0.80,0.91) |
| Fifth quintile® | | | | | | |

*(Table 5.2 Continued)*

*(Table 5.2 Continued)*

| Variables | Model-I Effect (b) (p-value) | $e^b$ | 95% C.I. for $e^b$ | Model-II Effect (b) (p-value) | $e^b$ | 95% C.I. for $e^b$ |
|---|---|---|---|---|---|---|
| *Place of residence* | | | | | | |
| Rural | | | | −0.23(0.00) | 0.79 | (0.75,0.84) |
| Urban® | | | | | | |
| *Caste* | | | | | | |
| Scheduled tribes | | | | −0.33(0.00) | 0.72 | (0.64,0.81) |
| Scheduled caste | | | | 0.03(0.39) | 1.03 | (0.97,1.09) |
| General castes® | | | | | | |
| *Religion* | | | | | | |
| Christianity | | | | 0.30(0.00) | 1.35 | (1.22,1.51) |
| Islam | | | | 0.32(0.00) | 1.37 | (1.28,1.47) |
| Rest ® | | | | | | |
| Model $\chi^2$ (d.f.) | 325.25 (1) | | | 1302.44 (18) | | |
| (p-value) | 0.00 | | | 0.00 | | |
| Deviance $R^2$ | 0.01 | | | 0.05 | | |

*Note:* ®denotes the reference category.

the general castes. Similarly, the older adults belonging to the religious communities, namely, Christianity and Islam are found to have 35 per cent and 37 per cent higher expected count when compared to the older adults belonging to the rest of the religious community.

## Burden of Impairments

Similar to the findings for the burden of chronic diseases, the socio-economic and cultural factors are found to be associated with this aspect of physical health also. However, unlike the former case, a fewer number of socio-economic and cultural factors show significant association with the burden of impairments. These factors are the age, the marital status, the financial dependence, the education, the living arrangements and religion (Table 5.3).

The widowed older adults have an excess of 9 per cent of the expected count when compared to the currently married older adults. Being

**Table 5.3**

*Parameter estimates for Poisson Regression of the burden of impairments for the older adults in India*

| Variables | Model-I Effect (b) (p-value) | $e^b$ | 95% C.I. for $e^b$ | Model-II Effect (b) (p-value) | $e^b$ | 95% C.I. for $e^b$ |
|---|---|---|---|---|---|---|
| Intercept | −4.98(0.00) | 0.01 | (0.01, 0.01) | −5.12(0.00) | 0.01 | (0.00, 0.01) |
| Age | 0.05(0.00) | 1.05 | (1.04, 1.05) | 0.04(0.00) | 1.04 | (1.04, 1.05) |
| *Gender* | | | | | | |
| Male | | | | 0.05(0.17) | 1.05 | (0.98, 1.13) |
| Female® | | | | | | |
| *Marital status* | | | | | | |
| Never married/ divorced/separated | | | | 0.03(0.84) | 1.03 | (0.74, 1.44) |
| Widowed | | | | 0.18(0.00) | 1.19 | (1.12, 1.27) |
| Currently married® | | | | | | |
| *Financial dependence* | | | | | | |
| Dependent | | | | 0.50(0.00) | 1.65 | (1.52, 1.79) |
| Partially dependent | | | | 0.31(0.00) | 1.36 | (1.23, 1.51) |
| Independent® | | | | | | |
| *Level of education* | | | | | | |
| Illiterate | | | | 0.20(0.01) | 1.23 | (1.06, 1.42) |
| Less than 10 years of schooling | | | | 0.21(0.00) | 1.23 | (1.07, 1.42) |
| 10 or more years of education® | | | | | | |
| *Living arrangements* | | | | | | |
| Alone | | | | 0.23(0.00) | 1.26 | (1.17, 1.37) |
| Co-residence® | | | | | | |
| *Household economic condition* | | | | | | |
| First quintile | | | | −0.07(0.15) | 0.93 | (0.85, 1.03) |
| Second quintile | | | | −0.05(0.34) | 0.96 | (0.87, 1.05) |
| Third quintile | | | | −0.01(0.87) | 0.99 | (0.91, 1.08) |
| Fourth quintile | | | | −0.10(0.03) | 0.9 | (0.82, 0.99) |
| Fifth quintile® | | | | | | |

*(Table 5.3 Continued)*

*(Table 5.3 Continued)*

| Variables | Model-I Effect (b) (p-value) | $e^b$ | 95% C.I. for $e^b$ | Model-II Effect (b) (p-value) | $e^b$ | 95% C.I. for $e^b$ |
|---|---|---|---|---|---|---|
| *Place of residence* | | | | | | |
| Rural | | | | 0.03(0.44) | 1.03 | (0.96, 1.11) |
| Urban® | | | | | | |
| *Caste* | | | | | | |
| Scheduled tribes | | | | 0.02(0.72) | 1.02 | (0.90, 1.16) |
| Scheduled caste | | | | 0.02(0.55) | 1.03 | (0.95, 1.11) |
| General castes® | | | | | | |
| *Religion* | | | | | | |
| Christianity | | | | 0.16(0.06) | 1.17 | (1.00, 1.38) |
| Islam | | | | 0.12(0.02) | 1.13 | (1.02, 1.25) |
| Rest ® | | | | | | |
| Model $\chi^2$ (d.f.) | 490.61(1) | | | 784.04(18) | | |
| (p-value) | 0.00 | | | 0.00 | | |
| Deviance $R^2$ | 0.03 | | | 0.04 | | |

*Note:* ®denotes the reference category.

financially dependent or partially dependent enhances the expected count by 65 per cent and 36 per cent, respectively, when compared to the financially independent older adults. For the illiterate older adults and for those older adults who had less than 10 years of school education, the expected count is about 23 per cent more than that for those older adults who had more than 10 years of education. Further, the older adults belonging to the religious groups, namely, Christianity and Islam are found to have 17 per cent and 13 per cent more expected count, respectively, when compared to the rest of the religious group.

# Discussion

The findings of this chapter confirm the association between the health status of older adults and the socio-economic and cultural factors. The differentials in the socio-economic and cultural factors correspond to the differentials in the burden of diseases and the burden of impairments among the older adults. On the one hand, the economic dependency of older adults is associated with a greater burden of chronic diseases/ impairments, whereas, on the other hand, the lower the economic status of a household, the lower is the burden of diseases. These findings are not in agreement in general with the other studies on older adults, carried out in different socio-cultural settings (Backlund et al., 1996; Berkman and Gurland, 1998; Grundy and Sloggett, 2002; Huisman et al., 2003; von dem et al., 2003; Matthews et al., 2006; Zimmer, 2008), as these studies show a positive association of health with the economic status of the household. However, the findings of this chapter are not directly comparable with other such studies because of the use of different indicators of health and the conceptual framework. This pattern is indicative of higher prevalence of chronic diseases and impairments among poor (financially dependent older adults). Underutilization of available health care services among them (Fried and Wallace, 1992; Mahal et al., 2000) may be responsible for such patterns. To reduce the effect of economic factors on overall health status of older adults, older adults with low or no income may be provided with adequate financial assistance.

The widowhood among older adults is found to be associated with ill health. This finding of the present investigation is in contrast to the study by Zimmer (2008) where the marital status was found not to be associated with health. The greater burden of diseases and impairments associated with the widowhood and increasing age might be less felt through social reforms and greater government and private institutional efforts towards intensive rehabilitation measures through hospitals and health bodies. The effect of education is discernible, but the associations point in opposite directions. The burden of chronic diseases decreases relatively with the fall in the level of education, whereas, the burden of impairments increases relatively with the fall in the level of education. The findings of this chapter, thus, do not totally agree with the findings of the studies in other developing countries (Liang et al., 2000; Liang, Liu and Gu, 2001; Zimmer et al., 2004; Zimmer and Kwomg, 2004).

The effects of only few modifiable socio-economic and cultural factors can be controlled through joint efforts of government and non-governmental organizations (NGOs). Financial dependence is one such factor. The health care facilities need to reach the financially disadvantaged older adults. There are other factors that are non-modifiable, for example, age and widowhood. Widowhood is associated with a greater burden of chronic diseases and impairments. The reasons for this association may be due to the fall in the social status that accompanies widowhood. In India, the issues related to older adults have found voice in the National Policy on older Persons (NPOP) that was adopted in 1999. With the prime focus of well-being, the NPOP enunciates a number of areas of concern, needing to be addressed through policy initiatives. These include pension cover for all, heavily subsidized health services and housing for older adults (Prakash, 2003). In addition to this is the enactment of the Maintenance and Welfare of Parents and Senior Citizens Bill, 2007, that has provisions for addressing the financial security and medical care of older adults. However, the fact remains that there are no separate health care facilities for the older adults in India (Kumar, 2003). Moreover, due to poverty, distance, lack of escort and immobility, the formal health care services remain unutilized (Kumar, 1996). As most geriatric morbidities are preventable and take effect over an extended period of time, a life course perspective to the health of older adults is needed (Kumar, 2003). In addition to this, the health care may be made available at the doorsteps of the older adults.

This chapter emphasizes the influence of the socio-economic and cultural environments on the health of older adults in India. The conceptual construct is wide enough to include a large number of potential correlates of health. Further, the empirical results indicate the appropriateness of the count models for quantifying the burden of ill health among older adults. This empirical finding needs to be tested in different cultural settings, other than the present one, for generalization. This chapter is limited to the physical aspects of health, that is, chronic diseases and impairments. Other important aspects of health, namely, emotional well-being and the self-rated health also need to be studied for a comprehensive exposition of the quality of life of the older adults. In addition to this, the data give information only on the self-reported diseases. Data on self-reporting may have the lacuna of under reporting as certain diseases like heart diseases need diagnosis to be ascertained. In such cases, the actual chronic condition might go underreported. Information at the time of the onset of a disease is not available for the given data. The assumption that the occurrence of a disease is independent of the occurrence of some other disease is a simplification of the real-life scenario. The complexities arising out of the existence of co-morbidities make the modelling arduous, unless such simplifying assumptions are introduced in the model. This chapter can at most claim to infer about the association of various socio-economic and cultural factors with the burden of ill health. The nature of the data does not permit the investigation of the causal pathways (Adama, Hurd, McFadden, Merrill and Riberio, 2003) to ill health. The variables included in the model can account for only a part of the information on the health of older adults. This is clear from the values of the deviance $R^2$ of the models for chronic diseases (deviance $R^2 = 0.5$) and for impairments (deviance $R^2 = 0.4$). The rest of the information may lie with the biological and behavioural factors that need further investigation. The importance of the socio-economic and cultural factors in explaining the health aspect of the quality of life of older adults could perhaps be better established through the choice of more appropriate variables and more apt modelling. Such studies, however, are valuable for designing appropriate intervention programmes for the older adults.

# Conclusion

The share of older adults in the population of India is projected to reach 12.4 per cent by 2026 (Registrar General and Census Commissioner, India, 2006). This trend is expected to continue in foreseeable future. Older adults are distinct from the rest of the population in various socio-economic aspects, such as work participation rates, likelihood of being married, financial dependence, the disease patterns and the needs of health care, to name a few. Hence, ensuring to the older adults a better quality of life is as necessary as addressing the issues such as malnutrition among children, maternal and child health, women empowerment and family welfare. In other words, issues related to the quality of life of the older adults need to be considered on equal footing along with other high priority issues. Health is an important integrant of the quality of life, and thus needs to be addressed in a long-term policy perspective. To put the matters explicitly, we need to know the need for geriatric care in India and how to fulfil the unmet need of geriatric care. Specially designed countrywide sample surveys are a prerequisite for obtaining reliable estimates of the need. Further, the quantum and the type of geriatric care required may differ from region to region, as the process of ageing is not uniform across the states of India. Therefore, region-specific socio-economic and health policies may be needed to mitigate the effect of financial constraints, widowhood, gender, caste and religion on the health-related quality of life of older adults.

# References

Adama, P., Hurd, M.D., McFadden, D., Merrill, A. & Riberio, T. 2003. Healthy, wealthy, and wise? Tests for direct casual paths between health and socioeconomic status. *Journal of Econometrics, 112*, 57–63.

Alam, M. 2006. *Ageing in India: Socio-economic and health dimensions*. New Delhi: Academic Foundation.

Alam, M. & Karan, A. 2011. *Elderly health in India: Dimension, differentials and determinants* (BKPAI Working Paper Series No. 3). New Delhi: United Nations Population Fund (UNFPA).

Antonovsky, A. 1967. Social class, life expectancy and overall mortality. *Milbank Memorial Fund Quarterly, 45*, 31–73.

Audinarayana, N. 2005. Self-reported chronic morbidity and perceived health status among the elderly in Tamil Nadu: Patterns, differentials and determinants. In S. Abedin (Ed.), *The elderly: emerging issues* (pp. 145–170). Dhaka: Bangladesh Association of Gerontology.

———. 2012. *Rural elderly in India*. Delhi: B. R. Publishing Corporation.

Backlund, E., Sorlie, P. D. & Johnson, N.J. 1996. The shape of the relationship between income and mortality in the United States: Evidence from the National Longitudinal Mortality Study. *Annals of Epidemiology, 6*, 1–9.

Berkman, C.S. & Gurland, B.J. 1998. The relationship among income, other socioeconomic indicators, and functional level of older persons. *Journal of Ageing and Health, 10*, 81–98.

Beydoun, M.A. & Poplin, B.M. 2005. The impact of socio-economic factors on functional status decline among community-dwelling older adults in China. *Social Science and Medicine, 60*, 2045–2057.

Cambois, E., Robine, J. & Hayward, M.D. 2001. Social inequalities in disability free life expectancy in the French male population 1980–1991. *Demography, 38*, 513–524.

Chattopadhyay, A. & Roy, T.K. 2005. Does retirement affect healthy ageing? A study of two groups of pensioners in Mumbai, India. *Asia-Pacific Population Journal, 20*, 89–113.

Deeg, D.J.H. 2007. Health and quality of life. In H. Mollenkopf & A. Walker (Eds), *Quality of life in old age: International and multi-disciplinary perspectives* (pp. 195–214). The Netherlands: Springer.

Fox, J. 1989. *Health inequalities in European countries*. Gower: Aldershot.

Fried, L.P. & Wallace, R.B. 1992. The complexity of chronic illness in the elderly: From clinic to community. In R.B. Wallace & R.F. Woolson (Eds), *The epidemiologic study of elderly* (pp. 10–19). Oxford: Oxford University Press.

Grundy, E. & Sloggett, A. 2002. Health inequalities in the older population: The role of personal capital, social resources and socio-economic circumstances. *Social Science and Medicine, 56*, 935–947.

Hayward, M.D. & Gorman, B.K. 2004. The long arm of childhood: The influence of early-life social conditions on men's mortality. *Demography, 41*, 87–107.

Huisman, M., Kunst, A.E. & Mackenbach, J.P. 2003. Socioeconomic inequalities in morbidity among elderly: A European overview. *Social Science and Medicine, 57*, 861–873.

Husain, Z. & Ghosh, S. 2010. Is health status of elderly worsening in India: A comparison of successive rounds of National Sample Survey, data. Available at: http://mpra.ub.uni-muenchen.de/25747/.

Kadushin, C. 1964. Social class and the experience of ill health. *Sociological Inquiry, 185,* 914–919.

Kaneda, T., Zimmer, Z. & Tang, Z. 2004. Differentials in life expectancy and active life expectancy by socioeconomic status among older adults in Beijing. *Disability and Rehabilitation, 27,* 241–251.

Kelly, M.P., et al. 2009. A conceptual framework for public health: NICE's emerging approach. *Public Health, 123,* 14–20.

Kitagawa, E.M., & Hauser, P.M. 1973. *Differential mortality in the United States: A study of socioeconomic epidemiology.* Cambridge: Harvard University Press.

Kumar, V. 2003. Health status and health care services among older persons in India. *Journal of Ageing and Social Policy, 15,* 67–83.

Kumar, V.S. 1996. Rural Elderly: health status and available health services. *Research and Development Journal, 2,* 16–22.

Liang, J., Liu, X. & Gu, S. 2001. Transitions in Functional status among older people in Wuhan, China: Socioeconomic differentials. *Journal of Clinical Epidemiology, 54,* 1126–1138.

Liang, J., McCarthy, J.F., Jain, A., Krause, N., Bennett, J.M. & Gu, S. 2000. Socio-economic gradient in old age mortality in Wuhan, China. *Journal of Gerontology: Social Sciences, 55,* 222–233.

Link, B.G. & Phelan, J. 1995. Social conditions as fundamental causes of disease. *Journal of Health and Social Behaviour, 36,* 80–94.

Lloyd-Sherlock, P. 2000. Population ageing in developed and developing regions: Implications for Health Policy. *Social Science and Medicine, 51,* 887–895.

Mackenbach, J.P., Kunst, A.E., Cavelaars, E.J.M., Groenhof, F., Geurts, J.J.M. & EU working group on socioeconomic inequalities in health. 1997. Socioeconomic inequalities in morbidity and mortality in western Europe. *The Lancet, 349,* 1655–1659.

Mahal, A., Singh, J., Afridi, F., Lamba, V., Gumber, A., Selvaraju, V. (2000). Who "benefits" from public sector health spending in India? Results of a benefit incidence analysis for India. Background paper for *Better Health Systems for India's Poor.* New Delhi: National Council of Applied Economic Research.

Matthews, R.J., Jogger, C. & Harcock, R.M. 2006. Does Socio-economic advantage lead to a longer, healthier old age? *Social Science and Medicine, 62,* 2489–2499.

Matthews, R.J., Smith, L.K., Hamock, R.M., Jagger, C. & Spiers, N.A. 2005. Socio-economic factors associated with the onset of disability in older age: A longitudinal study of people aged 75 years and over. *Social Science and Medicine, 6,* 1567–1575.

National Sample Survey Organisation. 2006. *Morbidity, health care and the conditions of the aged* (Report No. 507 (60/25.0/1). New Delhi: Ministry of Statistics and Programme Implementation, Government of India.

Prakash, I.J. 2003. Ageing, disability and disabled older people in India. *Journal of Ageing and Social Policy, 15,* 85–108.

Registrar General and Census Commissioner, India. 2006. *Population projections for India and states 2001–2026: Report of the technical group on population projections constituted by the National Commission on Population.* New Delhi: Office of the Registrar General and Census Commissioner.

Registrar General and Census Commissioner, India. 2011. *Provisional Population Totals Part 1 2011 India Series 1.*

Satyanarayana, K. & Medappa, N. 1997. Care of the aged—a long haul ahead. *Indian Journal of Medical Research, 106,* 265–272.

Sharma, S.D. & Agarwal, S. 1996. Ageing: The Indian perspective. In V. Kumar (Ed.), *Ageing: Indian perspective and global scenario* (pp. 12–19). New Delhi: All India Institute of Medical Sciences.

Siva Raju, S. 2002. *Health status of the urban elderly: A medico-social study.* Delhi: B. R. Publishing Corporation.

Smith, J.P. & Kington, R. 1997. Demographic and economic correlates of health in old age. *Demography, 34,* 159–170.

Sudha, S., Suchindran, C., Mutran, E.J., Irudaya Rajan, S. & Sarma, P.S. 2006. Marital status, family ties, and self-rated health among elders in South India. *Journal of Cross Cultural Gerontology, 21,* 103–120.

UNDP (United Nations Development Programme). 2012. *Human development report.* New York: United Nations Development Programme.

von dem K., Olaf, L.G., Cockerham, W.C. & Siegrist, J. 2003. Socioeconomic status and health among the aged in the United States and Germany: A comparative cross-sectional study. *Social Science and Medicine, 57,* 1643–1652.

Walker, A. & Mollenkopf, H. 2007. International and multidisciplinary perspectives on quality of life in old Age. In H. Mollenkopf & A. Walker (Eds), *Quality of life in old age: International and multi-disciplinary perspectives* (pp.3–13).The Netherlands: Springer.

WHO. 1978. *Declaration of Alma-Ata.* Available at: www.euro.who.int/AboutWHO/Policy/20010827.

———. 2007. *A conceptual framework for action on the social determinants of health.* Available at: http://www.who.int/social_determinants/knowledge_networks/2007.pdf.

Zimmer, Z. 2008. Poverty, wealth inequality, and health among older adults in rural Cambodia. *Social Science and Medicine, 66,* 57–71.

Zimmer, Z. & Amornsirisomboon, P. 2001. Socioeconomic status and health among older adults in Thailand: An examination using multiple indicators. *Social Science and Medicine, 52,* 1297–1311.

Zimmer, Z., Chayovan, N., Lin, H. & Natividad, J. 2004. How indicators of socioeconomic status relate to physical functioning of older adults in three Asian societies. *Research on Ageing, 26,* 224–258.

Zimmer, Z. & House, J.S. 2003. Education income and functional limitation transition among American adults: Contrasting onset and progression, *International Journal of Epidemiology, 32,* 333–360.

Zimmer, Z. & Kwong, J. 2004. Socioeconomic status and health among older adults in rural and urban China. *Journal of Ageing and Health, 16,* 44–70.

Zimmer, Z., Martin, L.G. & Li, H. 2003. Determinants of old age mortality in Taiwan. *Social Science and Medicine, 60,* 457–470.

# 6

# Ageing and Cross-cultural Variation in Health Issues*

*Satwanti Kapoor, Deepali Verma, Renu Tyagi,
N.K. Mungreiphy, Meenal Dhall, Prerna Bhasin,
Heemanshu Aurora and Anup K. Kapoor*

## Introduction

Our globe is in the stage of epidemiological transition, leading to intricate dynamics in population ageing—increasing the size and proportion of the population in advanced age groups—and the health and vitality of older people (Olshansky and Ault, 1986). The combination of high fertility and declining mortality during the 20th century has resulted in a large and rapid increase in elderly populations. But this rapid decline in mortality and the increase in life expectancy have chiefly been a result of the substitution of communicable diseases by degenerative counterparts with their profound and prolonged effects. These emerging age-related risks of metabolic disorders have further resulted in elevation of age-specific morbidity and mortality (Bhatt, Minal, Sonaliya, Solanki and Nayak, 2011). It raises a series of concerns for geriatric health, as chronic illnesses, such as cardiovascular

* The authors are grateful to all the subjects who volunteered for the present study. The financial assistance to AKK from University Grants Commission (Research Award) and SK (UGC-Career Award) is greatly acknowledged. RT is thankful to the Department of Science and Technology (DST) for the research grant. NKM is grateful to the University Grants Commission (UGC) for providing financial assistance through Rajiv Gandhi National Fellowship.

disease, arthritis and diabetes, rise with advancing age, which has been exacerbated by a transition in lifestyle factors. Consequently, today, the elderly experience increasing dependence on others for every small need, compromising their self-esteem.

Ageing, a universal phenomenon, is a progressive impairment of biological function, leading to loss of adaptive response to stress. Hence, the elderly are prone to ill health, physical and sensory impairment, heightened sensitivity and increased susceptibility to the diseases (Birren and Schaic, 1996). Though ageing is global, it differs in individualistic grounds and across various population groups with respect to age-related physiological and biological changes. This indicates the differential role of genetic and environmental factors such as physical activity, diet, boisterous living, health status, climate, environment and radiation, etc. According to Morgan, Armstrong, Huppert, Brayne and Solomou (2000), levels of health are poorer and levels of mortality generally higher, in urban as compared to rural areas. This suggests that even modest urban–rural differences in lifestyle have a profound impact on health and survival in later life.

India is projected to have the highest number of elderly in the world by the year 2025. In India, elderly population is 10 crore, forming 10 per cent of the total population, and it is estimated to reach up to 15 crore by the year 2020. This demographic dynamic is due to the control of communicable diseases and better health conditions, leading to increased longevity (Bhatt et al., 2011). The extension of human life, however, raises a question: Whether present and future cohorts of older people will be healthier than previous generations? Or whether increased longevity comes with deteriorating health, an increased risk of disability or poor quality of life? Disability and chronic illness are interrelated: The former represents an objective assessment of physical limitations while the latter corresponds to the development of long-term health conditions that may or may not have an impact on assessments of disability. Their relationship to quality of life signifies the impact of chronic conditions and/or disability on geriatric health (Armstrong, 2005). The changes in life expectancy and rates of chronic illness and disability provide us with the basis for understanding the changing circumstances in which chronic illness occurs and is treated. This emphasizes to facilitate a potential environment for the aged individuals and promote self-dependency that can limit the impact of chronic conditions (Bhawalkar, Dangore, Parikh and Tapkir, 2006). Hence, this chapter is an effort to evaluate the phenomena of differential ageing with special reference to health dimensions, if any, among adults from different populations experiencing differences in economy, lifestyle and habitual physical activity.

# Area and People

## Nolias

Nolias are constitutionally categorized under the other backward class (OBC). But they prefer to call themselves as 'sea tribes'. They have poor socio-economic status and sustain themselves by fishing and related activities. Almost all the households depend entirely on fishing for their livelihood. The men folk are engaged in fishing activities while women play an important role in the management of the household economy and are also engaged in the fishing trade. Among Nolias, the household is the unit of production as well as consumption. Except small children, every member in Nolia household contributes in production activities. Fish is the most important resource for them. Nolias are small-scale fishermen who have a subsistence economy. They have their own boats and nets. Their traditional way of fishing involves strenuous physical activity. Adult men go into the sea, women and children help them on the beach, and old people do mending of the fishing net along with training the young ones for fishing. The role of women folk is vital in their economy, as they dry the fish and go to market to sell it. The Nolias are Telgu fishermen who have migrated to the Ganjam district of Odisha, perhaps in end of the 19th century. For this chapter, various Nolia villages were covered, namely, Nua Boxipalli, Venkatraipur, New Venkatraipur, Boxipalli, Hatipada, Narainpur, Alipur, Mansulkota and Parvatipur (Kapoor, 2010).

## Rajis

Uttaranchal state, a district consisting of eight mountains in the Central Himalayan region, is the abode of the Raji, which is socially and economically the most underdeveloped tribal community of the

Uttaranchal. Sometimes known as '*Vanrawats*', meaning forest lords, they were recognized as a Scheduled Tribe in 1967 and as PTG in 1975 by the Government of India. The Raji is an extremely small tribe: 22 in number according to 1901 census. However, the 1971 Census recorded a population of 226, and a 1977 survey reported a total population of 338 (Tiwari, 1980). In 1988, the Raji population was 456 (Bora, 1988). The Raji is in a transitional stage between hunter–gatherer and a pre-agricultural economy. The shift is from food gathering to food production, wandering to sedentary lifestyle. In earlier days, Raji were dependent on hunting–gathering. In the post-independence era since 1948, the economy of the Raji has undergone several changes due to resettlement, dairy farming, agriculture, etc. At present, most of the male members work as labourers (but not throughout the year) and the females keep themselves busy cutting firewood and grass and selling these in the nearest markets, as well as food gathering and hunting.

Their social life is characterized by an individualistic pattern with no stratification into classes or caste. They follow the nuclear family system. Their education level is very low: 75 per cent of subjects in the age range of 20–25 years and 100 per cent of subjects in the age range of 61–80 years were illiterate (Kapoor, Tyagi and Kapoor, 2009). The staple food of the Raji is rice with wild vegetables such as the tuber, locally known as '*tarur*' (Kapoor, 1998). Few anthropological or developmental studies have been carried out so far on Rajis (Tiwari, 1980, 1986; Kapoor and Kapoor, 1985; Bora 1991; Kapoor and Patra, 2002). The studied population, the Rajis, is scattered over 12 villages in three districts, namely, Pithoragarh, Champawat and Udhan Singh Nagar, in an area of roughly 200 km. These villages are located at altitude ranging from 3000 ft from sea level. The following villages of Rajis were covered for this chapter, namely, Khirdwari, Kimkhola, Altari, Jamtadi, Madanpuri, Kuttachaurani, Bhoktiruwia, Chifaltara and Ganagaon.

## Tangkhul Naga

Tangkhul Naga is one of the sub-tribe of Naga tribe. Tangkhuls inhabit the North East region of India and also the western parts of Myanmar. In India, they are found in Nagaland, Manipur, Assam and Arunachal Pradesh, which are largely hilly areas. Tangkhul Nagas constitute the major bulk of the population of Ukhrul district of Manipur, the Northeastern most part of India, which is a mountainous region and isolated from the neighbouring states by a chain of hill ranges. Tangkhul Naga population is squarely concentrated in the Ukhrul district, though sizable populations are also found in Senapati district and Imphal valley that have originated from Ukhrul district. The data for Tangkhul Nagas were collected from the Ukhrul district of Manipur. They are patrilineal by descent and patrilocal by residence. Among Nagas, nuclear family is the most common type of family found, though there are a few joint and extended families. The Tangkhuls practice mostly tribe endogamy and clan exogamy. Traditionally, the main occupation of the Tangkhuls was farming and the source of income of the people was agriculture in which both terrace and wetland farming were practiced along with small-scale industries, animal husbandry, forest and river wealth. Now, with the advent of modern civilization, they are exposed to capitalistic trend of market competitions and urbanization. As a result, many of them have now shifted their occupation and have taken up business and jobs in both public and private sectors, though some of them are still engaged in farming (Mungreiphy and Kapoor, 2008a and 2008b).

## Rajputs

The data for Rajputs were collected from district of Sirmaur, which lies in outer Himalayan ranges, commonly called as Shiwalik between 70°-01'-12" and 77°-49'-40" E and 30°-22'-30" and 31°-01'-20" N. The villages covered for the study are: Ratoli, Ser, Halonipul, Talia, Neri, Sidori, Kot, Koti, Phagu, Deedag, Sanyio, Kulah, Dharoti, Miog, Pubiana, Jadoh, Shalana, Kothia Siana, Khadel, Jajar, Renuka, Ser, Jagas and Karuth. Another leading district in Himachal called Solan—which was carved out of the erstwhile Mahasu (Shimla) area of Pepsu (Punjab) and by merging princely states of Baghaat, Mangal, Kunuhar, Mehlog, Baija, Kuther and Handoor (Nalagarh) on 25 January 1971, when the state of Himachal Pradesh came into being—was also explored for data collection. The villages from which the data were collected were Jubbar, Chamian, Bandh, Shiva, Sheel, Ganguri, Upper, Ganguri lwer, Mudru, Kuthar, Jagit Nagar, Nauti, Anji, Kanda, Sunarahi, Kala Kumthan, Kote chanhole, Badiar, Bagi, Tamlong and Kalti. In Himachal Pradesh, data were collected from three districts, that is, Sirmaur, Solan and Rajgarh districts. The villages where data were collected were about 3,000–8,000 feet above sea level. Maize and wheat are the staple food of the people (Kapoor et al., 2010). The Rajputs of Himachal Pradesh are patrilineal and practice caste endogamy but *gotra* exogamy. The local inhabitants depend on agriculture for their subsistence and adopt several traditional practices conducive for farming in sloping terrains. Increasingly, most rural families have access to off-farm incomes to supplement the shortfall from agriculture. Many families have one or more member working in urban centres out of the state or in the military.

## Urban Population of Delhi

Delhi is situated between the Himalayas and Aravallis range in the heart of the Indian sub-continent. The studied group comprised of males and females from the urban dwellings of Delhi, capital of India. The data were collected among adults belonging to *Baniyas* and Punjabi population. The subjects in older age groups were drawn from family set-ups as well as from six old-age homes (institutions) in Delhi. Data for the subjects staying in family set-up were collected using a door-to-door survey from the North Delhi. For this chapter, subjects were matched for age and socio-economic status and data for the institutionalized (the elderly from old-age homes) and non–institutionalized (the elderly staying with family) categories were combined for analysis. The majority of the subjects belonged to the middle class socio-economic group. The dietary habits of both males and females were mixed type, including both vegetarian and non-vegetarian; however, most of them were vegetarians and had three meals a day. Lifestyles of elderly males and females differ markedly with respect to dietary habits and physical activity. The males were found to have more regular diet and better exercise level than their female counterparts who had relatively irregular diet and involvement in the most of the household activities. A small percentage (10%) of total sample included salad and milk in their diet on a regular basis. The education level for the total sample varied from illiterate to graduate. The rate of illiteracy was higher among elderly women than men (Tyagi, 2007).

# Materials and Methods

A cross-sectional study was conducted among 830 males and 985 females in the age range 20–80-plus inhabiting different regions of India—Nolias (Odisha), Rajis (Uttarakhand), Tangkhul Naga (Manipur), Rajputs (Himachal Pradesh) and Urban (Delhi). The sample was stratified by ethnicity into five age groups—20–49 years, 50–59 years, 60–69 years, 70–79 years and 80 years or older (Table 6.1). In this chapter, ageing trend in the blood pressure (BP) has been evaluated among these population groups. The age of the subjects was recorded by recall, pension paper if were in services, their birth cohorts, confirmation from family members and by recollection of significant socio-cultural and historical events. Socio-economic characteristics, including education, occupation, income, food habit, physical activity, etc. were qualitatively collected using an ethnographic approach. Study purpose was explained to all the volunteers prior to data collection and written consent was obtained from each subject. BP was recorded using an aneroid sphygmomanometer following standardized techniques by trained anthropologists.

The data were statistically analysed with SPSS 17.0. The basic characteristics are presented as mean and standard deviation. Analysis of variance was used to reveal the significant differences in the means of the variables stratified by age and population. The ageing trend in BP has been presented by the error bar graph with 95 per cent confidence interval (CI) for the mean. It is 95 per cent likely that the mean of the used sample will fall in the area bounded by two error bars. The values were considered signiûcantly different if $p \leq 0.05$.

**Table 6.1**

*Distribution of subjects*

| S.No. | Population | Males (N) | Females (N) |
|-------|-----------|-----------|-------------|
| 1 | Nolias (Odisha) | 155 | — |
| 2 | Rajis (Uttarakhand) | 63 | — |
| 3 | Rajput (Himachal Pradesh) | 130 | 157 |
| 4 | Tangkhul Naga (Manipur) | 238 | 294 |
| 5 | Delhi | 244 | 534 |

*N*= No. of subjects.

# Results

Tables 6.2 and 6.3 shows agewise mean systolic BP (SBP) and diastolic BP (DBP) among males of different population. Except Rajputs and Tanghkul Nagas, other populations showed increase in SBP and DBP

**Table 6.2**

*Age-wise mean systolic blood pressure (mmHg) among males of different population*

| Populations | N | 20–49 years Mean (SD) | 50–59 years Mean (SD) | 60–69 years Mean (SD) | 70–79 years Mean (SD) | 80+ years Mean (SD) | F-value | Sig. |
|---|---|---|---|---|---|---|---|---|
| Nolia | 155 | 121.8 (4.76) | 127.6 (9.84) | 131.1 (12.44) | 132.2 (12.75) | — | 5.92 | 0.001 |
| Rajis | 63 | 121.0 (4.45) | 128.8 (10.47) | 154.3 (54.38) | — | — | 6.24 | 0.003 |
| Rajput (HP) | 130 | 131.5 (12.67) | 136.8 (29.73) | 127.7 (33.22) | 135.5 (10.17) | 133.4 (21.85) | 0.6 | 0.661 |
| Tangkhul Naga | 238 | 124.3 (13.89) | 125.7 (22.47) | 138.1 (23.87) | 130.9 (25.59) | — | 3.87 | 0.01 |
| Delhi urban population | 244 | 121.3 (8.65) | 127.1 (18.09) | 130.3 (19.17) | 135.6 (19.44) | — | 4.45 | 0.005 |

**Table 6.3**

*Age-wise mean diastolic blood pressure (mmHg) among males of different population*

| Population | N | 20–49 years Mean (SD) | 50–59 years Mean (SD) | 60–69 years Mean (SD) | 70–79 years Mean (SD) | 80+ years Mean (SD) | F-value | Sig. |
|---|---|---|---|---|---|---|---|---|
| Nolia | 155 | 80.9 (2.94) | 84.5 (9.06) | 90.6 (13.46) | 90.4 (8.81) | — | 7.81 | <0.001 |
| Raji | 63 | 79.7 (4.08) | 85.8 (8.98) | 94.4 (9.54) | — | — | 17.13 | <0.001 |
| Rajput(HP) | 130 | 84.8 (8.24) | 82.6 (22.80) | 79.1 (18.74) | 89.1 (9.34) | 77.3 (13.68) | 1.94 | 0.108 |

*(Table 6.3 Continued)*

*(Table 6.3 Contineud)*

| Population | N | 20–49 years Mean (SD) | 50–59 years Mean (SD) | 60–69 years Mean (SD) | 70–79 years Mean (SD) | 80+ years Mean (SD) | F-value | Sig. |
|---|---|---|---|---|---|---|---|---|
| Tangkhul Naga | 238 | 78.1 (12.38) | 83.1 (13.96) | 81.7 (13.43) | 77.9 (17.52) | — | 2.01 | 0.113 |
| Delhi urban population | 244 | 87.7 (7.62) | 85.2 (11.65) | 86.9 (13.38) | 84.7 (13.05) | — | 0.64 | 0.591 |

with age. Nolias explicated a consistent increase and showed significant variation between different age groups ($p < 0.001$). Rajis showed an abrupt rise in the mean BP, both SBP and DBP (154.3 ± 54.38 and 94.4 ± 9.54, respectively) with noticeable variability at age 60–69 years and the difference was significant ($p < 0.01$). The urban males of Delhi demonstrated a steady increase in SBP with significant differences for various age groups ($p < 0.01$) and an inconsistent trend with age in DBP. Among Tanghkul Nagas, SBP increased in 60–69 years age group (138.1 ± 23.87) but declined in 70–79 years (130.9 ± 25.59) with significant difference at $p < 0.01$, while DBP increased in 50–59 years age group (83.1 ± 13.96) and decreased in 60–69 years (81.7 ± 13.43) followed by 70–79 years (77.9 ± 17.52) with statistically non-significant difference. Rajputs showed undulating trend of SBP and DBP without any significant difference between age groups. Figures 6.1 and 6.2 showed a pictorial representation of mean SBP and DBP, respectively, among males of different populations with CI to explain the variability in BP.

Tables 6.4 and 6.5 showed agewise mean SBP and DBP among females of different population. Among Nolias and Rajis, female data were not collected due to unavailability of subjects. Among females, the SBP increased significantly with age ($p < 0.001$). However, among Rajputs, constancy in the mean values between age group 60–69 years (127.4 ± 15.15) and 70–79 years (127.0 ± 12.56) demonstrated no ageing effect during this period. A similar trend was observed among females of Delhi in the age range 70–79 years (130.0 ± 20.28) and 80-plus years (130.9 ± 23.0). SBP was highest among Tangkhul Naga (143.5 ± 24.92) in the age range 70–79 years, followed by females of

**Figure 6.1**

*Mean systolic blood pressure (95% CI) among ageing Raji and Nolia males in comparison to urban Delhi males*

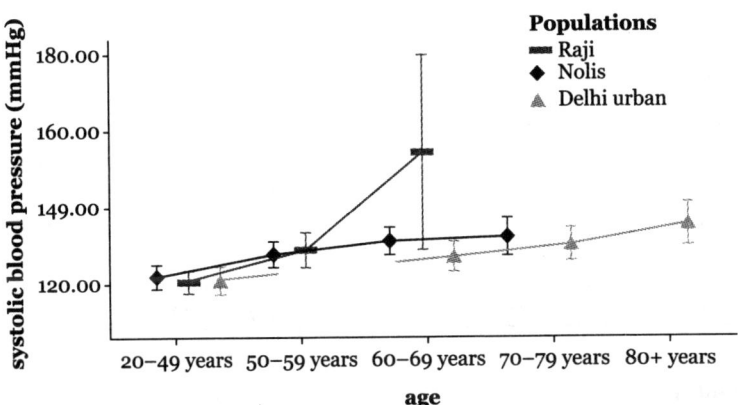

**Figure 6.2**

*Mean systolic blood pressure (95% CI) among ageing Rajput and Tangkhul Naga males in comparison to urban Delhi males*

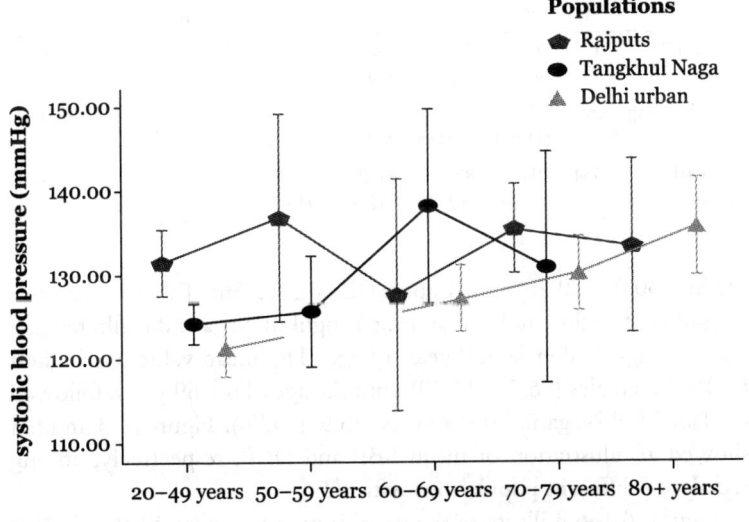

**Table 6.4**

*Age-wise mean systolic blood pressure (mmHg) among females of different population*

| Population | N | 20–49 years Mean (SD) | 50–59 years Mean (SD) | 60–69 years Mean (SD) | 70–79 years Mean (SD) | 80+ years Mean (SD) | F-value | Sig. |
|---|---|---|---|---|---|---|---|---|
| Rajput(HP) | 157 | 117.5 (12.05) | 124.1 (18.47) | 127.4 (15.15) | 127.0 (12.56) | 136.3 (10.77) | 6.82 | <0.001 |
| Tangkhul Naga | 294 | 112.2 (10.98) | 128.4 (22.98) | 134.6 (20.62) | 143.5 (24.92) | — | 38.88 | <0.001 |
| Delhi urban population | 534 | 117.4 (14.66) | 130.2 (20.37) | 131.5 (21.57) | 130.0 (20.28) | 130.9 (23.00) | 14.23 | <0.001 |

**Table 6.5**

*Age-wise mean diastolic blood pressure (mmHg) among females of different population*

| Population | N | 20–49 years Mean (SD) | 50–59 years Mean (SD) | 60–69 years Mean (SD) | 70–79 years Mean (SD) | 80+ years Mean (SD) | F-value | Sig. |
|---|---|---|---|---|---|---|---|---|
| Rajput(HP) | 157 | 76.0 (9.85) | 79.9 (11.52) | 79.5 (14.95) | 77.3 (8.18) | 78.6 (10.47) | 0.9 | 0.465 |
| Tangkhul Naga | 294 | 69.5 (11.91) | 82.6 (12.09) | 81.7 (12.33) | 85.9 (9.76) | — | 29.24 | <0.001 |
| Delhi urban population | 534 | 79.6 (10.74) | 87.5 (12.72) | 86.2 (12.79) | 80.7 (13.21) | 79.7 (13.83) | 10.27 | <0.001 |

Delhi (130.0 ± 20.28) and Rajputs (127.0 ± 12.56). Table 6.5 presents a significant decline in DBP among Tanghkul Naga and Delhi females except Rajputs after 50–59 years of age. The mean value was highest for Delhi females (86.2 ± 12.79) until the age of 60–69 years, followed by Tangkhul Naga in 70–79 years (85.9 ± 9.76). Figures 6.3 and 6.4 showed an illustration of mean SBP and DBP, respectively, among females of different populations with CI.

Figures 6.1–6.4 illustrate the variability in the mean SBP and DBP among males. CI provides a range of values for SBP and DBP that

**Figure 6.3**

*Mean diastolic blood pressure (95% CI) among ageing Raji and Nolia males in comparison to urban Delhi males*

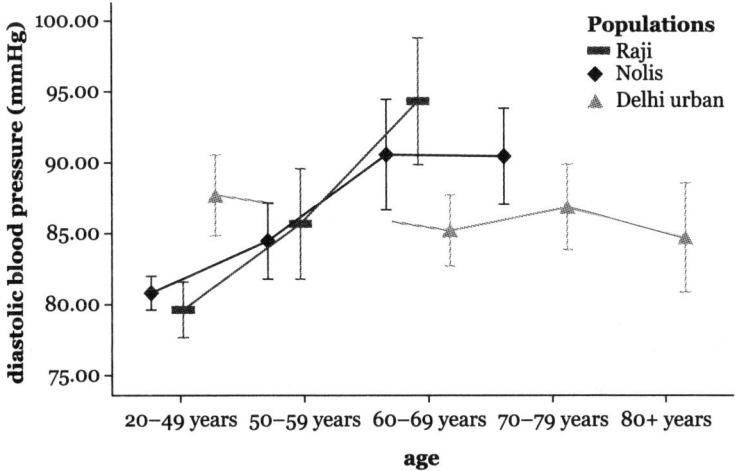

**Figure 6.4**

*Mean diastolic blood pressure (95% CI) among ageing Rajputs and Tangkhul Naga males in comparison to urban Delhi males*

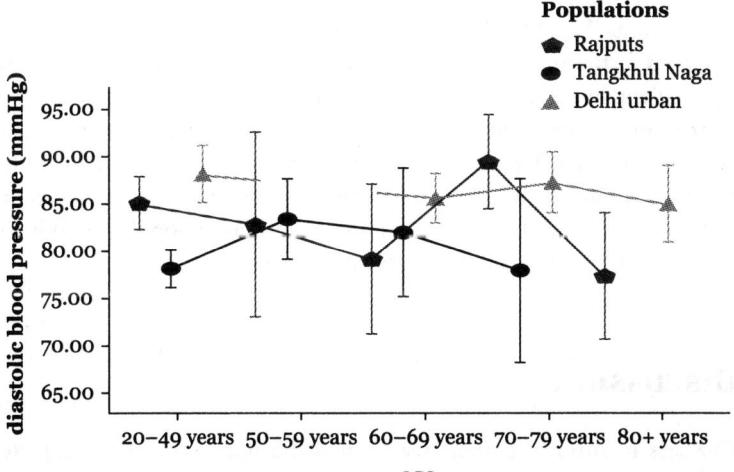

**Figure 6.5**

*Mean systolic blood pressure (95% CI) among ageing Rajput and Tangkhul Naga females in comparison to urban Delhi females*

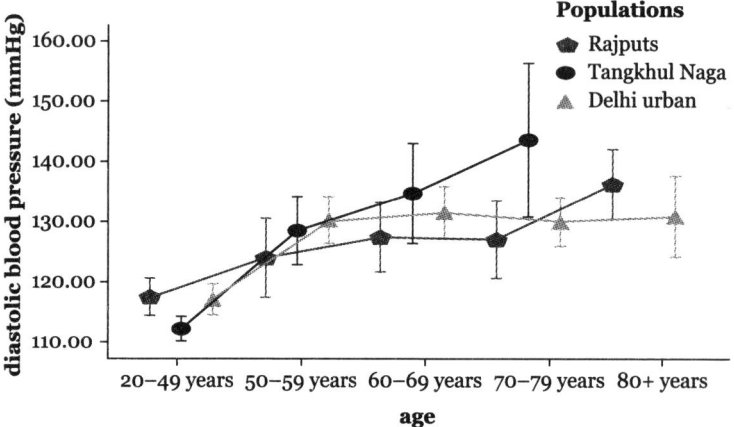

would have 95 per cent probability to include the true mean. The broader bar across mean with the advancing age represents the high variability in BP within a particular group. The variability was discernible among Raji males followed by Tangkhul Naga and Rajputs males. Delhi females showed consistency in mean BP with age (Figures 6.5 and 6.6), while among Tangkhul Naga and Rajputs females, an inconsistency was observed in the trend of mean BP. Variability is seen to increase with age that might be due to the smaller sample size or it simply shows a momentous increase within-group variation, a consequence of differential ageing. The considerable decrease in sample size at later stages of life is a subtle indicator of its ageing trend. A complete absence of data or a reduction in sample size implies how a particular population fails to reach a certain milestone in its ageing calendar.

## Discussion

Changes in survival curves have led to the notion of increasing life expectancy and verging of a larger proportion of the population in the age range where chronic non-communicable diseases become the major

**Figure 6.6**

*Mean diastolic blood pressure (95% CI) among ageing Rajput and Tangkhul Naga females in comparison to urban Delhi females*

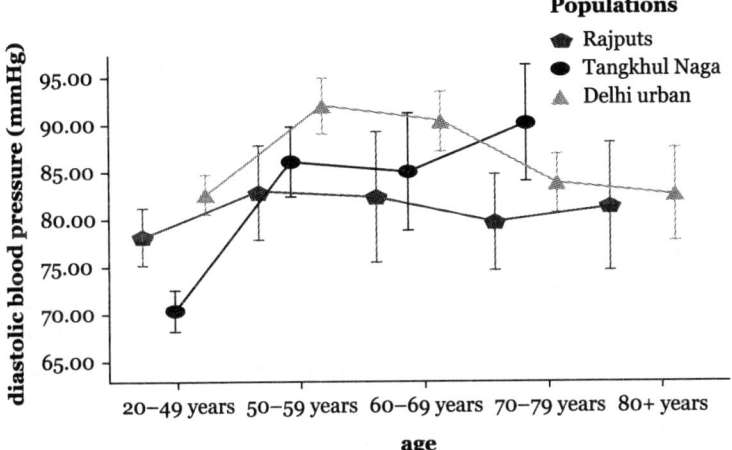

cause of morbidity and mortality (WHO, 2002). At the same time, the changeover in lifestyle with urbanization has been liable to be the cause of the increasing prevalence of metabolic disorders, often designated as epidemiological transition. Thus, the increased probability of survival has raised a question about limits to life expectancy and the potential for human lifespan—'Are we living healthier as well as longer lives, or are our additional years spent in poor health?'(Dobriansky, Suzman and Hodes, 2007).

This chapter underlines the ageing trend in BP among the population inhabiting varied geographical regions. Essential hypertension is a degenerative problem that effects function of many organs in the body, limiting functionality in adults as they age. The increase in BP (SBP and DBP) with age depicted in this chapter is consistent with other findings (Joshi, Kate and Shegokar, 1993; Mukhopadhayay, 1996; Kapoor and Tandon, 2003; Kusuma, Babu and Naidu, 2004). Discernible ageing effect on BP has been observed from 50 years of age in this chapter. Some investigators have theorized that ageing drives certain age-related changes in the blood vessels, creating an environment that promotes arterial stiffening, which contributes to the development of hypertension. But, during the later years of old age, there exists extent of variability in the trend that can be attributed to differential lifestyle, socio-cultural and biologically diversity among the population. The increase was however not localized to urban population and has been perceived to gravitate in traditional (Nolias) and transitional populations (Rajis, Rajputs and Tangkhul Naga). Despite conventional livelihood, the subtle changes observed in BP with age among tribal population parallels with those of urban inhabitants. However, several studies have revealed the consistency in BP during the later years of life among traditional living societies. The Yanomamo Indians, an unacculturated tribe inhabiting the tropical equatorial rain forest of northern Brazil, did not experience augmented BP with age in contrast to civilized populations (Crews and Mancilha-Carvalho, 1993). The mean BP for Kung Bushmen in northern Botswana remained same throughout life (Trusewell, 1972). Thus, the changes typically attributed to the normal ageing process are now emphasized to be linked to lifestyle or environmental factor (Scotch, 1963).

Nolia, a fishing community, has poor socio-economic status and was found to be undernourished with age (Kapoor et al. 2010). Despite these facts, the BP of Nolias increased with age, but remained within normal range. They follow traditional way of fishing for their subsistence that involves strenuous physical activity equivalent to physical activity level more than 1.4 (James, Ferro-Luzzi and Waterlow, 1988). Hence, this progression in BP may provide a selective advantage against the hypoglycaemia to the undernourished elderly Nolias. Morris, Sacks and Rosner 1993 reported that fish provides protective edge against hypertension, which happens to be the staple diet of Nolias (Kapoor et al., 2010).

On the contrary, Rajis (primitive tribal group), a traditional hunter–gatherers tribe, has now been forced to shift as labourers in agriculture/fishery or carpentry (Kapoor et al., 2009). This domineering transition in occupation might be responsible for an abrupt increase in BP during the later years of their life. In this age group, the Rajis are in the hypertensive category as per Joint National Committee VII (2003). Tension and anxiety were observed to be a causal factor for elevated level of BP among the elderly (Tyagi, 2000).

Contemporarily, Tangkhul Naga and Rajputs on exposure to the capitalistic trend of market competitions and urbanization have shifted their occupation to business and jobs in both public and private sectors (Mungreiphy and Kapoor, 2010; Kapoor et al., 2010). Rajis, Tangkhul

Naga and Rajputs are depicting a rural–urban transition. This partial transition allied with improvement in socio-economic status and sedentary lifestyle has resulted into 'acculturation stress' among tribal population and consequently has elevated the BP similar to those seen in western populations (Heymsfield, Allison, Heshka and Pierson, 1995). Furthermore, in urban population, the conventional living patterns among the elderly have changed drastically over a period of time. Medication for threatening diseases is easily accessible to urban population that might control the lifestyle problems of the elderly, but they cannot have healthy ageing, as it deteriorates the functioning of the body. Intricacies of traditional lifestyle can be stepping stones to graceful ageing. The confounding effects of urban–rural statuses are most evident in subjective health ratings of a population. The experience of good health appears significantly more widespread among those living in rural areas (Morgan et al., 2000).

A transition of the traditional joint family system to the nuclear families has given rise to the concept of institutionalization or old-age homes. Shifting to old-age homes has been found to initiate the psychological stress of staying away from the families, clearly reflected in deviance of the cardiovascular functions among the elderly staying in an old-age home (Tyagi, Kapoor and Kapoor, 2008). The traditional practice to live with their children in old age has not been necessarily with the intention of receiving support; often the rest of the family also benefits from the arrangement.

# Conclusion

Among urban population, the increase in BP with age, as revealed in this chapter, is indicative of sedentary lifestyle and obesity as disposing factors (Zamboni et al., 1997; Tyagi and Kapoor, 2010). Under nutrition, on the contrary, accompanied by loss of muscle mass and diminished immunity predisposes the elderly towards functional impairment (James et al., 1988) and hence high BP with age. It has been found that in rural/traditional populations, the prevalence of chronic energy deficiency is on rise with age, contrary to the urban populations where nutritional status dynamics is more in favour of overweight/obesity, yet both these conditions have been found to be significantly correlated to the rise in BP. Therefore, the differential trend in BP with age signifies a U-shaped relation between nutritional status and BP. These findings broaden the need of comprehending the health trends of a population before implementing any intervention programme. Thus, the heterogeneity among the elderly with respect to an environmental niche should emphasize on the consideration of physiological, psychological and social differences before implementing any changes in their dietary and lifestyle pattern. Being free of illness does not necessarily ensure a good quality of life during the process of ageing. Enhancement of independence, dignity and freedom of choice for elderly people is adding life to their years. Hence mobility, self-dependence, active lifestyle and social relations that are all correlates of traditional way of ageing are of great essence. It is not implied that we go back to the pre-modern era, but such lifestyle pattern needs to be maintained—in part through appropriate diet, apposite health care services along with an efficacious social environment that will lead to graceful ageing.

# References

Armstrong, D. (2005). Chronic illness: Epidemiological or social explosion? *Chronic Illness*, 1, 26–27.

Bhatt, R., Minal, S.G., Sonaliya, K.N., Solanki, A. & Nayak, H. (2011). An epidemiological study of the morbidity pattern among the elderly population in Ahmedabad, Gujarat. *National Journal of Community Medicine*, 2(2), 233–236.

Bhawalkar, J.S., Dangore, J.S., Parikh, R. & Tapkir, V.B. (2006). Comparative evaluation of health education in geriatric population in urban and rural areas. *Medical Journal of Padmashree Dr D Y Patil Medical College*, 1(1), 31–35.

Birren, J.E. & Schaie, K.W. (1996). *Handbook of psychology of ageing*. USA: Academic Press.

Bora, H.S. (1988). Cave dwellers of Himalayas—Raji a primitive tribal group of Uttar Pradesh.*Seminar Proceedings, Tribal Situation in Uttar Pradesh*, Yojana Bhawan, Lucknow (February 19–21).

———. (1991). The forest dwellers of middle Himalayas—Rajis—A primitive tribal group of UP Pithoragarh, Published leaflet.

Crews, D.E. & Mancilha-Carvalho, J.J. (1993). Correlates of blood pressure in Yanomami Indians of northwestern Brazil. *Ethnicity disease*, 3(4), 362–371.

Dobriansky, P.J., Suzman, R.M. & Hodes, R. J. (2007). *Why population ageing matters: A global perspective*. Washington, DC: National Institute on Ageing and National Institutes of Health, U.S. Department of Health and Human Services.

Heymsfield, S.B., Allison, D.B., Heshka, S. & Pierson, R.N. (1995). Assessment of human body composition. In D.B. Allison (Ed.), *Handbook of assessment methods for eating behaviors and weight related problems: Measures, theory, and research* (pp. 515–543). Thousand Oaks, CA: SAGE.

James, W.P.T., Ferro-Luzzi, A. & Waterlow, J.C. (1988). Definition of chronic energy deficiency in adults. Report of a Working Party of the International Dietary Energy Consultative Group. *European Journal of Clinical Nutrition, 42*, 969–981.

Joint National Committee (JNC) VII. (2003). Seventh report of the Joint National Committee on the prevention, detection, evaluation and treatments of high blood pressure. *Journal of American Medical Association, 289*, 2073–2082.

Joshi, P.P., Kate, S.K & Shegokar, V. (1993). Blood pressure trends and lifestyle risk factors in rural India. *Journal of Association of Physicians India, 41*, 579–581.

Kapoor, A.K. (1998). Dilemma of caste-tribe and tribe-caste transformation. In V.K. Pant & B.S. Bisht (Eds), *Backward communities: Identity, development and transformation* (pp. 119–138). New Delhi: Gyan Publishing House.

Kapoor, A.K., Dhall, M. & Tyagi, R. (2010). Nutritional status and ageing among Car Nicobarese and Nolia males of India. *The Open Anthropology Journal, 3*, 155–160.

Kapoor, A.K. & Kapoor, S. (1985). The secular growth trends among Himalayan population. *Anthrop Közl, 29*, 85–88.

Kapoor, A.K. & Patra, P.K. (2002). Raji—a food hunter and gatherer primitive tribe of Uttaranchal: A study of selection intensity. *Anthropologist, 4*, 253–256.

Kapoor, S. & Tandon, K. (2003). Physical activity, occupation, altitude. In A.K. Kalla & D.K. Bhattacharya (Eds), *Understanding people of India: Anthropological insight*. New Delhi: Department of Anthropology, University of Delhi.

Kapoor, A.K., Tyagi, R. & Kapoor, S. (2009). Nutritional status and cardio-respiratory functions among adult Raji males, a hunter and gatherer tribe of the Indian Himalayas. *Anthropological Science, 117*(1), 1–7.

Kapoor, S., Dhall, M. & Kapoor, A.K. (2010). Nutritional status and ageing among populations inhabiting varied geographical regions in India Biennial book of EAA. No.6 (pp. 85–100).

Kusuma, Y.S., Babu B.V. & Naidu, J.M. (2004). Prevalence of hypertension in some cross-cultural populations of Visakhapatnam district, South India. *Ethnicity and Disease, 14*, 250–259.

Morgan, K., Armstrong, G.K., Huppert, F.A., Brayne C. & Solomou, W. (2000). Healthy ageing in urban and rural Britain: A comparison of exercise and diet. *Age and Ageing, 29*(4), 341–348.

Morris, M.C., Sacks, F. & Rosner, B. (1993). Does fish oil lower blood pressure? A meta-analysis of controlled trials. *Circulation, 88*(2), 523–533.

Mukhopadhayay, B. (1996). Blood pressure profile of Lepchas of the Sikkim Himalayas, epidemiological study. *Human Biology, 68*, 131–145.

Mungreiphy, N.K. & Kapoor S. (2008a). *Overweight, Obesity and Socio-economic Change among Tangkhul Naga Tribal Women of Manipur, North East India*. pp 99–114, Research Proceeding in Anthropology published under UGC-SAP, Department of Anthropology, University of Delhi.

———. (2008b). Overweight, obesity and socio-economic change among Tangkhul Naga tribal women of Manipur, North East India. Available from Nature Proceedings at http://hdl.handle.net/10101/npre.

———. (2010). Socioeconomic changes as covariates of overweight and obesity among Tangkhul Naga tribal women of Manipur, north-east India. *Journal of Bio-social Sciences, 2*(3), 289–305.

Olshansky, S.J. & Ault, B. (1986). The fourth stage of the epidemiologic transition: The age of delayed degenerative diseases. *The Milbank Quarterly, 64*(3), 355–391.

Scotch, N.A. (1963). Socio-cultural factors in the epidemiology of Zulu hypertension. *American Journal of Public Health, 53,* 1205.

Tiwari, S.C. (1980). Population structure and changing subsistence pattern of the Raji—a hunting gathering community of the Indo-Tibetan Border. In I.P. Singh & S.C. Tiwari (Eds), *Man and his environment* (pp. 251–259). New Delhi: Concept Publishing Company.

———. (1986). Some aspects of religious practices among the Rajis of Kumaon. In L.P. Vidyarthi & M. Jha (Eds), *Ecology, economy and religion of Himalayas* (pp. 180–192). Delhi: Orient Publishers.

Trusewell, A.S. (1972). Blood pressure of Kung Bushmen in northern Botswana. *American Heart Journal, 1,* 5–12.

Tyagi, R. (2000). *Socio-biological aspects of ageing phenomenon among institutionalized and non institutionalized senior citizens* (Unpublished PhD thesis). Department of Anthropology, Faculty of Science, University of Delhi.

———. (2007). Body composition and nutritional status of the institutionalized and non-institutionalized senior citizens. *EAA Summer School eBook, 1,* 225–231.

Tyagi, R. & Kapoor, S. (2010). Functional ability and nutritional status of Indian elderly. *The Open Anthropology Journal, 3,* 200–205.

Tyagi, R., Kapoor, S. & Kapoor A.K. (2008). Environmental influence and health status of elderly. *The Open Anthropology Journal, 1,* 14–18.

WHO Secretariat. (2002, May 13–18). Adapted from documents A55/17 and A55/17 Add.1. Fifty-fifth World Health Assembly, Geneva, World Health Organization. Available at: http://www.who.int/gb/.

Zamboni, M., Armellini, F., Harris, T., Turcato, E., Micciolo, R., Bergamo-Andreis I.A., et al. (1997). Effect of age on body fat distribution and cardio-vascular risk factors in women. *American Journal of Clinical Nutrition, 66,* 111–115.

# 7

# Older People with Disability: Concerns and Policies

*Indumathi Rao, Tattwamasi Paltasingh
and Renu Tyagi*

## Introduction

The challenges faced by today's elderly include isolation, lack of health care facilities, economic dependency, abuse, neglect and disability, etc. It is beyond debate that elderly people with disabilities are the poorest of the poor in any community. The proportion of ageing population with disabilities is going up, but its status and security is on the decline in both developed and developing countries. Disabilities have different perspectives across regions, gender and culture. Disability can be defined as any restriction or lack of ability to perform in a manner or within the range considered normal for a human being (WHO, 2002). The Persons with Disability (PWD) Act has defined it as not less than 40 per cent of any type of disability (i.e., blindness, low vision, cerebral palsy, leprosy, hearing impairment, locomotor disability, mental illness and mental retardation or multiple disabilities) as certified by a medical authority (PWD, 2005). However, there is no uniform definition of the term 'disability'. Disability issues cut across all sectors and thematic areas of the community development. Elderly population with mild-to-severe disabilities is a global concern in the 21st century. The levels of moderate and severe impairments are higher in low-income and middle-income countries than in high-income countries. The elderly have to cope with health, socio-economic and associated problems, some of which may be chronic and require constant attention, thereby carrying the risk of disability and consequent loss of autonomy. Older persons with disabilities who are single go through several difficulties. This chapter discusses ageing and disability among the elderly in India while highlighting the existing policies and associated implications.

# Disability and Elderly: Demographic Evidences

The global prevalence of moderate and severe disabilities is expected to increase (WHO, 2004). Bangladesh had the highest prevalence rates of 5.6 per cent (WHO, 2002). There is a lack of proper data on the number of disabled and magnitude of the problem. In India, the National Sample Survey Organization (NSSO) data for the first time gave the demographic details of the disabled persons in the country (NSSO, 2002). There is no reliable and analytical demographic study conducted at the national level regarding the status of disabled in the country except the NSSO 58th round. The reason could be the lack of political will and social unpreparedness for the problem.

## Global Scenario

The worldwide proportion of the elderly to the total population is expected to increase from 10 per cent in 2000 to 15 per cent by 2025 and over 21 per cent by 2050 (United Nations, 2007). The number of people with disabilities is increasing due to population ageing and emergence of chronic diseases. About 15 per cent of the world's population lives with a disability. Today, about 30 per cent mortality is due to the cardiovascular diseases (CVDs) happening worldwide. About 80 per cent of such instances occur in the developing nations (WHO, 2011). There are overwhelming demands for more health and rehabilitation services for elderly population (Srivastava and Khan, 2008). The population growth trend of the elderly in India is somewhat similar to the world's trend. There has been a shift in the age structure of elderly population because of the combination of increased longevity and decreased mortality. People in developing countries such as India are likely to spend a greater fraction of their total lifespans in poor health, because the onset of both fatal and non-fatal diseases tends to occur at younger ages unlike developed nations. Though women have longer life expectancy compared with men, the women suffer with poor health for an extended period of their life (Kinsella and He, 2008; World Health Organization, 2011). The World Health Organization views ageing as a privilege and a societal achievement. However, age-associated impairment or disability seeks additional and careful attention. Hearing loss, vision problems, locomotor problems, mental illness and nutritional deficiency are the most common causes of impairment globally for all age group. However, among the elderly, dementia, chronic respiratory tract diseases and cerebrovascular disease are more common (WHO, 2008).

## Situation in India

The process of population ageing began in developed countries and it is slowly shifting to developing countries such as India where the population of the elderly increased from 24 million in 1961 to about 77 million in 2001. Consequently, health care, psycho-social and socio-economic factors associated with elderly population need increased attention (Prakash, 2003). However, there is a scarcity of the database regarding the nature and extent of disability among elderly population in India (Lakshmi, 2008). The NSSO has conducted two surveys on morbidity and health status of the elderly (aged 60 years and above)—that is, the 52nd round (July 1995–June 1996) and the 60th round (January–July 2004). Disability is found to be affecting 17 per cent of the 60-plus population in India (NSSO, 2003). In another study among the geriatric population of Mangalore city of Karnataka, prevalence of disability is found to be more than 65 per cent. Most common disability among these elderly is found to be speech and locomotor disability. Prevalence of disability was found to be higher (90.9%) among the 80 years and above age group. About one-third of the disabled elderly have chronic co-morbid conditions (Ganesh, Yadav, Sajjan and Kotian, 2008) adversely affecting their quality of life. Various levels of neural-psychiatric morbidity have been reported among the elderly (Varghese and Patel, 2004).

An increasing age tends to be associated with increased risk of disability among the elderly (Tas et al., 2007). Locomotor disabilities are the most prevalent type of disabilities affecting all ages. Mental disabilities are the highest in the working age population, whereas visual and hearing disabilities are the highest in the aged. Onset of visual and hearing disabilities and other severe type of disabilities are found to be highly concentrated among the elderly of 70 years and above (Patel, 2009). CVDs are responsible for most of the mortality and disability in India over the last few decades (Shah and Mathur, 2010; Patel et al., 2011). The NSSO survey has depicted information relating to the magnitude and type of disability, age at onset of disability, possible cause of disability, housing condition, village facilities, particulars of slum and consumer expenditure, employment and unemployment. As per NSSO (2006) Report, about 30 per cent elderly in India are suffering with health problem. Among these, 40 per cent of the elderly were suffering from visual, locomotive, auditory or vocal disability, while a significant proportion was suffering from chronic diseases. About 20 per cent of them were suffering from CVDs, 15 per cent with cough-related diseases and 9 per cent with diabetes (Husain and Ghosh, 2010).

# Regional and Gender Disparity in Disability

Age is associated with a 1–2 per cent decline in functional ability per year, with sedentary behaviour accelerating it. Difficulties in the basic activities, such as bathing, dressing, going to the toilet, continence, feeding and moving from chair to bed, are reported by a significant number of those over 70 and even more of those over 85 years. Common difficulties also include problems with using the telephone, housekeeping and handling money. Inability to go out unaided affects a significant number of the elderly over 75 years. Hearing and reading difficulty is more common over the age of 75 years (WHO, 2011). Social isolation and loneliness are likely to become an increasingly widespread problem among older people due to increased life expectancy, changing family structures and greater mobility of the working population. Older persons living alone are more likely to get dementia and may need outside assistance in the case of illness or disability and are at greater risk of social isolation in both developing and developed nations (Casey and Yamada, 2002).

In India, around 10 per cent of the population is found to be affected with some or other disabilities (Barbotte, Guillemin, Chau and Lorhandicap Group, 2001; Sharma and Praveen, 2002). In India, the disability prevalence rate has been found to decline for elderly population in both urban as well as rural areas during 1991–2001. As per census (2001), over 21 million people in India were suffering from one or the other kind of disability that is equivalent to 2.1 per cent of the population. Among the total disabled in the country, 12.6 million are males and 9.3 million are females. The number of disabled person is more in rural than urban areas. As per census (2001), disability among elderly males is found to be higher than elderly females. 'Seeing' followed by movement-related disability were found to be highest among elderly population in India (Table 7.1), whereas as per the NSSO survey, locomotor disability is reported to be the most common, both in rural and urban areas. Each type of disability is found to be more frequently occurring in rural areas as compared to the urban areas (Table 7.2).

The disability rate (i.e., the number of disabled per 100,000 populations) for the country as a whole is 2130. There is a high prevalence of disability and distress among elderly population of North India (Joshi, Kumar and Avasthi, 2003). In rural areas, about 38 per cent elderly males and more than 42 per cent elderly females are suffering from some or the other type of physical disability. As per the survey, two-thirds of the rural population are found to be affected due to disability unlike one-third of the urban population

**Table 7.1**

*Disability among elderly as proportion of total disabled people: India*

| Type of disability | Total (%) | | | Rural (%) | | | Urban (%) | | |
|---|---|---|---|---|---|---|---|---|---|
| | Total | Male | Female | Total | Male | Female | Total | Male | Female |
| Seeing | 2.6 | 2.6 | 2.6 | 2.8 | 2.8 | 2.8 | 1.9 | 2 | 1.9 |
| Hearing | 0.6 | 0.6 | 0.6 | 0.7 | 0.7 | 0.7 | 0.4 | 0.4 | 0.5 |
| Mental | 0.2 | 0.3 | 0.2 | 0.2 | 0.2 | 0.2 | 0.2 | 0.3 | 0.2 |
| Movement | 1.4 | 1.6 | 1.1 | 1.4 | 1.7 | 1.2 | 1.1 | 1.4 | 0.9 |
| Speech | 0.2 | 0.2 | 0.1 | 0.2 | 0.2 | 0.2 | 0.1 | 0.2 | 0.1 |
| Total | 4.9 | 5.2 | 4.7 | 5.3 | 5.5 | 5 | 3.9 | 4.2 | 3.6 |

*Source*: Census (2001).

**Table 7.2**

*Type of disability among elderly*

| Place of residence | Mental retardation | Mental illness | Blindness | Low vision | Hearing | Locomotor | At least one disability |
|---|---|---|---|---|---|---|---|
| Rural | 11 | 180 | 1,733 | 747 | 1,551 | 2,796 | 6,401 |
| Urban | 7 | 167 | 1,087 | 459 | 1,385 | 2,888 | 5,511 |

*Source*: NSSO (2003).

**Table 7.3**

*Percentage distribution of disabled elderly*

| | All | Rural | Urban |
|---|---|---|---|
| All | 45.86 | 45.76 | 46.21 |
| **Age group (year)** | | | |
| 60–64 | 36.07 | 36.23 | 35.49 |
| 65–69 | 41.74 | 41.57 | 42.36 |
| 70–74 | 51.05 | 51.45 | 49.55 |
| 75-plus | 60.75 | 60.45 | 61.74 |
| **Gender** | | | |
| Male | 46.83 | 46.28 | 48.83 |
| Female | 44.94 | 45.25 | 43.86 |
| **Educational Status** | | | |
| Below primary | 47.52 | 47.27 | 49.27 |
| Primary | 46.56 | 46.56 | 46.57 |
| Middle | 43.25 | 42.60 | 44.99 |
| Secondary | 42.59 | 41.31 | 44.98 |
| Higher | 42.88 | 41.89 | 43.79 |

*Source*: Pandey (2009): Computed based on NSSO (2003).

(NSSO, 2003). Highest percentage of disability is reported among the elderly in age group of 75 years and above. Men are more affected with disability as compared to women. The elderly who have studied below primary level are most affected with disability as compared to their better educated counterparts (Table 7.3). The proportion of aged persons reporting physical immobility was found to increase with the

**Table 7.4**

*Per 1,000 distribution of aged persons by state of physical mobility*

| Age group (years) | Rural | | | Urban | | | Rural + Urban | | |
|---|---|---|---|---|---|---|---|---|---|
| | Male | Female | Person | Male | Female | Person | Male | Female | Person |
| 60–64 | 66 | 96 | 82 | 98 | 100 | 99 | 75 | 97 | 86 |
| 65–69 | 112 | 140 | 124 | 207 | 90 | 141 | 136 | 122 | 129 |
| 70–74 | 318 | 323 | 321 | 304 | 242 | 269 | 315 | 303 | 309 |
| 75–79 | 191 | 261 | 222 | 150 | 364 | 251 | 181 | 288 | 230 |
| 80 & + | 241 | 399 | 317 | 202 | 269 | 249 | 235 | 360 | 301 |
| All | 157 | 201 | 179 | 181 | 154 | 165 | 162 | 187 | 175 |

*Source*: NSS 60th Round (2006).

age for all categories, being as high as 30.1 per cent for persons aged 80 or more. The rate is seen to be higher among females than males for all age groups in rural areas (Table 7.4).

In all, more number of females in rural areas than in urban areas and more number of urban men as compared to rural men are reported with physical immobility (NSSO, 2006). Vision problems followed by hypertension, joint pain, diabetes, hearing loss, respiratory problems and skin problems were found to be the major health problems among the elderly living in the urban areas (Tyagi, 2007). Disability due to vision (48.5%) emerges as the highest contributor followed by disability due to movement, mental, speech and hearing problem (Census, 2001). The prevalence of mental disability is more prevalent among elderly females than elderly males (Kumar et al., 2008). The health needs of 33.1 per cent of elderly are not fulfilled in India. Among them, a larger relative proportion is female (50% of female elderly are widows versus only 15% of male elderly who are widowers). The widows are reported to be disproportionately vulnerable to disability, illness and poor health care utilization (Rajan and Sreerupa, 2008).

Realizing the dearth of data on disability in the country, the census 2011 has extended the coverage by including two more categories of disabilities for this census (Subramani, 2012). About 46 per cent of the elderly suffer from at least one kind of disability. The age-specific disability rates and severity of disablement increase with age. The percentage of disability among the elderly in the age groups 60–64 years, 65–69 years, 70–74 years and 75 years and above are 36, 42,

51 and 61, respectively (NSSO, 2003). The same trend exists in both rural and urban areas. It is projected that the disability related with non-communicable diseases (NCDs) will increase and contribute to a higher proportion of overall national disability (Kowal et al., 2010). The percentage share of disability is found to be higher among elderly male than that of elderly female population. However, about 60 per cent of the elderly in India live disability-free lives, with highest proportion of such elderly from South India and the lowest from East India (Lakshmi, 2008).

There are strains and stresses in taking care of the elderly needs. The importance of taking care of elderly people has become more relevant in society due to the increase in nuclear families and breakdown of joint family system in India. There is a lack of basic rehabilitation services that are community based and easily accessible in a majority of villages in India. One can presume that elderly persons with disabilities in rural areas must be experiencing difficulties that further get complicated by poverty. A causal relationship between poverty and disability is reported by earlier studies (DFID, 2000; World Bank, 2007; Braithwaite and Mont, 2008). In India, poverty is reported to be the major cause of disability because of malnutrition, increased risk of infectious disease, limited access to medical care and lower educational level, etc. (Thomas, 2005). However, there is a paucity of data that focus relationship between poverty and disability in elderly population in India (Sengupta and Agree, 2003; Prakash, 2003). In addition to the socio-economic indicators, medical history and related information are also linked with frailty, health risks and disabilities among the aged (Albert, 2004). Despite realizing that disability is of major concern among elderly population, there is no exclusive scheme or programme particularly meant for the disabled elderly. Policy initiatives in India have just addressed the issue of disability in the recent policy on senior citizens, 2011. The inadequacy of the existing policy and welfare measures has been discussed in the next section.

## Policy Initiatives

The ancient wisdom and practices in our cultures gave due recognition and status to the elderly and their experiences. But in the present communities with vast urban and rural divide, it is rather difficult to imagine similar status of the elderly within the family. The World Assembly on Ageing is the first international instrument on ageing, guiding thinking and formulation of policies and programmes on ageing. It was endorsed by the United Nations General Assembly in 1982. The primary objective of this 'International Plan of Action' was to strengthen the capacities of the governments and the civil society to deal effectively with the ageing of populations and to address the developmental potentials and needs of older persons. This document includes 62 recommendations for action, addressing research, data collection and analysis, training and education, health and nutrition, protection of elderly consumers, housing and environment, family, social welfare, income security, employment and education, etc. Independence, participation, care, self-fulfilment and dignity are identified as the five broad areas of intervention. Different countries have responded in their own way towards the issues concerning elderly population. Countries such as India and Sri Lanka are more affected due to population ageing. They have introduced exclusive policies for its elderly population, while the government of the Maldives has not initiated any such action (MPF, 2009; CSO, 2011). The Bangladesh government adopted an inclusive Population Policy including older persons as vulnerable groups (Bangladesh, 2004). India is a signatory to the Declaration on the Full Participation and Equality of People with Disabilities in the Asia Pacific Region, that is, the Biwako Millennium Framework for action towards an inclusive, barrier free and rights-based society. The Framework aims to develop a national system of disability-related data collection and analysis, and establishment of a definition of disability to enable internationally comparative analysis (UN-ESCAP, 2006).

In India, the legislative framework for protecting the rights of disabled people is covered by four acts. (1) The Mental Health Act 1987 with consolidated and amended law relating to the treatment and care of mentally ill persons. (2) Rehabilitation Council of India Act 1992 that works to regulate the training of professionals in rehabilitation and sets out a framework. (3) Persons with Disabilities Act 1995 that aims to provide the equal opportunities, protection of rights and full participation of disabled people. This act aims to provide 3 per cent reservations for disabled people in poverty alleviation programmes, government jobs and state educational facilities, etc. (4) The National Trust Act 1999 that provides for the constitution of a national body for welfare of persons with autism, cerebral palsy, mental retardation and multiple disabilities (Thomas, 2005).

## National Policy on Disability

The National Policy for Persons with Disabilities Act 2005 gives way to the National Policy on disability, released in February 2006. The policy recognizes persons with disabilities as a valuable human resource for the country. The policy seeks to create an environment that provides them equal opportunities, protects their rights and enables their full participation in society (PWD, 2005). The focus of the policy is on prevention of disabilities, rehabilitation measures and counselling. The National Policy on disability focuses on issues such as education and economic rehabilitation of persons with disabilities, disabled women, disabled children, barrier-free environment, disability certificates, social security, involvement of the non-governmental organizations (NGOs), collection of regular information on persons with disabilities and more research in the field. However, the policy document ignored elderly population. In view of the increasing elderly proportion and associated disabilities with age, there is a requisite of an exclusive policy and action plan with a focus on disabled elderly.

## National Policy for Older Persons

The Directive Principles of State Policy in Article 41 of the Indian Constitution (propagated in 1950) enjoined the state with the responsibility of making effective provisions for public assistance in cases of unemployment, old age, sickness, disablement and in other cases of undeserved want. In 1999, the government of India adopted the National Policy for Older Persons (NPOP) that recognizes ageing as a national concern and the policy is aimed at ensuring that the elderly do not live unprotected, ignored or marginalized (CSO, 2011). The NPOP is an acknowledgement, for the first time, in a formal way by the government of India that the elderly have their own needs and it is the duty of the state to address these needs. The NPOP that recognizes the elderly as a huge human resource says that about six-tenths of the population in the age range 60–69 years can be expected to be in reasonably good physical and mental health, free of serious disability and leading an active life. It recognizes that a large number of the elderly are expected to be in need of care in old age. However, in the policy, the elderly with disability and chronic diseases were not given due attention (Prakash, 2003). The NPOP does not include the active collaboration of *panchyath raj* system and grants for community-based rehabilitation (CBR) services. A Review Committee for the NPOP is constituted and new national policy, 2011 has been formulated in view of the changing needs of senior citizens in the country (CSO, 2011).

## National Policy for Senior Citizens (NPSC–2011)

The national policy for senior citizens (NPSC), 2011 paid some attention to disability and associated issues among the elderly. The policy identifies that the women experience proportionately higher rates of chronic illness and disability in later life than men. Women suffer greater NCDs and experience lower social and mental health status, especially if they are single and/or widowed. Disability is given due consideration in financial aspects as well with the proposed coverage of oldest old under the Indira Gandhi National Old Age Pension Scheme. The policy envisions additional pension in the case of disability, loss of adult children and related responsibility for grandchildren and women. Disability among the elderly requires special attention while covering the health care issues in the policy. The NPSC-2011 visualizes creating an age-friendly, barrier-free access in buses and bus stations, railways and railway stations, airports and bus transportation within the airports, banks, hospitals, parks, cinema halls, shopping malls and other public places that senior citizens and the disabled visit (GoI, 2011).

## Tackling Disability: Need for Inclusive Approach

The needs of elderly people with disabilities are vast and diverse. It varies from the issues of isolation, lack of health care facilities, economic dependency, redundancy, abuse and neglect to over indulgence in family matters. Traditionally, the elders are respected in Indian homes and their care is still recognized as a family responsibility. It is necessary that intervention should prevent disintegration of the family and the community. Rapid globalization, urban migration, break-up of joint families, more engagement of women in paid jobs, social and economic pressures within the families and information technology are constantly adding new dimension to the issues concerning the elderly. Diseases and disabilities affect the elderly as well as their lifestyle patterns; therefore, the government health services need to be more equipped accordingly in terms of infrastructure and trained human resource. Welfare programmes can be planned with a special focus on the poor, lonely, disabled and chronically ill elderly. The quality of life of the elderly can be improved by reducing the burden of disease among them (Shashi, Mishra and Goswami, 2004). Initiatives such as Technology Interventions for Elderly, a programme initiated by the Ministry of Science and Technology (Government of India) for the disabled elderly, aims to create an enabling environment for the elderly. The programme supports various other programmes such as design and development of assistive devices, elderly friendly homes and the use of information and communication technology towards elderly care (Goyal and Dixit, 2009). Reaching and including the disabled people and their families in the design, implementation, monitoring and evaluation of all development programmes is desired as well as a necessity in the present time. The community will continue to have elderly people with disabilities with an improvement in the average life expectancy. Unless they become part of the development programmes or poverty alleviation programmes, the holistic development of a community cannot be achieved. Ageing and associated disabilities is natural; however, it needs preparedness on the part of individual, family, community and the governments.

NGOs are bringing issues and concerns to light and are addressing these issues at local level. Self-help groups (SHGs) or mutual aid groups, considered as an integral part of the CBR, can address the issues concerning ageing and disability, especially in rural/tribal areas in India. This needs an active collaboration of panchayati raj institutions (PRI) and funding support. Even older people with mild and moderate degree of disabilities can be productive and participative members of the community. We need both institutional and community-based care in India. The SHGs of senior citizens are very useful, and this has been successfully tested by NGOs in India. Such groups assist the senior citizens in the day-to-day life, such as payment of bills/escort services/ shopping assistance, etc. The group members have vast knowledge and skills to participate in community development activities. They assist senior citizens to avail health care and benefits such as rehabilitation services (CBR) pensions/assistive devices.

Keeping in view the declining support systems for the elderly, the community involvement needs to be encouraged to ensure care and support to the disabled ageing population. The Senior Citizens Forum, CBR Network (South East Asia), an SHG, adopts NPOP and extends its service for the welfare of senior citizens. More than 50 SHGs are working with different areas of Bangalore with an aim to facilitate meeting of senior citizens regularly. They aim to reduce their loneliness and to exchange their views, discuss their personal problems to seek solutions with other like-minded senior citizens. These SHGs arrange meetings with learned citizens, that is, doctors, social service personnel to share their experience and wisdom, and also conduct health check-ups to make them lead more meaningful life. Public policies should support community-based initiatives. However, some may need institutional care that should be provided closer to the community without uprooting them from the cultures in which they have lived all through their life. The elderly need to be encouraged to take up activities of cognitive engagement, physical exercise, balanced diet, no smoking or tobacco chewing and frequent health screenings (Albert, 2004). In India, there are discrepancies in understanding and the conceptualization of the term 'disability' that may be due to the social stigma attached to the disability. In addition, the term is not mentioned in the constitution or the millennium development goals (MDGs) that restricts the inclusion of people with disability (Lang, 2009; UN Enable, 2009).

Adoption of national policy of senior citizens has given a new ray of hope to elderly in India. However, there exist long gaps in the translation of the commitments made in the NPSC-2011 to the grassroots level reality. There is a need to shift from welfare approach to rights-based approach in addressing the needs of elderly people in general and elderly people with disabilities in particular. The disability policies in India have assumed the uniformity of disability experience while negating the varied nature of the disability. There are various types and degrees of disability with other socio-cultural factors including regional, geographical, class, caste, religion and gender. The policy document needs to envision greater inclusion of persons with disabilities while framing of such documents. In India, the medical, allied health professionals and people dedicated to the specialized services, who do not support inclusion, are mainly involved with the policymaking for the disability. There is a need to activate disability rights activists for getting social justice and full participation of the disabled people (Ghosh, 2012).

# Best Practices: Local and Global

Accessible transport is an important factor in reducing poverty, as it can facilitate the participation of people with disabilities including the elderly in economic, social and political spheres. An accessible transport system promotes independence and choices for disabled elderly (UNDP, 2010). There is a system of support and services available within the community with housing adaptation and the development of technological systems in different countries such as Italy, United Kingdom, Spain, Japan, Sweden, Canada, The United States and Israel (Brick and Lowenstein, 2011). Public-supported long-term care insurance programmes for senior citizens are functional in Netherlands, Israel, Germany, Austria and Japan. The US Foster Grandparents Programme has been replicated in a number of other countries. There is Hospice care for the terminally ill worldwide including India (Rajagopal and Venkateswaran, 2003; Randhawa, Owens, Fitches and Khan, 2003; Velayudhan et al., 2004). In India, more than 138 organizations are providing hospice and palliative care services in 16 states or union territories. These services are usually concentrated in large cities and regional cancer centres. Older Adults Technology Services programme has organized the USA's largest and most successful municipal technology initiative for senior citizens in New York City in partnerships with over 40 community organizations. This programme has achieved national recognition as a model for engaging, training, and supporting older adults to use computers and broadband access to improve their health, social engagement, access to services and the quality of life (OATS, 2009). Israel has pioneered the tele-health technology, such as remote cardiac monitoring. Services such as distress call buttons, occupational therapy for the housebound elderly, transportation for the disabled, loan of medical, rehabilitative and technological equipment are available in Israel (Brick and Lowenstein, 2011).

## Conclusion

Most of the countries, especially in Asian continent, are facing the dual challenge of a rapidly greying population and inadequate financial resources to support it. Age-related disability is a serious issue that needs to be tackled with more preparation. Most of the existing programmes meant for persons with disabilities have not included the concerns of senior citizens. India has signed and ratified the UN convention on the persons with disabilities in 2006 that adopts a right-based life cycle approach. The NPSC, 2011 has addressed the disability issue among the elderly to some extent that had been overlooked in earlier NPOP, 1999. The policies must recognize this fact to frame better disability-friendly policies and strategies. A barrier-free society, including buildings, living places and transportation systems for public use, is desired as it enables diverse groups, especially the elderly for an effective inclusion. The rights-based perspective is lacking in the policies, especially when it refers to vulnerable groups. Therefore, rights-based vision needs to be adopted while addressing all issues concerning older persons (Rao, 2010). There have to be schemes that can assist voluntary organization, welfare associations and community working for the senior citizens. The NGOs and community-based organizations can be encouraged to provide social support to the older population through establishment of day care centres, providing aids and appliances to disabled people and reaching out services at the time of necessity. In view of the varied diseases and disabilities affecting the elderly as well as their lifestyle patterns, the social support in health services needs to be more equipped in terms of infrastructure and human resource training. The disabled elderly constitutes a distinct group; therefore, an exclusive policy for this group to address their issues is required. India needs to address issues of ageing using an inclusive approach that needs a partnership between government, corporate sectors, civil societies and other stakeholders. However, there is a need to address and implement this issue adequately at both national- and state-level policies.

# References

Albert, S.M. (2004). *Public health and ageing: An introduction to maximizing function and well-being.* New York: Springer Publishing Company.

Bangladesh. (2004). Bangladesh population policy 2004. Dhaka: Ministry of Health and Family Welfare, Government of the People's Republic of Bangladesh.

Barbotte, E., Guillemin, F., Chau, N. & Lorhandicap Group. (2001). Prevalence of impairments, disabilities, handicaps and quality of life in the general population: A review of recent literature. *Bulletin of World Health Organisation, 79,* 1047–1055.

Braithwaite, J. & Mont, D. (2008). *Disability and poverty: A survey of World Bank poverty assessments and implications.* Washington, DC: World Bank.

Brick, Y. & Lowenstein, A. (2011). Global Ageing: Issues and Actions. *Journal of International Federation on Ageing, 7*(2).

Casey, B. & Yamada, A. (2002). *Getting older, getting poorer? A study of the earnings, pensions, assets and living arrangements of older people in nine countries*(Labour Market and Social Policy Occasional Papers, No. 60). Paris: OECD.

Census. (2001). New Delhi: Office of Registrar General.

CSO—Central Statistics Office. (2011). *Situation analysis of the elderly in India.* New Delhi: Ministry of Statistics and Programme Implementation, Government of India.

DFID. (2000). *Disability, poverty and development.* London: Department for International Development.

Ganesh, K.S., Yadav, A., Sajjan, B.S. & Kotian, M.S. (2008). Epidemiology of disability among geriatric population in the semi urban area of Mangalore city, Karnataka. *Indian Journal of Gerontology, 22*(1), 35–42.

Ghosh, N. (2012). *Disabled definitions, impaired policies: Reflections on limits of dominant concepts of disability* (Occasional Paper 34). Kolkata: Institute of Development Studies.

GoI. (2011). National policy for older persons. (2010). (Article 51), New Delhi: Ministry of Social Justice and Empowerment, Government of India.

Goyal, V.C. & Dixit, U. (2009). Assistive and enabling technologies for elderly in India. *International Congress on Gerontology and Geriatric Medicine 2009,* AIIMS, New Delhi, 27 February.

Husain, Z. & Ghosh, S. (2010). *Is health status of elderly worsening in India: A comparison of successive rounds of National Sample Survey data.* Available at http://mpra.ub.uni-muenchen. de/id/eprint/25747. (Accessed on 7 May 2014).

Joshi, K., Kumar, R. & Avasthi, A. (2003). Morbidity profile and its relationship with disability and psychological distress among elderly people in Northern India. *International Journal of Epidemiology, 32,* 978–987.

Kinsella & He. (2008). *An Ageing World* and United Nations, *World Economic and Social Survey 2007: Development in an Ageing World.*

Kowal, P., Kahn, K., Ng, N., Naidoo, N., Abdullah, S., Bawah, A., et al. (2010). Ageing and adult health status in eight lower-income countries: The INDEPTH WHO-SAGE collaboration. *Global Health Action Supplement, 2*: 11–22.

Kumar, S.G., Das, A., Bhandary, P.V., Soans, S.J., Kumar, H.N.H. & Kotian, M.S. (2008). Prevalence and pattern of mental disability using Indian disability evaluation assessment scale in a rural community of Karnataka. *Indian Journal of Psychiatry, 50,* 21–23.

Lakshmi, P.G. (2008). Condition of disabled elderly in India. *HelpAge India–Research and Development Journal, 14*(2), 27–33.

Lang, R. (2009). The United Nations convention on the right and dignities for persons with disability: A panacea for ending disability discrimination? *ALTER—European Journal of Disability Research, 3*, 266–285.

MPF. (2009). Investing for future population (Department of National Planning paper for the Maldives Partnership Forum (MPF), 23–24 March.

NSSO—National Sample Survey Organization.(2002). Office of the Chief Commissioner for Persons with Disabilities. New Delhi: Ministry of Social Justice and Empowerment, Government of India.

———. (2003). 58th Round. *Disabled persons in India.* New Delhi: Ministry of Statistics and Programme Implementation, Government of India.

———. (2006). 60th round. *Morbidity, health care and the condition of the aged* (Report No. 507). New Delhi: Ministry of Statistics and Programme Implementation, Government of India.

OATS—Older Adults Technology Services. (2009). Response to request for information: Broadband initiatives program and broadband technology opportunities program. Available at ww.ntia.doc.gov/legacy/broadbandgrants.

Pandey, M. (2009). *Poverty and disability among Indian elderly: Evidence from household survey* (ASARC Working Paper 09). New Delhi: Institute of Economic Growth.

Patel, S. (2009). An empirical study of causes of disability in India. *Internet Journal of Epidemiology, 6*(2). Available at https://ispub.com/IJE/6/2/4308

Patel, V., Chatterji, S., Chisholm, D., Ebrahim, S., Gopalakrishna, G., Mathers, C., et al. (2011). Chronic diseases and injuries in India. *Lancet, 377*, 413–428.

Prakash, I.J. (2003). Ageing, disability, and disabled older people in India. *Journal of Ageing and Social Policy, 15*(2–3), 85–108.

PWD. (2005). Persons With Disabilities (Equal Opportunities, Protection of Rights and Full Participation) Act, 1995. New Delhi: Ministry of social justice and empowerment, Government of India.

Rajagopal, M.R. & Venkateswaran, C. (2003). Palliative care in India: Successes and limitations. *Journal of Pain and Palliative Care Pharmacotherapy, 17*,121–128.

Rajan, S.I., & Sreerupa. (2008). Disease, disability and healthcare utilization among the aged. In S.I. Rajan, C. Risseeuw & M. Perera (Eds), *Institutional provisions and care for the aged: Perspectives from Asia and Europe* (pp. 39–54). New Delhi: Anthem Press.

Randhawa, G., Owens, A., Fitches, R. & Khan, Z. (2003). Communication in the development of culturally competent palliative care services in the UK: A case study. *International Journal of Palliative Nursing, 9*(41), 24–31.

Rao, I. (2010). Impact of national policy on older persons on older people with disability. *Research and Development Journal, 16*(3), 19–22.

Sengupta, M. & Agree, E.M. (2003). Gender, health, marriage and mobility difficulty among older adults in India. *Asia-Pacific Population Journal, 53*, 65.

Shah, B. & Mathur, P. (2010). Surveillance of cardiovascular disease risk factors in India: The need and scope. *Indian Journal of Medical Research, 132*, 634–642.

Sharma, A.K. & Praveen, V. (2002). Community based rehabilitation in primary health care system. *Indian Journal of Community Medicine, 117*, 139–142.

Shashi, K., Mishra, P. & Goswami, A. (2004). Morbidity among elderly persons residing in a resettlement colony of Delhi. *Indian Journal of Preventive and Social Medicine, 35*(1&2), 1–9.

Sri Lanka. (2002). Sri Lanka: Statement at the Second World Assembly on Ageing.

Srivastava, D.K. & Khan, J.A. (2008). Disability needs attention now! *Indian Journal for the Practising Doctor, 5*, 3–4.

Subramani, L. (2012). Census-2011: Sensitive to disabled population. *Deccan Herald*. Available at http://www.deccanherald.com/content/63000/census-2011-sensitive-disabled-population.html

Tas, U., Verhagen, A.P., Bierma-Zeinstra, S.M.A., Hofman, A., Odding, E., Pols, H.A.P., et al. (2007). Incidence and risk factors of disability in the elderly: The Rotterdam study. *Preventive Medicine, 44*, 272–278.

Thomas P. (2005). *Mainstreaming disability in development: India country Report*. Available at www.disabilitykar.net

Tyagi, R. (2007). Socio-health profile of aged population. In R.K. Pathak, A.K. Sinha, B.G. Banerjee, R.N. Vasishat & C.J. Edwin (Eds), *Bio-Social issues of health* (pp. 550–555). Delhi: Northern Book Centre.

UNDP. (2010). *A review of international best practice in accessible public transportation for persons with disabilities*. Kuala Lumpur, Malaysia: Ministry of Women, Family and Community Development & UNDP.

UN Enable. (2009). Convention on the Rights of Persons with Disabilities and Optional Protocol. UN-ESCAP (2006). United Nations ESCAP. Disability and the Biwako Millennium Framework for Action. Available at: www.unescap.org/epoc.

United Nations. (2007). *World economic and social survey: Development in an ageing world*. New York: United Nations.

Varghese, M. & Patel, V. (2004). The graying of India: Mental health perspective. In S.P. Agarwal (Ed.), *Mental health. An Indian perspective 1946–2003* (pp. 240–248). New Delhi: Elsevier.

Velayudhan, Y., Ollapally, M., Upadhyaya, V., Nair, S., Aldo, M. et al. (2004). Introduction of palliative care into undergraduate medical and nursing education in India: A critical evaluation. *Indian Journal of Palliative Care, 10*: 9–14.

WHO. (2004). *Global burden of disease report*. Geneva: WHO. Available at: www.who.int/healthinfo/global_burden_disease/GBD_report_2004.pdf.

———. (2008). *The global burden of disease: 2004 update*. Geneva: WHO Press.

———. (2011). *World report on disability*. Geneva: WHO.

WHO Secretariat. (2002). Adapted from documents A55/17 and A55/17 Add.1. Fifty-fifth World Health Assembly, Geneva, World Health Organization, 13–18 May. Available at http://www.who.int/gb/

World Bank. (2007). *People with disabilities in India: From commitments to outcomes*. Washington, DC: Human Development Unit, South Asia Region, World Bank.

# 8

# Prospective Approach to Healthy Ageing

*Pawan Kumar and A.M. Khan*

## Introduction

The challenge related to ageing and longevity has come into limelight along with a rapid demographic transition, which has resulted in unprecedented transition in the structure of the society. It means that family as a stable base of elderly care is changing in its form and contents, and becoming fragile to undertake the responsibility of total care of the elderly. This demands a shift in the existing perspective towards the elderly, and hence there is a need for an active participation of the elderly to be suitably built into the system. Therefore, they need to be placed into the framework of producing something rather than being passive recipients of welfare programmes. Longevity of life, reduction in the risk of death and universal reduction in fertility have resulted into increasing trend in the population growth of the older people. During the early history before 1900, the average length of life ranged between 20 and 35 years. By 1900, the life expectancy reached to 45–50 years in the industrialized countries. After 100 years, the life expectancy reached to 65 years for the world as whole and 80 years in some advanced countries. The birth rate during 19th century fell down fast, from 6–8 children per woman to the estimated 2.6 children worldwide; during 2000–2005, the total fertility had fallen below 2 children per woman in more than 67 countries in the world, including some developing countries. In India, the growth rate of 60-plus population is almost three times higher than the growth of the general population. The increase in 80-plus population is almost five times (WHO Regional Health Forum, 2012). As per United Nations (2002) projections, the population of the world stood at around 6.1 billion in the early 21st century and is likely to increase to 9.3 billion by 2050. The population of ageing globally is likely to multiply fourfold, from 595 million to 2 billion by 2050. The same phenomenon of increase is expected in both growth rates of the elderly and their proportion in the coming decades. The proportion of elderly population is expected to increase from 10 per cent in 2000 to 15 per cent in 2025 and 21.1 per cent in 2050. Countries such as China and India are not only at the forefront in terms of the absolute number of the world population, but also in terms of the absolute number of elderly population.

The population ageing is occurring across the globe as a result of the transition from a 'high fertility mortality regime' to a 'low fertility mortality regime' (Hayward and Zhenmei, 2001). The developed regions of the world being ahead of the developing countries with respect to demographic transition have already experienced its consequences; and the developing world is currently facing a similar situation. Although the proportion of the elderly (60 and above) seems to be relatively small in some of the developing countries, these countries still have more elderly persons in absolute terms because of their large population base. The Indian aged population is currently the second largest in the world next to that of China. The absolute number of 60-plus population in India is expected to increase from 77 million in 2001 to 137 million by 2021 (United Nations, 2005). Elderly population in India showed a gradual rise over the years, from 5.4 per cent in 1951, it grew to 6.4 per cent in 1981 and close to 7.45 per cent in 2001 and around 10 per cent in 2011. The growth rate of the elderly for the period 1991–2001 is close to 40 per cent, more than the general population growth rate. There are several challenging issues related to the ageing population. The composition of work participation gets affected. The positive windows of opportunity for work go down (World Bank, 1994; United Nations, 2005), reducing the productivity and growth of the economy (Rainwater and Timothy, 1999). Population ageing has economic and social implications in a long run and it creates an imbalance within generations (Keynes, 1936). Its few implications are discussed in the following sections.

# Epidemiological Transition and Implications

Changes in age composition affect both individuals and families through a higher occurrence of widowhood due to age difference in marriage and living arrangements for family members (Schafer, 1999). Financial inadequacy seems to be of a higher degree among elderly women compared to their male counterparts (Dak and Sharma, 1987; Nandal et al., 1987). The presence of frail elderly persons in the house breaks down the existing resource-sharing mechanism, resulting in the reduction of both 'overall welfare and individual welfare' (Sen, 1984). The research revealed that elderly persons suffer from social, economic and health insecurities in old age and fall short of the basic amenities (Rajan, Mishra and Sarma, 1999; Rajan, 2004; Alam and Karan, 2011). It results in epidemiological transition in the nature and type of ailments. It is accompanied by changes in the patterns of diseases and morbidity across time (Omran, 1971). With the changes in the pattern of illness, there is a prime shift in the services demanded and their accessibility to the aged. Burden of disease and lack of access to proper care are major challenges for individual elderly. Studies in the Western Europe and United States show that a fast decline in mortality of older people is creating a nightmare with high incidence of morbidity due to the occurrence of chronic diseases (Haines, 1995). The morbidity pattern is changing across the world; non-communicable diseases are increasing rapidly. The changing pattern of morbidity, particularly during old age, has created bigger challenges, and has also burdened the existing health care system (Kane et al., 1990; Kumar and Khan, 2012). There are evidences of unhealthy ageing from almost all the developing countries of Asia, Africa and Latin America. Various studies also show that the health risk of the elderly is mainly confined to access to health care that result in unhealthy ageing (Robeldo, 1985; Sokolovsky, 1991). The health risk of an aged person in a household can result in catastrophic shock in the family that can make households more exposed to poverty. The health problems of the elderly are largely affected due to their socio-economic and emotional insecurities. Health care for the elderly is the most important service to be made easily accessible, affordable and acceptable to all the old people. Involvement of old people into productive activities contributes to healthy ageing. Negative images of old age are linked with the socially and culturally defined norms. Globally, 70 per cent of all older people now live in low-income or middle-income countries. Health care systems need to find innovative and sustainable ways to cope up with the demographic shift. As reported by John Beard, director, World Health Organization's (WHO's) Department of Ageing and Life Course, 'With the rapid ageing of populations, finding the right model for long-term care (LTC) becomes more and more urgent.' The demographic shift is also being accompanied by changing social patterns, including smaller families, different residential patterns and increased female labour force participation. These factors often contribute to an increased need for paid care (Institute of Medicine, 2001). So, the care of the elderly is a major challenge for the family. It is more likely that institutionalized paid care for the elderly will replace familial care in the changing social settings that affect familial relations. The precise implications of population ageing for future levels of health and health care utilization would depend on whether the increases in life expectancy experienced in general are accompanied by suitable policies and programmes (Gruenberg, 1977; Kramer, 1980; Manton, 1982).

# Health Care and Ageing

Primary health care services at present mainly focus on physical diseases. They do not encompass other three components of health as per definition of WHO, which defines health as a state of physical, social and emotional well-being and not merely an absence of disease and infirmity. The profile of health problems of the elderly is loaded with social, emotional and economic insecurities. Any health care system devoid of these would remain meagre and notional, no matter whatever claim is made by the concerned department and country. The primary health care system has been envisaged as a base of elderly health care. It has to be fully redesigned in its services, taking into consideration the rapid epidemiological transition from communicable to non-communicable diseases. As Hooyman and Kiyak (2002) noted in their textbook on social gerontology, LTC is dealt with a wider array of services and assistance programmes. While wider selection of options for LTC is certainly beneficial to both the elderly and their families, it also poses a situation for families that can be sometimes stressful. So, the message in the society regarding LTC should be that just putting grandma or grandpa, mother or father into any old-age home/nursing home is not desirable, whereas determining the needs and desires of the elderly individual and matching them with the correct type of care should be the goal.

Both societies and state should own the responsibility of LTC and create and strengthen the system in future. In this context, Person–Environment (PE) Congruence Model takes into account a person's compatibility with his/her environment and assumes that the impact of the environment is mediated by the individual's abilities and needs (Hooyman and Kiyak, 2002). As such, it becomes an issue to ensure that the elderly individual being placed in a LTC facility is in equilibrium with the environment. In order to ensure such things, it is important to look at the location of the facility, the rules and regulations and the services provided. The PE congruence is defined as the degree to which individual and environmental characteristics match (Kristof-Brown, Zimmerman and Johnson, 2005). The characteristics may include an individual's biological or psychological needs, values, goals, abilities or personality, while environmental characteristics could include job demands, cultural values, rewards or various environmental conditions such as shelter, heat or food availability (Cable and Edwards, 2004). The PE fit can be understood as a specific type of person–situation interaction that specifies match between corresponding person and environment dimensions. The PE Congruence model also assumes that individuals are motivated to find environments that are congruent with their needs. In a broader sense, this model assumes that a positive outcome will result when specific personal needs or preferences are consistent with environmental demands and resources (Muchinsky and Monahan, 1987).

LTC demands a variety of services, both the medical and non-medical, to older people suffering with chronic illness or disability. This is the situation of life when older persons cannot take care of themselves and institutional care becomes a necessity. The family may face enormous constraints to provide LTC, which is an indispensable reality. It would require a long-term planning, decision-making, designing, financial provision, human resource development and execution of decisions to make the services available to the vulnerable elderly (Kumar and Khan, 2014). Informal care is by far the most prevalent form of LTC throughout the world. With increasing longevity of life, the demand of LTC is much higher, whereas availability of informal caregivers (by mostly the family members, relatives and friends) is declining due to structural and functional changes in the family. So, there is conflicting situation and designing of LTC becomes a major challenge in the context of smaller families, longevity, separate and more independent living situations for older people and workplaces away from home. Presently, in LTC, spouses and adult children, especially daughters and daughters-in-law, are the most common informal caregivers. They typically come to this role under unavoidable circumstances without knowing a great deal about (a) how the care should be provided, (b) how to navigate an often-complicated financing and delivery system, (c) the likely course of disability and illnesses and (d) how to cope emotionally with the strains of caring for a highly disabled individual. These need to be built into the society using multi-facet approach. Paid services either at home or in institution can play some relieving role; thus, they should be inducted in LTC.

Designing LTC needs due focus on the activities of daily living (ADL) and instrumental ADL (IADL). Individual elderly face problems in brushing teeth, bathing, dressing, etc. (ADL) and immobility (IADL). Individuals suffering from dementia need different types of care (Institute of Medicine, 2001; Hooyman and Kiyak, 2002). In LTC, the facilities have a great deal of concerns with these. Nutritional requirements and risk management are very important features. Nutritional concerns stem from the wide variety of individuals present in the facility. Some elderly are plagued with nutrition-related illnesses, such as diabetes, some may have problems with their weight (over or under) and others still may have allergies to certain foods. Obviously, due to the major health impairment, proper nutrition care facility is extremely important. Other deficiencies such as a mineral or vitamin deficiencies are also responsible for a number of illnesses. Poor immune system and bone strength are bigger issues and LTC is needed in many such cases. Risk management is another internal issue that must be addressed with sincerity by LTC employees and management (Institute of Medicine, 2001). LTC typically provides living accommodation for people who require on-site delivery and round-the-clock supervised care. Such arrangement includes professional health services, personal care and services, such as meals, laundry and housekeeping. These facilities can be classified in different categories, such as nursing homes, personal care facility, and residential care facility, and so on. It is estimated that 90 per cent of all home care is provided informally by a loved one without compensation. However, there are a large number of issues currently plaguing in LTC of the elderly. The government's financing has a long way to go into creating LTC facilities. The issues plaguing LTC of the elderly must include retirement plans, health care plans, social support systems and financial management. It is common for LTC to provide custodial and non-skilled care, such as assisting with normal daily tasks, such as dressing, bathing and using the bathroom. Increasingly, LTC involves providing a level of medical care that requires the expertise of skilled practitioners to address the often multiple chronic conditions associated with older populations. LTC can be provided at home, in the community, in assisted living facilities or in nursing homes. It may be needed for persons of any age over 60 years (WHO, 2003). States needs to institute and strengthen programmes for health care and palliative/terminal care through the use of pharmacological and non-pharmacological interventions. Giving special attention to patients suffering from dementia/Alzheimer's disease through community health care (at day care centres) is suggested for health care of the elderly.

## Caregiver's Concerns

Caregiver's well-being is an extremely important issue in LTC because it determines the quality of care. Stresses affecting the caregiver's are: financial (costs of care, conflicts between job and care and excessive absence at work), physical (headaches, weight changes, sleep disturbances and self-neglect) and emotional (depression, anxiety, loneliness, resentment, anger and strained family relationships). To overcome these, there is a need for strong supportive services to the caregivers. These services are adult day care, respite care, volunteer help at home, medical aid, community support, etc. If at home, care giving is to continue for a longer time with less priority to the supportive care facilities, then the care givers would face difficulties to continue their services. So, caregivers need more support in one form or another in order to efficiently carry out the primary care giving role (WHO, 2003).

## Economic Constraints in Care

The developed countries today are in an advantageous position because of dealing with the problems of old-age care for a longer period and also having the State provisions for the old-age security measures. The situation in developing countries is quite different, and therefore the lessons learnt about western models of old-age care are likely to have limited implications. The implication for social and economic lives of the elderly is far reaching in the Asian countries. Under western model, the state takes care of the physical health problems of the elderly, whereas eastern model is largely based on family care. As evident, developed nations had committed for old-age care as a State responsibility in their constitutions, although they are now finding it difficult in view of the increasing imbalance in the resources to be generated by the young population and the resource to be consumed by the older people. The scenario will remain same for all the countries if they fail to recognize the gravity of problem of ageing and also fail to make an application of innovative strategies. This chapter highlights the prospective approach to healthy ageing. In this context, few strategies are discussed in the following section.

# The Future Perspective of Healthy Ageing

The existing perspective of old-age care needs futuristic outlook. The planning and policy makers need to realize that the trend of the elderly growth and decline in fertility is going to create a serious imbalance between producers of the resources and consumers of the created resources, hence efforts are required to keep the persons into enabling environment where the elderly remain engaged in producing something rather than retiring from the productivity. The second futuristic outlook is to prepare people from an early stage of life towards a healthy and active ageing. Preventive and promotive outlook and suitable policies and programmes would help the countries to reduce the expenditures that the elderly needs in case of multiple disabilities and diseases. Self-care among the elderly needs to get sufficient space in the policy and programmes. Some of futuristic perspectives are discussed in the next section.

# Reimaging of Old Age as Social Construct

The picture of old age is portrayed as a burden, helpless, powerless, passive, pessimistic and depressive, and with a host of emotional problems like alienation, loneliness, etc. Most of these images are basically transmitted from the society itself. The image of old age is socially and culturally defined concept, thus varies cross culturally. The images that the elderly develop are a reflection of what the society and country at large expect. The elderly simply reciprocate to what they experience. It is true that there is a decay of body cell with age. However, it does not justify the negative images that the society beholds for the elderly. For example, the children are no more considered as a burden, they are recognized as a source of prosperity. The situation for the elderly is contrary. Should we believe that nature itself creates discrimination at different stages of human life? Or it treats each stage as unique, distinctive and incomparable; we need to find answers of all these. The society itself has created classification of age and inflicted discrimination by attaching preferential values to each stage of life. So, the rational society needs to understand the laws of nature and change its own mindset regarding preferential values attached to child, youth and old age. All the stages of life are equally good and incomparable. The sun rays are brighter in the middle of the day and same become dull at the time of sunset. Do they lose their importance? The answer is no. Sunset light is as significant as it is in mid-day. The same thing is true with human being, child, old age and youth. Each stage inherits its own values of life. Therefore, each stage of life is to be viewed and recognized in its own form. The society needs to learn, accept and appreciate each stage of life without comparing. In the society, stage-specific stereotype is prevalent phenomenon and that is why negative imaging in the elderly is a social construct of reality. Transforming negative images of old age to positive direction is a major challenge. It requires a multipronged approach. Government's interventions towards this direction need to be scientifically designed and suitably carried out in the society through formal and the informal education system with the help of the civil society and community at large. There is a need to educate the society at large that each stage of life is unique and distinct, carrying special features of life that are incomparable, and each stage of life should have equal opportunity for healthy living.

Three stages of life classified in this context are: (1) childhood with image of future source of power and productivity, (2) youth as a present source of power and productivity and (3) old age with an image of loss of productivity and power. It has been theorized that the centre of healthy ageing lies in retaining the 'identity of productivity' during old age. Once it is lost, the quality of care cannot be ensured in view of growing changes amongst younger generations (Khan, 2003). On one hand, older persons are viewed as a custodian of wisdom, experience and maturity, on the other hand, old age is considered as a state of miseries, dependency, helplessness, hopelessness, burden, sickness, sadness, etc. Even National Policy on Older Persons (NPOP) has depicted old people as burden, thus, substantiating the same image that the society beholds (Khan, 2003). Negative images in the society affect the happiness of older persons. Therefore, the best course of intervention is to change the images of negativity at large, and it is possible that the elderly can be made to realize and recognize their potential for active ageing. It is also possible to mould the perception of the society towards older people. The society could be prepared to accept old age as a distinctive stage of life, incomparable to any other state. People could be educated in self-care, as an indicator of active ageing. Old-age images of miseries transfer from one generation to another generation and children are the source of transmitting it. Therefore, the re-imaging process needs to begin from the early stage of life. The secret of healthy ageing lies in the appropriate understanding of re-images of ageing by proper interventions (Khan, 2008).

## Old Age as Resource

The perspective of old as a burden needs to be converted into old as a resource. As per old-age classification, the majority of older people fall into young-old category, and this group is to be engaged into a productive framework to prevent the problem so as to contribute to the society. The form and content of engagement of the elderly can be decoded into social and cultural contexts. The focus of a long-term approach should be on the younger generation to prepare them through their socialization and education to inculcate positive emotions and images for the care of older people. The old-age planning needs to get a place in the mind of the younger generation from the early stage of life. While preparing to meet the challenges of ageing, our old views about the elderly require a proactive outlook of Bose (2000) who said:

> Elderly are assets and not liabilities; elderly care is not a charity; Ministry of Welfare has no role; a new Ministry of Elderly should be created. The elderly with their life time's experience are the best persons to train the younger generation at the lowest cost.

The elderly also need to realize and recognize that they are capable of managing themselves provided they develop the capacity of knowing themselves and to accept their hidden potentiality. This requires socially enabling environment. Welfare-oriented schemes can only supplement the healthy ageing process. Age of forced retirement needs drastic change if the ability, competence and productivity of young-old people are taken as criteria. Many developed countries have shifted the retirement age from 60 to 65 and 70 years, and it is continuously increasing along with the longevity of life.

## Right for Natural Claim

A large number of elderly people do not get due care despite having sufficient property (in terms of housing saving). Sons (natural owner of the parent's property) behave indifferently; they rather abuse them and deprive their parents from basic care. They disown them and even throw their parents out of their home. So, the right to have a natural claim on the property of parents without providing quality care should be withdrawn. The children inflicting undesirable and highly condemnable torture of any nature towards their elderly parents should be deprived of the parent's resources. There are areas of immediate concern for the policymakers, these are: (1) ensuring adequate health care, economic and social support; (2) appropriate age-friendly health care policy and social services; (3) special policy concern for those who carry double responsibility of taking care of their children, their parents and even grandparents; (4) legal bindings for those who deny the responsibility of good health care to their parents and grandparents; (5) preparing youth on positive values of family care; (6) preparing the elderly to practice healthy lifestyle and (7) specific policy and programmes for rural, urban and slum elderly who have lost family care support due to migration or other circumstances.

## Empowerment

According to Ramamurthy and Jamuna (2004), empowerment of the elderly refers to building a capacity of the elderly and enabling them to use this capacity to negotiate and procure their needs. The empowerment means not only possessing the power but being able to use it effectively to one's advantage. They have listed three dimensions of empowerment. These are: (1) financial dimension, (2) health and (3) personal and social. Legal dimension is equally important in the context of empowerment. Positivity to old age is to be brought into the ambit of empowerment. Short- and long-term strategies to address healthy life of the elderly of today and tomorrow need professional, social and political discourses. The society's role in older person's dignity and freedom should be central themes of discussion. The discourses should focus on empowerment of social, economic, health care, emotional and recreational need of the elderly. Old-age planning and development programmes should have a focus on different categories of the elderly such as the old–old and centenarians who suffer with multiple disabilities. Poor elderly should be extended maximum support by the government. The involvement of senior citizen organizations in the empowerment process is required. Educational and training programmes need to be undertaken by involving professionals, planners, administrators, social workers and others working in non-governmental organizations (NGOs) of repute. The theme for the World Health Day 2012 is 'Health and Ageing' with the message that 'good health adds life to years'. The focus of activities is on (1) how good health throughout life can help older men and women to lead contended and productive lives and (2) how the elderly become resource base for their families and communities (WHO Regional Health Forum, 2012). These two themes require new look.

## Building Cities Elderly Friendly

The global ageing is forcing city planners around the world to create an effective support system for the older populations. Planners need to believe that by 2050, almost 2 billion people will be aged 60 and over, it is approximately double to what it was in 2006. This will mark one of the most historic demographic shifts in human history and for the first time, people over 65 years will outnumber those under the age of 5 globally. Another feature is that the most dramatic population shifts will occur outside the developed world, that is, in low-income or middle-income nations. The National Institute on Ageing estimated that most 'developed' nations took approximately 25–115 years in reaching to 14 per cent of the nation's population over 65. The developing nations would take around 35 years in reaching to the same level. One can imagine how massive infrastructural, individual, and family-based challenges would be emerging in the 21st century. The very first message that should go into the society at large within shortest time is that ageing concerns each and every one of us—whether young or old, male or female, rich or poor—no matter where we live (WHO Regional Health Forum, 2012). The implications of this historic shift are not known to the city planners at present. That is why growing cities are less friendly to the older people. The city planners need to ensure that older people will remain independent, socially engaged and enjoy a high level of well-being as long as possible. Simple changes to a city environment, such as offering computer classes, creating a map of public toilets or lengthening the time of crosswalk signals, have the potential to transform the lifestyles of older adults in a manner that enhances well-being and comfort in an ageing world. However, redesigning urban environments to foster the health, social engagement and productivity of older people can be a challenging task (WHO Regional Health Forum, 2012).

## Conclusion

The migration and breakdown of family from joint to nuclear can be responsible for growing distances (both physical and psychological) between young and the old. It adversely affects the care givers' presence and family support to the elderly. These are inevitable realities in the era of globalization. Therefore, the challenge is how to safeguard genuine needs of elderly care in the family, community and institutions. So far, our country's NPOP has focussed more on what they can benefit from the government in the material form. It does not focus on the quality care of all elderly. The elderly themselves have to fight with ageism by establishing a new model of active and healthy ageing. There is a need to give special attention in National Policy towards the empowerment of the elderly to facilitate their involvement into productive and developmental activities.

The health care of the elderly needs comprehensive, holistic and mix of public–private partnership because no profit organizations including NGO, trusts, charities and private health care institutions can play a significant role. While designing public–private mix model, rehabilitation care, respite care, LTC, palliative and terminal care for oldest old need special recognition of State. Private players would not find big market area for restoration of vision, hearing problems, hospice and palliative care for terminally ill persons, and it should remain a major concern for State. An integrated educational programme for health care of the elderly need short- and long-term programmes in order to empower people for self-care. This needs to include family as a major stakeholder. NGOs need encouragement of State in building elderly friendly environment to manage stereotyped ageing, that is, ageism that is a potential barrier in creating the environment for healthy ageing. The elderly also need to realize and recognize that they are capable of managing themselves. Age of retirement needs critical introspection by the country; it should be made flexible considering the ability, competence and productivity of the elderly that is likely to reduce the burden of the State. This concept of young elderly as resource rather than burden needs policy, programme and effective operationalization in future.

# References

Alam, M. & Karan, A. (2011). *Elderly health in India, dimensions, differentials and determinants, building knowledge based population ageing in India* (Working Paper: 3). New Delhi: UNFPA.

Bose, A. (2000). *Empowerment of Elderly* (Seminar Report). New Delhi: NIHFW.

Cable, D.M. & Edwards, J.R. (2004). Complementary and supplementary fit: A theoretical and empirical integration. *Journal of Applied Psychology, 89*, 822–834.

Dak, T.M. & Sharma, M.L. (1987). Changing status of the aged in North Indian villages. In M.L. Sharma & T.M. Dak (Eds), *Ageing in India* (pp. 43–55). New Delhi: Ajanta Publications.

Gruenberg, E.M. (1977). The failures of success. *Milbank Memorial Fund Quarterly Health and Society, 55*(1), 3–24.

Haines, M.R. (1995). Disease and health through the ages. In J. Somon (Ed.), *The State of Humanity* (pp. 51–60). Oxford: Basil Blackwell.

Hayward, M.D. & Zhenmei, Z. (2001). The demographic revolution in population ageing: A century of change, 1950–2050. In R.K. Binstock & L.K. George (Eds), *A book of Ageing and the Social Sciences*, (5th Ed., pp. 69–85). New York: Academic Press.

Hooyman, N. & Kiyak, H.A. (2002). *Social gerontology: A multidisciplinary perspective* (6th Ed.). Boston, MA: Pearson Education Company.

Institute of Medicine. (2001). *Improving the quality of long term care.* Washington, DC: National Academy Press.

Kane, R.L., Evans, J.G., McFadyen, D. (1990). *Improving the health of older people:A World View.* New York: Oxford University Press.

Keynes, J.M. (1936). *The general theory of employment, interest and money* (Vol. VII). London: Macmillan.

Khan, A.M. (2003). Managing mind-set of young and old; healthy ageing. *Indian Journal of Gerontology*, *17*(1 &2),189–196.

———. (2008). Issues related to ageing and social empowerment in India. In K.N. Bhatt (Ed.), *Population, environment and health emerging issues.* Jaipur: Rawat Publication.

Kramer, M. (1980). The rising pandemic of mental disorders and associated chronic diseases and disabilities. *Acta Psychiatrica Scandinavica*, *62*(285), 282–297.

Kristof-Brown, A.L., Zimmerman, R.D. & Johnson, E.C. (2005). Consequences of individuals' fit at work: A meta-analysis of person–job, person–organization, person–group, and person–supervisor fit. *Personnel Psychology*, *58*, 281–342.

Kumar, P. & Khan, A.M. (2012). Epidemiological transition and emerging conflicts in health care. *Global Research Analysis*, *1*(1), 96–97.

———. (2014). Human resource development for health care of elderly. In T. Paltasingh & R. Tyagi (Eds), *Emerging Issues in Gerontology-Relevance and Possibilities.* New Delhi: Bookwell Publishers.

Manton, K.G. (1982). Changing concepts of morbidity and mortality in the elderly population. *Milbank Memorial Fund Quarterly Health and Society*, *60*(2), 183–244.

Muchinsky, P.M. & Monahan, C.J. (1987). What is person–environment congruence? Supplementary versus complementary models of fit. *Journal of Vocational Behavior.* *31*(3), 268–277.

Nandal, D.S., Dhatri, R.S., Kadian, R.S. (1987). Ageing problems in the structural context. In M.L. Sharma & T.M. Dak (Eds), *Ageing in India: Challenge for the Society* (pp. 106–116). New Delhi: Ajanta Publications.

Omran, A.R. (1971). The epidemiologic transition. *Milbank Memorial Fund Quarterly. Health and Society.* *49*(I), 509–538.

Rainwater, L. & Timothy, M.S. (1999). *From relative to real income: Purchase power parties and household micro data, problems and prospects.* Papers and Final Report of the Third Meeting on Household Income Statistics. Ottawa, Canada: Statistics Canada, pp. 139–163. Available at: http://www.lis.ceps.lu/canberra/ottawareport/ottasession5.PDF.

Rajan, S.I. (2004). *Chronic poverty among the elderly* (Working Paper 17). New Delhi: Chronic Poverty Research Centre, IIPA.

Rajan, S.I., Mishra, U.S. & Sarma, P.S. (1999). *India's elderly burden or challenge.* New Delhi: SAGE Publication.

Ramamurthy, P.V. & Jamuna, D. (2004). *Handbook of India Gerontology.* New Delhi: Serials Publication.

Robeldo. (1985). *Unhealthy Ageing in Mexico,* CCRA Paper.

Schafer, R. (1999). *Determinants of living arrangements of the elderly.* W99-6, Joint Centre for Housing Studies. Cambridge: Harvard University.

Sen, A.K. (1984). *Resources, values and development.* Oxford: Oxford Blackwell.

Sokolovsky. (1991). Health Transition and Public Policy in USSR. CSRA paper, Moscow.

United Nations. (2002). *International Plan of action on ageing 2002.* UN: Division for Social Policy and Development.

————. (2005). *State of world population.* New York: UNFPA.

WHO. (2003). *Key policy issues in long term care.* World Health Organization collection on long term care. Geneva: WHO.

WHO, Regional Health Form. (2012). South East Asia region. *Special issue on Ageing and Health.* 16 (1).

World Bank. (1994). *Averting the old age crisis: Policies to protect the old and promote growth.* Washington, DC: World Bank.

# Section IV

## Gender and Culture

# 9

# Gender-sensitive Intervention for Elderly Women

*Tattwamasi Paltasingh and Renu Tyagi*

## Introduction

Gender is an important factor to determine the steady well-being of the society. Gender relations structure the entire life cycle, from birth to old age, influencing access to resources, opportunities and shaping life at every stage. Ageing is a process that encompasses a broad spectrum of experiences. A shift towards global population ageing and feminization of ageing is witnessed. The population of elderly women is growing rapidly and they are affected by this trend in both developed and developing countries. In India since independence, there is a relatively higher ratio of females to males in elderly population than the general population. Despite this demographic trend, women continue to endure unequal and inadequate access to health, education, employment and resources across cultures. In old age, the life of women is full of physical, social, emotional and financial insecurities. Often they are subjected to discrimination on grounds of age or gender. The impact of gender inequalities throughout a woman's lifespan in respect of education, employment opportunities and health care services widens at every stage of life and becomes more evident during the old age. As a result, older women are more likely than older men to suffer due to poverty and deprivation of basic needs. In the traditional Indian culture, a human lifespan is 100 years. In ordinary social intercourse, people would be considered old when their children were married and had grandchildren, regardless of their chronological age. Marriage of a son and arrival of a daughter-in-law into the joint family often reflect a major transition in the life of a woman. Menopause and the arrival of grandchildren usually are considered to be the advent of old age for women. There is a trend for women to consider themselves old at a younger age than men. In India, multigenerational living arrangements have been an integral part of the rural and the urban scenarios. During the last century, the socio-economic and value systems have slowly eroded. There is an increasing participation of women in the workforce, the emergence of more nuclear families and increased migration for better education and career prospects. Hence, the impact of ageing on gender-related issues requires serious discussions and analysis.

Broadly, the chapter would address the issues related to gender and ageing. It discusses and analyses the gender disparities among the elderly in an Indian situation. The first section of the chapter focuses on demographic transition in favour of females. The next section elaborates the prevailing gender disparities in terms of education, employment opportunities, cultural practices, health facilities and economic vulnerability. The chapter would reflect on issues like widowhood in association with the social norms that govern marital age and other customary practices that dictate the vulnerable position of the older women. The section on the lifetime contribution of women highlights their socio-economic support towards family and the society. Subsequent section provides a critical appraisal of the existing policy and other such interventions that have been proved to be inadequate in addressing the gender issues, followed by a brief conclusion.

# Global Population Ageing and Feminization

Ageing is a process that encompasses a broad spectrum of experiences. The 21st century has been witnessing the shift towards global population ageing. The number of older people in 2050 is estimated to be over 2 billion, that is, 22 per cent of the global population, an unprecedented doubling of the present 11 per cent of elderly population. The majority of this elderly population is comprised of elderly women (55%). About 80 per cent of elderly men are married as compared to only 48 per cent of married elderly women. There are 82 men for every 100 women at 60 years of age; however, there are only 55 men for every 100 women at the age of 80, witnessing majority of older women than older men (UNFPA, 2008).

In India, the population of older people reached to 100 million at present and by 2050, the figure is estimated to rise to 326 million (HelpAge India, 2012). The total population of the senior citizens (60+) was 7.7 crore, including 3.8 crore males and 3.9 crore females (Census of India, 2001), which is projected to increase by 2026 with profound social implications. India is one of the few countries in the world where men outnumber women at all ages till about 70 years; however, after 70 years of age, this trend reverses with more women than men (Dandekar, 1996). There is a relatively higher ratio of females to males in elderly population than in the general population. Feminization of elderly population is a noticeable phenomenon (Census of India, 2001). Further, the life expectancy of the elderly has gone up from 32 years in 1947 to 67 years in 2001. One of the main social effects of the extension of life in later years is an extended period of widowhood for women. The percentages of widows are disproportionately higher than that of widowers due to the cultural practice of men marrying younger women and widow remarriage being uncommon. The rate of divorce is negligible in this age group. According to NSS 42nd round, there were 654 widows and 238 widowers per 1,000 old persons in rural areas. The respective figures were 687 and 200 for urban areas. More than 65 per cent of Indian women live without a spouse as compared to 29 per cent of older men. About 40 per cent of the elderly (60% men and 19% women) were working. In rural areas, 66 per cent of elderly men and more than 23 per cent of aged women were participating in the economic activities, while in urban areas, only 39 per cent of elderly men and about 7 per cent of elderly women were economically active. The majority of the economically dependent elderly are financially supported by their own children, followed by the spouse. The female old–age dependency ratio is increasing over time (NSSO, 2008).

Older women are more likely to confront the challenge of loneliness to a greater extent due to their longer life expectancy, higher likelihood of being widowed, living alone and declining health (Hall and Havens, 2005). Ageism and elder mistreatment are of great concern for both elderly women and men; however, elderly women suffer worse than elderly men (Karkal, 1999), thereby making such issues more challenging for the ageing women. In a recent survey report of Help Age India, the metropolitan cities Mumbai and Delhi witnessed significant percentage of elder abuse (about 30%). The highest percentage of elder abuse is reported from Bhopal in Madhya Pradesh (more than 77%), followed by Guwahati in Assam (60%). Elderly women were found to have poor knowledge and awareness than elderly men about the available reporting and redressal mechanisms regarding elder abuse. Services such as police helplines and Parents and Welfare Act are rarely used by the elderly (HelpAge India, 2012).

The impact of gender inequalities throughout a woman's lifespan is reflected in old age, and it often results in unfair resource allocation, maltreatment, gender-based violence and prevention of access to basic services. In many cases, the women are marginalized and deprived of participation on equal terms in the social, economic, cultural and political activities of their society. As many women age and their independence declines, they become more vulnerable to abuse, exploitation and violence. Many older women face neglect, as they are considered no longer economically or reproductively useful and are seen as a burden on their families. In addition, widowhood, divorce, lack of caregivers for older women, postmenopausal difficulties, absence of geriatric medicine and health care are other grounds of discrimination that prohibit older women from enjoying their human rights. Socio-economic insecurity, medical problems and emotional insecurity increase their vulnerability (UNFPA, 2008). The emotional turmoil, the sense of anxiety, fear, anger and desperation that she faces in her early years take its toll during the later years of life.

# Gender Discrimination and Unequal Access

Gender is an important variable that influences the quality of life at all ages. Elderly people, and particularly elderly women, are marginalized without any state protection (Gopal, 2006). It is assumed that the women's primary involvement is in reproductive labour, unpaid household work and caregiving, and such notions often restrict women's employment opportunities, mobility, educational attainment and skills development. Gender and age discriminations, accompanied by physical and emotional vulnerability, make the life of an older woman difficult. Low social status, discriminatory practices, early marriage, multiple pregnancies and poor attention to health issues are responsible for the poor health status of older women. Societies assign different age expectations according to gender, socio-cultural norms and role assignments. Loneliness, socio-economic insecurity, medical insecurity and human rights are the major issues for elderly women, especially in the developing nations.

## Unequal Education and Limited Employment Opportunities

India represents wide gender gaps when it comes to education and employment opportunities, and these gaps have existed for a long time in the country. Socio-cultural norms and economic factors still prevent girls from getting education opportunities. Among elderly population, only 50 per cent of elderly men and 20 per cent of elderly women aged 60 years or more were literate through formal schooling (NSSO, 2008). Elderly women have high levels of illiteracy. There is a wide gender gap in education that is predicted to continue (United Nations, 2005). This further limits the ability of elderly women to be active members of their society and interferes with their access to fundamental human rights (Gomez, 2002). In India, most of the women are concentrated in low-wage, insignificant and demanding jobs, or part-time employment with few benefits and little security. Though their work embodies a lifetime of learned expertise and experience, women during her lifetime spend more time on combined unpaid and paid work than men. More than 78 per cent of the elderly workforce is engaged in agricultural activities, which for women marks an 84 per cent (Census of India, 2001).

## Gender and Cultural Practices

Discrimination against older women is often based on deep rooted cultural and social bias. Most women perceive themselves as 'old' by the time they are 50 years old. This perception of self as 'old' is based on the presence of grandchildren, widowhood, shrinkage of social roles and postmenopausal status (Prakash, 1997). In their life cycle, women earn less and experience inequality at work in the family and the society. For those women whose lifestyle is based on the husband as the main breadwinner, the economic situation deteriorates once they become widows, because their main source of income is reduced or ceased with the death of the spouse. A common phenomenon of ageing in South Asia, that is, desire for an elderly person to give up on the worldly pleasures and withdraw from this life is noticed. At the same time, the love and respect of these old women, sense of duty and feelings of devotion of the sons for their mother and the services carried by the daughters-in-law are also observed (Lamb, 2000; 2002).

## Economic Issues and Unequal Property

Old-age pension (OAP) schemes for elderly women are very restricted, including women only from below poverty line (BPL) category. This categorization is also not very inclusive. These women receive an amount of ₹200 pm only as the OAP that is not sufficient. These schemes do not include the women from lower middle and middle-class families. Their economic needs are not paid serious attention. Property right should always be made joint for men and women, as in India, there is no automatic transfer of the property right to wife on its own after the death of husband. This is very important because most women are outliving their husbands in the twilight years of their lives. For instance if a husband is suffering with a disease like dementia that causes memory loss, etc., the children and others can take advantage of the situation and the needy elderly woman is left behind. In many traditional societies including India, women have limited access to rights of inheritance or property ownership, and most of the women do not receive the benefits of pension schemes or provident funds. Therefore, they depend on the family or the state for financial support and living arrangements. Elder women continue to endure unequal and inadequate access to wealth, property and resources across cultures. Elderly women, especially widows, face substantial gender differential in the ownership of property and assets, in role and participation in the family as compared to aged men in India, hence influencing their access to the basic necessities of life (Paltasingh and Tyagi, 2012). In many cases, the women are marginalized and deprived of participation on equal terms in the social, economic, cultural and political activities of their society. Their ownership of, or access to, land may be restricted due to discriminatory inheritance laws and practices.

## Gender Discrimination in Health

The quality of life of elderly people is closely related to their health. In India, the caregiving duties assigned to women are significant, yet invisible part of women's domestic labour. The responsibilities of caring for a sick spouse, children, grandchildren and relatives often fall to women and that can have consequences for physical and psychological health of the women. In addition, the physical immobility has declined for elderly men and women (CSO, 2011). Women have longer life expectancies than men globally due to female hormonal protective factors, risk factors related with male working conditions, lifestyles and higher risk of injury. Women generally live longer, they experience greater morbidity and have less access to health care than men (WHO, 2004). The non-communicable disease such as heart disease and stroke are significant causes of death and disability in women worldwide (WHO, 2005), especially poor women (Leeder et al., 2004). Ageing women are more vulnerable to age-related diseases, especially breast cancer, memory disorders (e.g., dementia and Alzheimer), osteoporosis and rheumatoid arthritis, making them more dependent on care services. Old-age problems such as osteoarthritis and osteoporosis are associated with limited quality of life and disability. Postmenopausal women are more susceptible to osteoporosis and cardiovascular diseases (Karkal, 1999). Osteoporosis, a degenerative disease of bones, is the second most common metabolic disease in India (Rizvi, 2012). There are more than 6 crore people with osteoporosis in India (Delhi Osteoporosis Foundation, 2010). The incidence of osteoarthritis increases 20 times among women as compared to 10 times among men in 60–90 years of age (Melton et al., 1993). Poor access to primary health care services among elderly women could be explained on account of lack of transportation facilities, their low literacy levels and poor socio-economic status. The relation between poverty and ill health has been universally established. Poverty affects older women more in the rural areas. In densely populated urban areas and poverty-stricken rural areas where basic amenities are inadequate, health care of the general population and specifically of the older population poses a great challenge.

Indira Gandhi Rashtriya Swasthiya Bima Yojana covers elderly women. However, its coverage is very limited with coverage of only 100 districts of India. A large part of India is not covered. Insurance for women should start much earlier because the insurance companies are not interested to cover elderly women. In most of the Indian hospitals, there are no gerontologists who can exclusively provide their services to the elderly, especially elderly women, whereas in developed countries, there are exclusive geriatric wards and geriatricians. Elderly women get depressed with deteriorating or reduced physical ability, changing physical appearance, migration of children and difference in generations, ideas. In many Indian families, women are not involved into decision-making process. Often they are reduced to play the role of a care taker in the family. They have both health and emotional insecurities that further get intensified due to lack of social security measures.

## Exclusion of Elderly Women

In the mainstream gender discourse, older women are not taken into consideration. Most of the research on gender/women studies has focussed on the problem related to relatively younger women, such as domestic violence in the family, battered women and her experience and confrontation, education, generic health issues, etc. The research and academic work on elderly women have gained inadequate attention. Elderly women suffer various types of social exclusion. For instance, remarriage and companionship are not a stigma for elderly men but the same is not applicable for elderly women.

## Widows Issues

Fifty-four per cent of elderly women are widows; remarriage is the exception rather than the rule for the widows in India. About 10 per cent of widows marry again (Chen, 2001). India is perhaps the only country where widowhood exists as a social institution. Widows' isolation, deprivation and stigmatization are aggravated by ritual and religious symbolism. The exploitation of widows, for example, those abandoned by their families to the temple sites such as Mathura, Varanasi and Tirupati, has been documented. Thousands of India's widows live in gloomy poverty at these places. An estimated 20,000 widows in Vrindavan alone struggle to survive. Among those, the elderly ones are left to beg and chant for donations from pilgrims and tourists (United Nations, 2001). These women are not in touch or contacted by their family members.

## Crime Against Elderly Women

The rate of crime committed against elderly women has increased since last few years (Ahuja, 2007). Assam has reported the highest rate of crime against women at 89.5 per cent as compared to 41.7 per cent crime rate at the national level during the year 2012. The crime against women during the year 2012 has increased by 6.8 per cent over the year 2011 and by 24.7 per cent over the year 2008 (NCRB, 2012). Female victims are more in number than males (Patel, 2010). There is an urgent need to motion our Criminal Justice System of India in maintaining law and order situation of the country so that one should feel safe and secure.

# Women's Positive Contribution

Older women must not be viewed as only the recipients of family income generated by the male members but recognized for their positive contributions made throughout their lives, both to their families and to the society at large. Older women often play a crucial role as caregivers and main support in handling the family responsibilities. Human Development Report revealed that women were accounting for more than half the total time worked in the world and that they carried out more work in total (in terms of physical units of time) than men. Three quarters of men's working time were spent on paid activities, while only one-third of the women's working time was paid. In other words, women do more work than men; however, the current economic and political system does not record or reward it (UNDP, 1995). Women are heavily represented in the area of health care and pre-school activities, at the same time, they are disadvantaged in receiving the financial gain. The work includes both paid activities and unpaid activities including the subsistence, domestic, informal, volunteer sectors and traditional formal employment (Benería, 2003). Societal well-being and economic growth depend on both the paid and the unpaid work done by women and men. However, the women are largely represented in the unpaid activities.

These analytical approaches point towards an asymmetrical distribution of workloads within households and excessive burden on women. Work has been further classified into domestic work—that includes processing of goods and the care and maintenance of the household, caring for children, the elderly and the sick. There is often some requirement for which the work is carried out, for instance, the linkage between the domestic and public spheres needed as an outcome of family responsibilities, such as taking children to school, paying bills, or carrying out other necessary activities such as shopping, buying medicines, etc. (Picchio, 1992). These activities are often interpreted as support services. Caregiving work is of vital importance for the sustainability of the system and it includes civil society institutions, the State, the market and families. The family plays the significant role in the care of the elderly. In all instances, women play the most important caregiving role, whether it is inside or outside the home, paid or unpaid. Elderly women, who live longer and are less likely to get a pension from the contributory systems, can be benefited from the non-contributory pensions to reduce poverty and vulnerability (United Nations, 2011).

# Policy Initiatives: Gender Dimension

Given the predominance of women in the ageing population, gender-sensitive policies and programmes are needed to address the specific concerns of elderly women. Policies and practices should encourage social support and discourage social exclusion. This can be achieved by involving elderly women at all levels of planning while removing the social barriers to participation.

## CEDAW Convention and Older Women

The Convention on the Elimination of All Forms of Discrimination against Women (CEDAW) is a medium to protect the human rights of older women due to the problems confronted throughout their lifespan. At the Second World Assembly on Ageing, 2002, held in Madrid, the special needs of older women were highlighted. The Committee recommended that the physical, financial and emotional needs of older women should be addressed and older women's access to health care should be improved. The discrimination faced by older women in various countries with a wide range of areas has been addressed. For instance, in Japan, older women's medical issues, and in Mozambique, the lack of documentation in identity were mentioned. In January 2010, at the 45th CEDAW session in Geneva, older women's issues were raised from all eight countries, especially in Malawi, where the issues included witchcraft allegations, mob trials and killing of older widows in order to grab their property (CEDAW, 2010). Despite being signatories to the UN-CEDAW, many countries still discriminate against elderly women through unequal rights regarding marriage, divorce, nationality issues, property inheritance, employment, elder abuse and health care, etc. (United Nations, 2005).

## NPOP, NPSC (National Policies and Other Interventions)

In India, the appraisal of state and national initiatives for providing social security to older women points to the serious lack of will to address their concerns. The National Policy for Older Persons (NPOP) 1999, the first policy on older persons formed by the Ministry of Social Justice and Empowerment, does not pay adequate attention to gender issues. In the NPOP 1999, the sections on healthcare, nutrition, shelter and education do not have any specific reference to women's situation (Gopal, 2006). Problems concerning widows and destitute older women are not given due attention (Prakash, 2003). The NPOP has also ignored the older populations that are poor and belong to the lower middle class family. The pension benefits and other financial benefits do not cater to the needs of the people who are not employed in an organized sector job or unemployed. It has an element of urban bias. The women are not mentioned with reference to the property rights. The policy does not explain the financial aspects of its implementation (Sujaya, 1999). The elderly is a heterogeneous group, and it is more practical to develop a plan of action for a specified group of people, instead of a single policy directed at the entire elderly population (Chattopadhyay, 2004). In National Policy for Senior Citizens-2011 (NPSC-2011), the gender-specific issues are mentioned, though not adequately. The NPSC-2011 has envisioned the elderly requirement in better way; however, its finalization and effective implementation are awaited for betterment of the elderly.

There is a need to increase interaction opportunities for special categories of the elderly like lonely and disabled elderly; to encourage intergenerational activities, older women to volunteer for work; to strengthen the capacity of law enforcement and justice officials to respond to complaints for prevention and amelioration of violence against women; to establish support services in the community and to support collaborative efforts with the non-governmental organizations (NGOs). The policies need to adopt a rights-based approach that allocates older women their due share of resources fulfilling the United Nations Principles for Older People, that is, independence, participation, care, self-fulfilment and dignity. Parents, teachers, business leaders, NGOs and older women themselves have major roles to play in changing misconceptions and negative attitudes towards elderly women. It is particularly important to encourage the media to make ageing women more visible by highlighting their contributions, needs and rights. Older people networks, self-help and advocacy groups will help empower older women and strengthen their capacity to represent their own interests (WHO, 2007). There is a need for better assistance, support and safety nets for elderly women (Gopal, 2006). The largest segment of old-age security, that is, pension schemes, includes Employees State Insurance Scheme (ESIS), provident fund, pension and deposit-linked insurance scheme, etc., whereas the non-contributory schemes include Workmen's Compensation Act (1923), National Social Assistance Programme (1995) and the Payment of Gratuity Act (1972), etc.

The National Social Assistance Scheme, introduced in 1995, includes the National Old Age Pension Scheme (NOAPS) and National Family Benefit Scheme, etc. The old age pension scheme (NOAPS) is 100 per cent centrally sponsored scheme, giving assistance to the states for the poor elderly (Rajan, 2001) and available for both male and female destitutes above 65 years of age. In addition, a few states such as Tamil Nadu and Gujarat have destitute widow and destitute deserted widows pension schemes for those in the age group of 40–64 years. Kerala and Odisha have a pension scheme for destitute widows, whether old or young, and physically disabled. The central government has initiated a grants-in-aid scheme to voluntary organizations for providing day care centres for the elderly and construction of old-age homes since 1983–1984. However, the benefits of the available schemes and programmes for the elderly have been questioned several times due to their poor awareness, small budget, inappropriate identification of beneficiaries, restricted accessibility, difficult procedures and irregular payment, etc. The organized sector with merely 4 per cent of the workers includes only 15 per cent women. The elderly in India, however, require a mix of financial support and services that combine their living and dependency requirements (Gopal, 2006). There is a requirement of gender-sensitive plans and policies that can benefit elderly women who are discriminated on account of being old, women and widows (Paltasingh and Tyagi, 2012).

## Suggestions and Conclusion

A social health insurance system can be evolved for older persons, especially for elderly women with universal coverage. Increasing health problems demand special attention by the policymakers and practitioners towards the gender implications of long-term care policies and programmes. More attention needs to be given towards prevention and management of crime against the elderly, disabilities and economic vulnerability to improve the elderly women's quality of life and to reduce the health care costs. Self-help groups' formation, involvement of elderly women as resource person, exclusive helpline services for elderly females, an appropriate amount of OAP service at the doorstep, small income generation projects and sensitization programmes for the younger generation are needed for an improved quality of life of elderly females (Srivastava, 2010). Policymakers need to recognize this reality and take it into account.

More awareness and sensitivity about health, emotional and social issues among elderly women, their families, the public at large, through electronic and print media are required. Awareness among the elderly about special legislative provisions needs to be generated. Incorporation of a gender perspective in all policy actions on ageing, as well as elimination of discrimination on the basis of age and gender, is a great challenge. Gender-sensitive conventions need to be continued with newer outlines and more frequency for promoting senior women's requirement.

Some financial incentives to families caring for the older persons may further encourage the elderly care in family set-up. Travelling concession, arrangement of day care or recreation centres at suitable distances and provision of fully subsidized care for poor and 80-plus elderly through innovative health insurance scheme, especially for elderly women, are some of the initiatives that could be taken up to support the elderly care. Women must be aware of the status of their own health including bone structure and density, joints health, heart/lung/endocrine health, blood pressure, cholesterol level, etc. to determine possible health risks and the ways to tackle or abate these risks. A young woman should always plan out old life during young age and maintain physical, economic, social opportunities that can be used in later life (CHETNA, 2007). There is a need for the women to realize their rights. The voice of the older women needs to be incorporated in policy formulation, planning and implementation. Happy ageing depends on a person's ability to maintain meaning in life, despite physical decline, ageism, etc. In order to empower older women and change their stereotyped perceptions, governments, intergovernmental organizations and NGOs, including the mass media, should initiate collaborative efforts. Older women need not be viewed as victims of the existing patriarchal structures. Their positive economic and social contributions to their families and to the society throughout their lives should be acknowledged. Elderly women are tremendous source of resources through many productive activities. They can form a group among themselves that can help those learning new things from each other's experience. The NGOs like SEWA have introduced some activities for such women. They can have their own agenda to make themselves busy in a positive and productive manner. Elderly women can take care of their own life to make it meaningful and pleasant. They can identify their potentials and purpose in life to be productively engaged in life.

# References

Ahuja, R. (2007). *Crime against women.* Jaipur: Rawat Publications.

Benería, L. (2003). *Gender, Development, and Globalization: Economics as if All People Mattered.* London: Routledge.

CEDAW. (2010). *Report on older women and protection of their human rights.* Geneva: Office of the United Nations High Commissioner for Human Rights.

Census of India. (2001). New Delhi: Office of Registrar General of India.

Chattopadhyay, A. (2004, October 23). Population policy for the aged in India. *Economic and Political Weekly,* pp. 4694–4696.

Chen, M.A. (2001). *Perpetual mourning: Widowhood in rural India.* Oxford: Oxford University Press.

CHETNA. (2007). *She too counts: Critical need for gender responsive healthcare for the elderly.* The National Workshop on Gender Responsive Social Protection—Health Security for the Elderly.

CSO. (2011). *Situation analysis of the elderly in India.* New Delhi: Central Statistics Office, Ministry of Statistics & Programme Implementation, Government of India.

Dandekar, K. (1996). *The elderly in India.* New Delhi: SAGE Publications.

Delhi Osteoporosis Foundation. (2010). Osteoporosis. Available at: www.antya.com and www.drchopra.com.

Gomez, R.L. (2002). VI Meeting of the Mexican Society of Demography, Mexico.HelpAge International. *State of world's older people.* London: HelpAge International.

Gopal, M. (2006). Gender, Ageing and Social Security. *Economic and Political weekly, 41*(22): 4477–4486.

Hall, M. & Havens, B. (2005). *The effect of social isolation and loneliness on the health of older women.* Winnipeg: Prairie Women's Health Centre of Excellence.

HelpAge India. (2012). *Elder abuse in India: A Helpage India report.* New Delhi: HelpAge India.

Karkal, M. (1999, October 30). Ageing and women in India. *Economic and Political Weekly,* pp. 54–56.

Lamb, S. (2000). *White sarees and sweet mangoes: Ageing, gender and body in north India.* Berkeley: University of California Press.

———. (2002). Love and ageing in Bengali families. In D.P. Mines & S. Lamb (Eds), *Everyday life in South Asia* (pp. 56–68). Bloomington: Indiana University Press.

Leeder, S., Raymond, S., Greenberg, H., Liu, H., Esson, K. (2004). *Race against time: The challenge of cardiovascular disease in developing countries.* New York: Centre for Global Health and Economic Development.

Melton, L.J, Lane, A.W., Cooper, C., Eastell, R., O'Fallon, W.M., Riggs, B.L. (1993). Prevalence and incidence of vertebral deformities. *Osteoporosis International, 3,* 113–119.

NCRB. (2012). Crime in India 2012 Compendium. Delhi: Ministry of Home Affairs.

NSSO. (2008). *Socio-economic profile of aged.* New Delhi: Government of India.

Paltasingh, T. & Tyagi, R. (2012). Demographic transition and population ageing: Building an inclusive culture. *Social Change,* SAGE, *42*(3), 391–409.

Patel, M. (2010). Crimes against the elderly. *Indian Journal of Gerontology, 24*(3), 395–403

Picchio, A. (1992). *Social reproduction: The political economy of the labour market.* Cambridge: Cambridge University Press.

Prakash, I.J. (1997). Women and ageing. *Indian Journal of Medical Research,* 106, 396–408.

———. (2003). Ageing, disability, and disable older people in India. *Journal of Ageing and Social policy, 15*(2–3), 85–108.

Rajan, I.S. (2001, February 24). Social assistance for the poor elderly: How effective? *Economic and Political Weekly*, 613–617.

Rizvi, S.N.A. (2012). Osteoporosis. In Y.P. Munjal (Ed.), *API text book of medicine*, (9th ed., The Association of Physicians of India, pp. 309–312). New Delhi: Jaypee Brothers Medical Publishing (P) Ltd.

Srivastava, V. (2010). *Women Ageing: Social Work Intervention*. Jaipur: Rawat Publications.

Sujaya, C.P. (1999, October 30). Some comments on national policy on older persons. *Economic and Political Weekly*, pp. 72–74.

UNDP. (1995). Human Development Report. New York: Oxford University Press.

UNFPA. (2008). *Women, ageing and health: A framework for action. Focus on Gender.* World Health Organization and UNFPA.

United Nations (2001). *Women 2000. Widowhood: Invisible women secluded or excluded.* New York: United Nations Division for the Advancement of Women. Department of Economic and Social Affairs.

———. (2005). *Gender equality: Striving for justice in an unequal world.* Geneva: United Nations Department of Economic and Social Affairs, Population Division.

———. (2011). Human Rights Council. *Report of the Independent Expert on the question of human rights and extreme poverty, Magdalena Sepúlveda Carmona* (A/HRC/14/31). New York: United Nations.

WHO. (2004). *World Health Report—Estimated healthy life expectancy (HALE) at birth and age 60, by sex, WHO member states, 2002.* Geneva: World Health Organization.

———. (2005). *Preventing chronic diseases: A vital investment.* Geneva: World Health Organization.

———. (2007). *Women, ageing and health: A framework for action. Focus on gender.* World Health Organization and UNFPA.

# 10

# Ageing Women in India: Policy Response

*Mala Kapur Shankardass*

## Introduction

It is more than a decade since the Indian government announced the National Policy on Older Persons (NPOP), which coincided with the celebration of the International Year of Older Persons declared by the United Nations. The policy document declared in January 1999 was followed by the next year, that is, 2000, being declared as the National Year of Older Persons. These events held lots of promises and hopes for the older men and women in the country, especially since there was recognition that the older people were a fast-growing segment of the population. In fact, the last census, 2011, indicated that not only is the population 60 years and older increasing rapidly but since universally women outlive men for a few more years, older women will be a majority in the older population. The life expectancy of women both at birth and at age 60 is slightly higher as compared to the men in India as it is in many more countries, both in the developed and the developing world. By highlighting demographic trends, the 1999 policy document compares the increase in expectation of life for women and men. It refers to the increase of 11 years for women from 58 years to 69 years, in contrast to 9 years from 58 years to 67 years for men during the period 1986–1990 and 2011–2016. Improved life expectancy contributes to an increase in the number of persons 60 years and above, and in a 25-year period starting from 1991, the population of older persons, defined as those 60 years and above, is projected to double itself according to the Policy statement. In India, population projections support the fact of feminization of the ageing population. Census data disaggregated by gender indicates 7.1 per cent of older men as compared to 7.8 per cent of older women (Census 2001). The decadal growth rate of female elderly is 42.2 per cent as compared to only 28.6 per cent for elderly males. Sex ratios favouring women in later years are projected to rise further by 2016 and beyond. In India within the ageing population, the total number of women is higher than that of men, both among the older population, 60-plus, as well as among the oldest old, the 80-plus as it is in many developing and developed countries. As per 2011 census data, there are 1,022 older women compared to 1,000 older men at age 60, and at the ages of 65, 70, 75 and 80, there are 1,310, 1,590, 1,758 and 1,980 older women, respectively per 1,000 older men. This demographic reality leads to specific challenges of population ageing from a gender perspective. But, the 1999 NPOP and its implementation in the following years have not addressed this concern sufficiently. In fact, the policy statement (Government of India, 1999) itself has particularly been deficient in a number of ways in addressing concerns pertinent to ageing women in the country. The 1999 policy document at the outset is gender neutral, undermining to a large extent the interests of ageing women. The 'coming of age' of women in the Indian society calls for special initiatives to absorb ageing women in the development process, which remains a missing link in the policy.

In order to successfully address the challenges of feminization of the ageing population, gender-responsive initiatives and measures, such as policies and legal frameworks, programmes and projects, to promote well-being of the older men and women need to be explored. It is hoped that the government that is in the process of revising the existing policy will attempt at avoidance of gender neutrality and gender-biased language in the new policy document. The draft document of the revised policy does reflect on gender and its interface with life stage.[1] It will be extremely fruitful if the new policy response, which is in making, will allow for the specific needs of the ageing population to be addressed from a gender perspective, thus making the policy document more effective. The Madrid Plan of Action on Ageing (MIPAA) adopted by UN member countries in 2002, to which even India was a signatory, calls for gender concerns to be included in policies and action plans of countries (United Nations, 2002). In recent years, in view of the feminization of older persons, many international organizations, including the United Nations, World Health Organization, etc., have called for changes in social and fiscal strategies for encouraging social inclusion and health promotion for older women (ESCAP, 2010). In this chapter, some lacuna in the 1999 policy document with regard to focus on older women is highlighted and the need for action in areas overlooked as well as the need to celebrate the feminization of ageing is outlined. As women enjoy healthier and longer lives, and constitute both a larger accumulated number as well as proportion of the older population, it is both desirable and necessary to make issues of current and future cohorts of ageing women central to the development agenda. In fact, reference of older women, specifically as a category requiring urgent attention was missing, though in general, vulnerabilities of elderly women were mentioned in the policy document. The chapter focuses on important issues that need policy response and action to contribute significantly in improving the quality of life of older women in the country, especially from a life course perspective. There is an urgent need for a more sensitive and inclusive new policy for older persons with emphasis on gender perspectives.

# Gender Concerns in 1999 National Policy for Older Persons

The 1999 policy document fails to sufficiently highlight gender issues. It merely makes a few references to the marginalization of older women based on gender, though the policy statement reflects on few basic and inter-linking concerns, vis-à-vis older persons. There are almost negligible concrete recommendations, which consider older women's particular circumstances on account of gender and age in the policy document. It even does not specifically indicate the directions, the needs to be addressed and the relative roles of government and non-governmental institutions in facilitating areas of operation and action specifically for ageing women, except in certain sections of the policy, and that too, in brevity (Shankardass, 2003).

The mandate in the policy has no reference to women as they age. The main document that has three sections under many headings and subheadings indicates an overall concern with greater vulnerability of women in old age, but the section on 'Proposed principal areas of intervention and action strategies' makes no reference to ageing women under some important topics. The policy ignores gender differentials in many components of concern. For instance, under the heading of shelter, issues pertaining to women are not considered, even though women have specific housing and shelter needs, especially as widows and in particular because of the disadvantaged position they occupy as women in the society. Lack of or poor-quality shelter without ownership rights, no access to individual water connection/toilets, lack of safe drinking water, unsanitary living conditions add to older women's vulnerability to the poor quality of life (Arif, 2013). Similarly, in reference to the health and nutrition component in the document, there is no reference to women, despite the fact that research across the world since last two to three decades indicates gender differentials in old-age diseases, problems and health-seeking behaviour (WHO, 1998). It is a universal fact that women compared to men have lower health status and nutritional deficiencies. Indian studies as part of the National Commission on Macroeconomics and Health (2005) indicate that under-nutrition and various types of nutritional deficiencies are widely prevalent among older people, which lead to the common problems of chronic energy deficiency, nutritional anaemia and osteoporosis, especially among women.

Physically, ageing takes a greater toll on women than on men. Women experience proportionately higher rates of chronic illness and disability in later life than men. It is observed by researchers across the world that older women compared to older men have greater problems related to non-communicable diseases and also have lower social and mental health status, especially for single woman and widows. Older women live with numerous gender-specific chronic conditions, such as osteoporosis, arthritis, post-menopausal problems and depression, which are often disregarded as 'women's problems' and not treated as geriatric problems requiring treatment and management. Further, for women especially, old age connotes reduced sexual appeal and in denial of their sexuality, classified as 'asexual' (Shankardass, 2000). The National Sample Survey Organization (2006) data indicate ageing women with more health needs as compared to men, for instance, restricted mobility due to low bone density, orthopaedic problems due to osteoporosis, depression, back strains, uterus and breast cancer, visual and hearing acuity, diabetes and cognitive impairment. Further, ageing women and especially the widows are mostly anaemic, unhealthy and malnourished. Also, in the case of terminal illness, they are under acute mental, emotional and financial stress because they cannot pay for the long-term required drugs (Puri, 2007).

In the section on 'other areas of action', also in the 1999 policy document, there is no reference to women as much as it is missing under the headings of 'research', 'training of manpower' and 'media' too (Shankardass, 2003). In India, it is a known fact that illiteracy among women is much higher than that of men. There is a need to have special proposals for adult education of women, given the low levels of literacy among them, but there is no emphasis on education of ageing women in the 1999 policy, which is a ground for lack of empowerment among them. Low levels of literacy among older women also contribute towards their low economic and social status in the society. All education and training schemes at national, regional and state levels should be adapted to encourage older men and women to participate as an empowering strategy.

A major critique of the 1999 policy document is that it has been weak in implementation. As the policy document itself states in the last and the third section 'the policy will make a change in the lives of senior citizens only if it is implemented.' The nine paragraphs of proposals and action plans for implementation of the policy make no reference to the adequate representation of women on the bodies, bureaus, councils, associations, etc. among the different implementing agencies. It is no surprise that with the decision-making powers not in the hands of the women or with their involvement, due attention to ageing women has not received the importance that it deserves in the last few years.

## The Neglect of Older Women and Widows

Women in general are increasingly neglected in their old age due to factors such as dependency, ageism, urbanization, migration and changing family structures (Bagchi, 1997). The 1999 Policy Statement in section II has given significance to such and similar trends, as highlighted in paragraph 17, that advocate the need to give special attention to older females so that they do not become victims of triple neglect and discrimination on account of gender, widowhood and age. Further, in paragraph 23, it emphasizes the need for expansion of social and community services for older persons, particularly women, and enhances their accessibility and use by removing socio-cultural, economic and physical barriers and making the services client oriented and user friendly. This is the only section in which reference to older women as a special category emerges, but it remains only a statement of concern with little emphasis on interventions and action plans. There is a strong need for effective intervention strategies from a life course perspective to improve the quality of life of older women. In the Indian context, as it is in many other developing countries, older women are particularly disadvantaged because they face structural, social and economic inequalities throughout the course of their lives (Shankardass, 2002). In a patriarchal system that our country supports, women are treated as subordinates, and as Sujaya (2000) points out this subordination 'takes the shape of discrimination, disregard, insult, control, exploitation, oppression and violence—within the family as well as in the workplace and in the larger society', where ageism prevails endlessly. The policy should have considered this seriously in outlining its action plans. The older women become particularly vulnerable to living a life without the basic comforts and dignity.

The plight of older women in the country is of serious concern because of their numbers but is also urgent due to the conditions they live in, particularly, as widows. A number of studies reveal that widowhood leaves women often as destitute. In India, the prevalence of widowhood is asserted to be the highest in the world for all age groups (Chen, 2000). The National Policy in paragraph 6 acknowledges the incidence of widowhood being much higher among females aged 60 and above than among the males of the same age group, because it is customary for women to get married to men older by several years. Also, they do not remarry and live longer. The document states that in 1991, there were 14.8 million widowed females, 60 years and above compared to 4.5 million widowed males. In other words, there were four times as many widowed females as widowed males in the later age groups. The increase in the incidence of widowhood for women as they move up in age requires due consideration, as it has implications for financial, emotional and social securities, a fact, which does not receive sufficient attention in the policy document in terms of interventions and action plans. Using National Sample Survey data of 2004, Pandey and Jha (2011) found that poor economic conditions have a mediating effect on the relationship between widowhood and health. Their study showed that widowhood has an adverse effect on health—both directly and through reduction in their employment opportunities and economic freedom.

In an ageing country with regard to widowhood, there are two special concerns. The first relates to improving the quality of life of widows as they age, and the second relates to the emerging needs of those widowed in later years. Research indicates a higher proportion of older women than men, especially widows experiencing loneliness and dependency on children, social deprivations and exclusion. Gender-based division of labour in the society also leads to older women's lack of involvement in leisure and recreational activities, and being burdened with household chores for longer span of time compared to older men. Clearly, women and men experience ageing differently. Both have their sets of concerns that for older women are exacerbated by a lifetime of gender-based discrimination, often due to deep-rooted cultural and social bias. It is further compounded by other forms of discrimination based on social class, caste, disability, literacy, employment and marital status.

According to census 2001, 75 per cent of older persons are living in rural areas; 48.2 per cent are women, of which 55 per cent are widowed. In the age group of over 70 years, 23 per cent of men are widowers while the corresponding figure for women is 92 per cent. The numbers are only increasing due to armed conflicts, natural disasters, communal riots and the traditional marriage patterns. Only, 28 per cent of widows are eligible for pension and only 11 per cent actually receive the payments to which they are entitled. In addition is the fact that the pension obtained is grossly inadequate and the process of claiming the entitlement and of disbursement has many flaws. What is needed are social safety nets that are important to address old-age-related contingencies, as well as multiple deprivations, especially faced by widows and other vulnerable groups of older women, and which facilitate the removal of chronic vulnerability. Certain studies also indicate that poverty rates in households with older people are up to 29 per cent higher than in households without an elderly member (HelpAge International, 2005).

In India, as in many other Asian developing countries, it is observed that for many adult women, the experience of old age is very different from their counterparts in the developed regions, in that they become 'old' much before the benchmark of 60 years (Shankardass, 2000). The burden of performing the majority of the care work in the home and the community sets in old age and related disabilities faster. Also, non-recognition of their contribution at the household, community level and to the economy increases their gender- and age-related vulnerabilities. The disadvantages faced by women throughout their life course, especially when cumulative, spell poverty and exclusion of women in old age (HelpAge International, 2005). It is important that national policy works towards creating an enabling environment for older women to focus on their personal growth and development.

A policy document must reflect an understanding of the rural–urban differences between the status of older men and women, and further on differentials due to the marital status. The emerging concerns of the divorced and separated ageing women, as well as those of ageing never married, whose percentage is no doubt nominal, but on the increase, can no longer be ignored. For ageing women, being in single status brings in financial problems, reduction in standards of living, compulsions to work due to economic pressures, isolation from social life and deprivation of property and ownership. Ageing single women continue to face social ostracism and stigma in life. Also, older women, in particular, are vulnerable to 'property grabbing' by family members or others. Older women's destitution and poverty are a sequel to denial of property rights to them. Making a distinction between older women and older men on the one hand, and younger women on the other, marks their legal status. Daughters who are widowed, divorced and deserted are often illegally excluded from inheriting property under patriarchal norms. Assurance of legal rights to women is imperative in the present scenario, but the policy statement does not refer to this aspect (Shankardass, 2003). It only pertains itself to outlining in the proposed principal areas of intervention and action strategies a pointer in paragraph 26 of the 1999 policy document—'Widows will be given special consideration in the matter of settlement of benefits accruing to them on the demise of the husband.' However, there is no concern in the 1999 policy document for reviewing the unsatisfactory status of women's property rights, though all over the country, it is visible that there is an urgent need to do so. The report submitted by the gender sub-committee to the Chairperson of the committee for revision of the national policy in 2011 makes note of this fact. The reality that the women are facing today in the country is that their access to property, residence and maintenance is not assured and is connected with their marital status. Further, women's space and entitlements shrink as she ages. There is a general disregard in the society of older women's legal entitlements. Identification of women's vulnerability in this regard needs the impetus to improve the overall situation of ageing women. There is no concrete recommendation in the existing policy document, which addresses their particular circumstances on account of gender and age. The rights of older women, which are cursorily included under the Hindu Adoption and Maintenance Act as well as under Section 125 of the Criminal Penal Code, need to be strengthened, as often these are not enforced due to various social cultural reasons.

There has been insufficient focus on the implications of different legislative measures and legal provisions for ageing women and this needs to be rectified within a policy framework. While there are certain amount of safeguards, which protect women, though, their low literacy level, insufficient legal knowledge and awareness, structural, social and economic dependency make them vulnerable to inadequate use of these measures. The recent 'The Maintenance and Welfare of Parents and Senior Citizens Act, 2007 is a good legislative tool, but its use by women has been limited since its implementation. Ageing women have practical difficulties in going against their family members and seeking justice for their independent existence. Also, very little consciousness is there at the individual and societal level about the rights of women as workers, both in the organized and the unorganized sector as well as women's entitlement within social security schemes and health provisions. Epidemiological research from different regions of India indicates high prevalence of mental disorders among older women and widows. There is seen to be higher prevalence rates for neuroses, affective disorders and organic psychoses among ageing women compared to men (Puri, 2007). All these issues need to be addressed in our understanding of law and policy frameworks, as it applies to ageing women and have impacts on their quality of life.

## Abuse of Older Women and Other Vulnerabilities

Older women as compared to older men are vulnerable to abuse by spouse, children, siblings, family and also the society because of the high level of economic dependence of older women. All over the world, including India, it is seen that there is increasing incidence of abuse of older women. Main forms of abuse of older women include neglect, physical abuse, sexual abuse, psychological (also called emotional, verbal and non-physical) abuse, and financial (also called material) abuse or exploitation (United Nations, 2013). In India, more and more research is indicating that older persons, and more so women, are subject to an increasing number of cases of abuse and violence across the country and among the different socio-economic groups (Bose and Shankardass, 2004; Shankardass 1997, 2010). In recent years due to terrorism and communal riots, many older persons are also affected by the conflict, but seldom are their needs either recognized or supported in policy responses. Another aspect, which requires attention, but is often neglected or overlooked, is the impact of natural disasters and displacement of older persons, and specifically for ageing women. Floods, droughts and earthquakes, the natural calamities occurring in the last few years have had many adverse consequences for older men and women. Gendered aspects of risks and vulnerabilities in old age with regard to security—social, financial, health; disasters and emergencies; care, support and ageing experience and cohort differences—must be recognized in policy plans, and rehabilitation and recovery programmes should be addressed at different levels.

Several researched documents report the prevalence of abuse of single persons more than that of those living with spouses. In an analysis of National Family Health Survey phase-II, Agrawal (2012) found that the elderly who are living alone are likely to suffer more from both chronic illnesses, than those elderly who are living with their family, even after controlling for the effects of a number of socio-economic, demographic, environmental and behavioural confounders. In Indian society, there is a greater likelihood of men being cared for by their spouses and female relatives than it is for women. But the violence against ageing women and their neglect do not find a special reference in the policy document. It merely acknowledges the widow's rights of inheritance, occupancy and disposal that are at times violated by their own children and relatives. However, the policy provides a promise for the introduction of a clause in the Indian Penal Code for protecting older persons from domestic violence, specifically in the context of deprivation of their rights of inheritance, occupancy, etc. In this direction, older people should be made aware of their rights and existing legal protection, with media being roped in to bring awareness. There is a need for a policy framework that contributes towards safeguarding the rights, interests and welfare of ageing women in the male-dominated society. Policy collaboration among government and non-governmental organizations should be adopted to enhance the socio-economic status of the ageing and also to eliminate any kind of violence and discrimination against them, with special attention to the needs of older women. It is a welcome step that recent legislation, The Protection of Women from Domestic Violence Act of 2005, recognizes violence against older people; however, its enforcement is limited (Shankardass, 2013).

There has to emerge a positive acceptance of assisting ageing women as well as men and their families in rebuilding their homes, strengthening their caring capacity and restoring income-generating activities. Relief response must recognize and support both the vulnerabilities and the contributions of older persons, the women in particular, who have a more socially acceptable role as caregivers. It is an area of concern, requiring greater focus in research and in administrative processes for streamlining services and the provision of facilities for older persons whose needs are special.

## Rural–urban Division and Economic Dimensions

The 1999 policy document makes extremely limited reference to the concerns of older men and women residing in the rural areas. The policy document recognizes that three-fourths of the older population live in rural set-ups, but fails to make note of the increasing incidence of female-headed households due to rural–urban migration and the impact of this on the quality of life of ageing women. It is pertinent that policies for empowerment of women give due consideration to the specific economic and health needs of ageing women in rural settings who remain involved with agricultural activities. This is due to various compulsions, and as a result, they invariably continue to work till death. The 1999 policy overlooks the special concerns of women involved in agricultural activities and neither does it indicate any commitment for improving the position of workers in the unorganized or informal sector, except for working towards fulfilling the objective of covering all older persons below the poverty line under the old-age pension scheme. This is an ambitious task but it loses its significance if not attained within a specific time frame. The policy does not outline any deadline for achieving its goal and objective.

Providing social and financial securities is an important agenda for any ageing society. But in India, the Ministry of Social Justice and Empowerment, the nodal agency for dealing with ageing concerns, also recognizes that 90 per cent of older persons, and more so older women, are not covered by any social security measures (NISD, 2000). Poverty alleviation programmes directed at older men and women alone cannot provide a solution to the income and social security problems of the aged. The majority of the women workers sink below the poverty line in their old age, simply because they have not accumulated enough savings during their working years. The 52nd round (1995–1996) of the National Sample Survey Organization indicates that less than 18 per cent of older women had financial assets in rural India as compared to 57 per cent of older men. The position of older women in urban areas is better, with 38 per cent having financial assets. It is worth remembering that certain employment rules have safeguarded women's rights, particularly the right to the husband's pension and provident fund, etc. But, on the contrary, the right of men in organized sector jobs to secure their old age through service benefits is sacrosanct. It is even protected from the wife, who in her old age cannot execute a decree of maintenance through the attachment of the husband's retirement dues. The husband's retirement leaves most wives dependent, invariably at the mercy of children. The financial dependency on husband is also a risk factor for moving into a poverty situation since the social security emerging out of retirement benefits is not linked to the rising living index (Shankardass, 2003).

So far the policy and programmes in the country have paid piecemeal attention to the economic empowerment of ageing men and women. There are limited facilities for re-employment, part time jobs and for credit provisions in later years. While the 1999 policy states that age-related discrimination in the matter of entitlement to credit, marketing and other facilities will be removed, in 14 years of its implementation, nothing much has been done in this regard, it nonetheless pays no due attention to prevailing sex-related discrimination in economic and financial matters. Older women are in particular at a disadvantage in applying for credit schemes and are negatively impacted by the structural adjustment programmes in the country. The existing policy recognizes that structural adjustment policies may affect workers in some sectors more adversely, especially those in the household or small-scale industry, but ignores the emerging data indicating women's greater participation in this sector.

# The Path Ahead and Conclusion

The 21st century has brought in greater emphasis on gender and human rights perspective in policymaking and action plans impacting the quality of life of older men and women. There is also hope of bringing attention and taking up fresh initiatives to include older person and specifically ageing women in the development process. Ageing of women in India provides special challenges and opportunities for development. Longer and healthier lives of an increasing number of women in the country bring tremendous potential for older women to be a resource for economic and social developments.

It is important that the revised policy framework adopts a radical change of perspective that would change the orthodoxy that overlooks gender concerns, replacing it with a strategy to integrate older women. The National Policy for the Empowerment of Women states that the principle of gender equality is enshrined in the Indian Constitution in its Preamble, Fundamental Rights, Fundamental Duties and Directive Principles. The Constitution not only grants equality to women across the lifespan, but also empowers the State to adopt measures of positive discrimination in favour of women. The emphasis on gender perspectives in a national policy document is crucial in this light. There is an urgent need for a more sensitive and inclusive policy for older people, with emphasis on gender perspectives.

In Indian society, there are glaring differentials in literacy, employability, wages, earning capacity, income insecurity and economic status between older men and women. The high morbidity of older women, but longer life expectancy as compared to older men, the differential access of older persons to health care based on gender as well as on rural–urban locations and the high proportion of widows in the 60-plus group, all serve to highlight the many points of interventions from a gender perspective and should be taken up at policy level. Older men and women are a heterogeneous group and have diverse needs based on caste, economic well-being, level of education and rural/ urban setting, and this must be recognized in policy, programmes and action plans for an effective outreach. The goal of a policy document should be to have a gender perspective at all levels including planning, programming, budgeting, maintaining and evaluation while addressing issues arising out of population ageing. Gender dimensions should be widely disseminated so as to encourage appropriate responses.

# Endnote

1.  In 2011, the Ministry of Social Justice and Empowerment formed a Committee under the Chairmanship of Dr Mohini Giri to bring out a revised National Policy on Older Persons to be adopted by the Government in the coming months. The draft of the revised policy titled National Policy for Senior Citizens 2011 was submitted for approval to the Ministry of Social Justice and Empowerment, but it is yet to be accepted for adoption. The Committee formed four sub-committees to comprehensively deal with the concerns of older people and incorporate the same in the new policy. One of the sub-committees was on the gender perspectives of which the author of this chapter was the Chairperson.

# References

Agrawal, S. (2012). Effect of living arrangement on the health status of older in India. *Asian Population Studies, 8*, 87–101.

Arif, R. (2013). Status of widows in India with particular reference to elderly women. *HelpAge India–Research and Development Journal, 19*(3), 6–14.

Bagchi, K. (Ed.). (1997). *Elderly females in India—Their status and suffering.* New Delhi: Society for Gerontological Research and HelpAge India.

Bose, A. & Shankardass, M.K. (2004). *Growing old in India: Voices reveal and statistics speak.* New Delhi: B. R. Publishing Co.

Chen, M.A. (2000). *Perpetual mourning widowhood in rural India.* New Delhi: Oxford University Press.

ESCAP. (2010). *Regional review draft report: A gender perspective on ageing in Asia Pacific—Social inclusion and health promotion in the millennium development goals,* Bangkok: Economic and Social Commission for Asia and the Pacific.

Government of India. (1999). *The National Policy on Older Persons.* New Delhi: Ministry of Social Justice and Empowerment, Shastri Bhavan, GoI.

HelpAge International. (2005). *MDGs must target poorest says older people: Supplement to ageing and development.* London, UK: HelpAge International.

National Commission on Macroeconomics and Health. (2005). *Burden of disease in India: Background papers.* New Delhi: National Commission on Macroeconomics and Health. Ministry of Health and Family Welfare, GOI.

National Sample Survey Organization. (2006). *Morbidity, health care and the condition of the aged* (Report No. 507) Jan–June, 2004. New Delhi: Ministry of Statistics and Programme Implementation, Government of India.

NISD. (2000). Add life to their years. *Social Defense, 50,* 145.

Pandey, M.K. & Jha, A.K. (2011). Widowhood and health of older in India: Examining the role of economic factors using structural equation modeling. *International Review of Applied Economics, 26,*111–124.

Puri, K. (2007). The Maintenance and Welfare of Parents and Senior Citizen's Bill 2007 and the ageing women and widows. *Research and Development Journal, 13*(3), 37–43.

Shankardass, M.K. (1997). The plight of older women: Victims of domestic violence. In K. Bagchi (Ed.), *Elderly females in India—Their status and suffering.* New Delhi: Society for Gerontological Research and HelpAge India.

———. (2000). *Women and ageing in south east Asia region countries—Report for World Health Organization.* Delhi: SEARO Office, Women, Health And Development Unit.

———. (2002). Voices of older poor in India. *Situation and voices: The older poor and excluded in South Africa and India.*(Population and Development Strategies Series Number 2). New York: UNFPA.

———. (2003). Concerns for ageing women in India. *Bold, Quarterly Journal of the International Institute on Ageing, 13*(3), 19–24.

———. (2010). Elder abuse and adult protection. In S. Johnson & S.I. Rajan (Eds), *Ageing and health in India.* Jaipur: Rawat Publications.

———. (2013). Addressing elder abuse: Review of societal responses in India and selected Asian countries. *International Psychogeriatrics, 25* (8), 1–6.

Sujaya, C.P. (2000). National policy on older persons, *Seminar,* 488.

United Nations. (2002). *Madrid international plan of action on ageing.* New York: United Nations.

———. (2013). *Neglect, abuse and violence against older women.* New York: Division for Social Policy and Development, Department of Social and Economic Affairs, United Nations.

WHO. (1998). *World health report.* Geneva: World Health Organization.

# 11

# Imagining Old Age: Cultural Interpretations

*Subhadra Mitra Channa*

## Introduction

Ageing is commonly viewed as something that happens to the body and is natural to all human beings in a biological sense. Yet, cross-cultural studies reveal that the process of ageing and of age itself can be viewed in very different ways by people in various societies, and perspectives on ageing also change with times and social and economic conditions. Other factors such as class, occupation and education may also intervene in what people perceive as ageing. In this chapter, there is a discussion, with examples, regarding what ageing means in different contexts and in different cultural perspectives. This chapter aims to address the issues of ageing in the context of the debate, privileging either biology or culture. With respect to ageing, two major areas need investigation: firstly, the concept of age being cognitive rather than physiological in character and, secondly, the experience of ageing in gendered terms. While the former targets attitudes, the latter is more in the nature of social expectations and role performance. For example, one generation back in India, a 40-year-old woman was considered elderly and she was often socially a grandmother by this age. But in urban areas and with education and much higher age at marriage, a woman of 40 is considered young or not yet past the prime of her life. Thus, concepts such as 'elderly', 'old', 'young', etc. are strongly informed by culture and historical contexts of time and space and not actually determined by chronological age. Then, again lifestyle factors, such as nutrition, living conditions and occupation, make important contributions to even the physical process of ageing. Those living under vulnerable and harsh conditions tend to age faster than those with favourable life circumstances.

With reference to the intersection of age and gender, one may look at the widely prevalent social custom found in most parts of the world, of men being older than their wives or a normal heterosexual relationship involving mostly an older man and a younger woman. Such a practice considered 'normal' in many societies is embedded in other values and cosmologies, such as patriarchy, the role expectations of men and women and also the cultural models of ageing. In a patriarchal society, a man is supposed to be the bread winner, and therefore has to be of a certain age before he can marry. The woman on the contrary is supposed to be 'supported' 'by her husband and it is preferred that she be younger so that the expected power hierarchy can be maintained'. A wife should be obedient and submissive to her husband and an age gradient helps. But in cultural translation, it is not attributed to power hierarchy but to such cognitive categorizations, such as 'women age faster' or 'a man is never old'. On the physiological side, for example, much cultural weightage is given to female menopause but not to the medical menopause found in men. Cultural models of role expectations also fit into the practice, for example, a woman is supposed to care for her husband, nurse him and take care of him physically, a man can get by only providing monetary support. In Bengal, for example, up to the middle of the 20th century, the age gap between a husband and wife was normally from 10 to 20 years, the wife being far younger to her husband. The pragmatic reason was that as the husband ages, the younger wife should be able to take care of him, but manifestly, the plea was that women age much faster, similar to the folk saying, '*kuri perule buri*' (a woman past 20 is old). Thus, in whichever way we look at it, ageing seems to be much more than a biological concept, although one cannot quite overlook the physiological part. As Staples (2011: 558) points out that bodies do have their constraints, and that 'personal biologies' do have a constraining effect on 'who we are or might aspire to be' (ibid.). Thus, when we are talking of cultural constructions, it is more in the nature of a cultural interpretation of 'what is'. A child, for example, cannot *be* an adult but may be treated as one. Even though a woman may consider herself 'young' at 40, her biological clock will interfere with her reproductive capacities. Thus, both biology and culture are significant in determining age interpretations, although in this chapter, the constructed and interpreted dimensions are more emphasized than the 'biological' ones. However, differences that exist at the cultural level are of the collective mind and to be assessed separately from individual differences that are beyond the scope of this chapter. Here, we shall discuss only collective attitudes towards ageing, age and the passage of time as well the intersection of gender and age.

# Social and Cultural Variables Affecting the Process of Ageing

The physiological process of ageing is a natural process through which all living beings pass. From birth till death, some natural processes of ageing take place in all living beings. With minor variations, such physiological phenomenon may follow a certain pattern common to the entire human species. For example, Hofer and Sliwinski (2001: 342) write, 'Covariance between chronological age and cognitive variables (e.g. memory and speed) is rarely unique—single or common factor ageing theories are sufficient to account for cognitive age effects'. Yet, the concept of age or ageing remains diverse, subjecting to a huge variation in terms of the meaning that is assigned to how different cultures view the process of transformation of a human being over a life cycle. Thus, there is a clear interface between the physiological aspects of ageing and the cultural interpretations of it, and it can be observed that the latter tends to influence the former in a significant way. Just as Cruikshank (2009) puts it, 'ageing in North America is shaped more by culture than biology, more by beliefs, customs and traditions than by bodily changes. In other words, it is socially constructed'. To understand the cognitive aspect of ageing, one needs to refer to some of the theoretical understandings about what constitutes reality and the distinctions between the 'objective' reality and the 'subjective' interpretations of it.

Phenomenologists, such as Husserl, had introduced the notion of a 'life world' that leads to the understanding that human beings 'collectively create and inhabit a shared world of constituted meaning or experience' (Ulin, 2001: 3). The very fact that meaning is subject to a common experience and shared understanding makes it obvious that the boundaries of such life worlds cannot extend infinitely to include everyone. Yet, it is debatable as to who is included within the range of a specific range of experience and who is excluded? People share certain life worlds and often inhabit more than one intersecting worlds; some experiences can be shared with some people and not with others, while some are universal, yet subject to situational interpretations. A phenomenological understanding based upon the subjective creation of worlds of meaning implies that humans prefigure the world they live in. Since the same human beings may occupy different life worlds simultaneously, they may present different aspects of their selves differently in different situations.

This is definitely antithetical to the world of science that tries to generalize every experience and object through a commonly shared nomenclature. Science has a reductionist framework that believes in one answer to every question. However, the current explanations even in the field of science have begun to give credibility to the realm of subjectivity, for example, the recognition by modern medicine of the psychosomatic components of diseases and the notion of situated knowledge as given by feminists such as Donna Harraway (Scheffler, 1982; Kakar, 1982; Harraway, 1988).

Let us take a concept such as adolescence that has received so much attention in anthropological literature (Mead, 1949). According to Mead, the adolescent trauma that was seen in the American society of her times was not due to any psycho-biological changes in the human teenager, but in the kind of social values that prevail in the American society, one that puts too much pressure on the growing adults to make choices for themselves rather than have their life mapped out for them. Among the societies of the South Seas where she had done fieldwork, precisely to test certain hypotheses generated from the culture and personality approach, she found that there was no particular trauma experienced when children grew to be adults. In fact, there is no particular physical milestone that marks out adulthood, as children take on adult tasks gradually and from a young age and slowly make a transition. Both boys and girls were allowed to slowly pick up adult work by imitation and by helping their elders. Sexuality was not something that was kept a secret and even small children were allowed to watch babies being born and not shielded from any life cycle events including death. In other words, there was no separate world of children and adults, and as Mead has recorded, the children did not grow up abnormal or maladjusted because they had exposure to sexual activity and such events as childbirth and death, from which average American child was shielded by the adults. Because they had no clearly marked out childhood, they therefore had no adolescent trauma and grew up with no particular tension.

In India too, before the age of modernization, child marriage and generally close joint family living did not keep the children out of the day-to-day affairs, although in the big households, they may have been shielded from direct exposure to sexuality. Young children in India even today, especially from rural areas and from economically deprived sections, do not have much of a childhood and are engaged in adult work such as taking care of younger siblings and even earning money for the family from a young age. To have a period of adolescence is thus linked to the privilege of having a childhood in the first place. Thus, in affluent societies such as the USA or among the upper classes in India, children may have both a period of childhood and a slower period of growing up with a clearly marked adolescent period. But poorer children or those not belonging to urban areas may just grow up quickly with very little marked childhood. Thus, even some widely accepted collective assumptions like that about 'adolescent trauma' prevalent in some parts of the world may be seen as culturally produced myths, depending more upon social and political contexts than upon actual physiology. Similarly, the notion of what is appropriate in terms of 'age' is also directly controlled by cultural circumstance. Thus, the questions 'when is a person an adult?' and 'when is a person adult enough to be procreative or sexually active?' seem to be changing with historical times and spatial contexts, rather than questions that are linked to biological process of ageing.

We all have known from our grandmothers that they were married and were probably even mothers before they reached the age of 16. Let us now compare the phenomenon of this kind of marriage that was a part of normative and accepted behaviour of those times in a certain historical situation with what is widely condemned as teenage pregnancy in the USA. The physiological phenomenon is the same that a girl gets pregnant at puberty, but the cultural interpretation in terms of ageing is very different. While in pre-modern Bengal, for example, a 13-year-old girl was considered appropriately grown-up and capable of being a wife and mother, in modern day USA, she is considered an adolescent delinquent and subjected to a social/psychological scrutiny that labels her as aberrant. The separation of time and space is not the only difference that one needs to consider while considering differences in the collective construction of meaning, but the entire network of meanings in which the particular event is situated. To understand the process of the appropriateness of the age of becoming a mother, we must look into the related processes of getting married and setting up a household, the meanings attached to these and also to the political and economic settings, in short of being social adults. It is generally observed that even in richer countries, such as the USA, the section of girls who become teenage mothers or have teenage pregnancies belong to the weaker sections of the society. Consequently, not only these populations have a shortened childhood, the process of ageing is also speeded up due to poverty, childbearing and lack of knowledge. An apt example is the book Random Family (2003), a true narrative of life in the backyards of New York City that shows how children grow up by the time they are 10 and 11 to engage in sex and crime; also, there seems only gender difference in role performance but not in ageing. The girl child and the boy child are equally vulnerable, except in different ways.

Different historical periods also show differing sense of ageing and we are finding that the process of ageing is getting delayed in most societies. For example, in urban areas of India, among the better off and better educated classes, ageing is now much slower; people appear to be much younger than they were a generation or two back. As Mujahid and Siddhisena (2009: 17) indicate, the life expectancy in the South Asian region is going up steadily. They predict, 'Further increases are projected and by 2050 it is expected that life expectancy in all countries (of South Asia), except Afghanistan, will exceed 75 years in Afghanistan it will be 63 years while in Sri Lanka, it will exceed 80 years'.

Thus, as life expectancy increases, people's attitude towards ageing will also change as it is already changing. Nowadays, among the educated and upper classes, age at marriage is increasing for both boys and girls. There is a prolongation of both childhood and youth, and people at least in some sections of the Indian society are entering late into marriage. Late age at marriage means that there is a prolonged youth, as in India, anyone unmarried is considered 'young' and any one married as 'mature'. Consequently, those with older children are regarded as 'older' compared to those with young children. People generally feel old in comparison to the maturity of their children, and as soon as children get married, parents would inevitably be regarded as 'old' and of an older generation. Since getting married late is an important variable as far as the cultural process of ageing is concerned, let us look into some of the key factors that affect age at marriage.

In the early 20th century in India, getting married was for the sake of social continuity of *jati* and *kula* (or in other words caste norms) and to protect the honour of women and of their natal families. The physical age of getting married, especially for a girl, was not determined by the fact of the physical maturity, but by the needs of honour and the availability of an appropriate groom, the social status of her natal family and various other considerations revolving around the merits of the girl and boy and their respective families. Thus, a girl was grown up and socially, collectively and publicly declared to be mature when all other conditions leading to her marriage were fulfilled. This growing up was not measured against her biological age, although it could be influenced by her physical growth. All over India, pre-pubescent marriage of girls from upper castes/classes was widely practised, and while in some places such as in Northern India, the practice of child marriage was supplemented by that of '*gauna*' (the second part of marriage where a girl was actually sent off to her husband's house after reaching puberty), in some places such as in Bengal, the child bride was sent off to her affinal home immediately.

In modern times, the values of caste are getting somewhat weak in comparison to other values, such as education, economic status, etc. Thus, girls and boys are getting married at much later ages. There are also legislations that have banned pre-pubescent marriages. But, more than laws, it is the social values regarding marriage that have changed. Education and career options for women have greatly impacted the age of marriage for girls across the rural and urban divide also. Thus, adulthood and marriage come later for many more persons than it came a generation or two back. Further, an educated woman who is capable of earning her living is, for her family, no longer expected to be much younger than her husband; in fact, in modern times, the age gaps are also decreasing among the same communities where they were very high in earlier times. In fact, although many people may not still prefer an older bride, yet values and norms are changing according to family and individual status. Women, who are capable of 'maintaining' their good looks/health till fairly advanced age are also putting an end to the widely prevalent myths of 'women age faster'.

Thus, when we are discussing the process of ageing, a very important consideration is to decide when a person becomes an adult? This transition from childhood to maturity is important in deciding the later effects of ageing as well. If there is a prolonged period of childhood, then the process of overall ageing is also slowed down. For example, if we compare the generations, then in most parts of the world including India, the age of marriage and consequently of maturity is going up. As discussed, our grandmothers were married at much younger ages. They also consequently were termed as older women at ages much earlier than how old age is viewed today. Thus, Prakash (1997) reports that 'most women in India perceive themselves as 'old' by the time they are 50 years of age. This perception of self as old is based on the presence of grandchildren, widowhood, shrinkage of social roles and menopausal state.' In urban India, many educated women may be getting married at around the age of 30, whereas in earlier times, a woman would be almost a grandmother at this age and a woman of 40 considered quite old. A modern woman of 40 may be feeling and behaving as quite young, especially when she maintains herself both physically and mentally as a young woman. Thus, the way one's life cycle matures affects the social process of ageing.

It is interesting to note that while women's age is often seen in terms of her ascendency in the social relations, such as becoming a mother and grandmother, etc.; quite often the man's age is viewed in perspective of his occupational status. Thus, men who are 'retired' from their work feel much older. Those who are able to work even in advanced age tend to keep their social ageing in check.

## Time as a Relative Concept

In most preliterate societies, there is no consciousness of chronological age. In fact, if we give it a thought what we call as age is also a culture-specific way of reckoning some of lateral time dimensions, such as division of time into months and years. For most people, without a calendar, there is only a cycle of events, ecological or historical. The days and nights are marked by various events, as are the years or annual events, such as the cycles of weather and rain, summer and winter. In most of rural India, people are still considering age as life cycle events or referring to some external context by which they can identify the chronology of a person's birth, or growing up. Most students of anthropology can recall that when they meet people in the field it is difficult to assess their chronological age, as very few have any idea of what is meant as 'age' and even fewer have any idea of their own age. Most people can recall only some event that marked their birth, what Munk (2011: 293) has called 'birth myths'.

Thus, like adolescence is a non-existent age category for most people, growing old can also mean many different things. While working in rural areas, I always found that ageing was mostly reckoned by what stage of a kinship position one was rather than what their actual age may be. For example, unmarried boys and girls were considered immature. Conversely, only those who were considered mature could be married, and again, this is not always a matter of actual age. Thus, when I asked about the age at which a person should get married, I was told that when a person can take care of himself/herself and perform all tasks to be appropriately performed by adults. This excluded, for example, anyone who was physically or mentally incapable of performing adult tasks, even if that person was chronologically an adult, he/she could never be a socially acceptable adult.

A sheep-herding community in the Himalayas (Channa, 2002) were well versed in the skill of counting, unlike some other preliterate communities who have limited skills of counting; these people were adept in counting in the hundreds, for they can always count the sheep (quite literally). They could mostly tell the chronological age of a person fairly accurately, yet they considered people belonging to different age categories more by their evolution in terms of a relational framework. Thus, all women who were having grandchildren came into the category of grandmothers or older women. Thus, age groups were more divided into categories such as unmarried, mothers, grandmothers, etc.

Everyday language or speech is a close indicator of culture and its complexities. We all know that simple labels are not conveyors of actual meanings. Thus, in India, we find that even when people are well aware of chronological age, in day-to-day conversations, phrases like 'she is the mother of young children' or 'he has reached a stage when his children are all married' are used more to indicate age or rather age categories. Yet, at another level, even a few days difference may indicate a changed social status, especially where a hierarchy between siblings is to be established. Thus, how age is reckoned is also context specific and associated with other social practices and values. Thus, becoming old may be more a phenomenon of the life cycle situation, rather than one of mere age. For example, as all of us know we never feel we are really old if we have living parents or older relatives, even older siblings. An eldest sibling will mature faster and be far more responsible because of the social categorization of always being the eldest. Likewise, the youngest of a set of siblings may have the privilege of remaining young for a longer time period. Each Hindu child reads in the Ramayana that the four sons of King Dasarath were in chronological order, but in actual terms, they were practically born simultaneously, and in any modern society would have been considered as quadruplets and not four hierarchically arranged brothers. In a recent article in the Statesman, Kampchen (2012: 6) writes that in a Hindu family, the chronology of birth is so important that in case of twins also, the one that is born a few minutes earlier is treated as an elder sibling and referred to as such. This is because there is cultural emphasis on hierarchy in a joint, upper caste, Hindu family with the mindset of having two siblings, one as the older and other as the younger one. This has also been stated in the religious book of the Hindus that is, the Ramayana.

We can compare this strict chronology to the societies with the age grade systems where instead of having people graded according to the minutes of their birth, a large number of children may be herded together to perform what is known as a puberty ritual. Such rituals have been recorded and analysed extensively by anthropologists like Victor Turner (Turner, 1967) and others. In these societies, all those children whose puberty rituals are performed together for one age set, irrespective of their actual age that may vary as much as 4–7 years, depending upon how frequently such rituals are socially performed, belong to the same age grade as regarded as equal and treated socially to be of the same category in terms of performing social roles. Thus, here we have a lumping together of children of various actual ages into one category and being considered for all practical purposes to be of the same age. In highly economically stratified societies, such as our modern class-based cities, a family's economic status may also determine the process of growing older. Again, it is a common scene to see a teenaged child of a privileged family being taken care of by a servant of approximately the same age group. Thus, a rich child will have his/her needs taken care of, breakfast provided, shoes polished and school bag packed by another child of roughly the same age group, but who has to work for a living, and thus misses out on childhood. The actual physical process of ageing is dependent on nutrition and lifestyle. Thus, we all know that life expectancy varies across cultures and classes. But what is even more important than class and economic status interfaces with the philosophy towards ageing and especially towards old age that is culturally cultivated and which provides meaning to the process of ageing.

## Ageing Across Cultures

It is said that one understands one's own culture best in comparison to another culture. While teaching a class at the University of South Carolina, I realized how different an average American's attitude is to old age as compared to that of average Indians. The text in question was an excerpt from Lamb's (2000) *White Sarees and Sweet Mangoes*, a study of ageing in Bengali culture (Lamb, 2002). It described a common phenomenon of ageing in South Asia, namely the desire for an elderly person to give up on the worldly pleasures and withdraw from this life. At the same time, it described the love and respect that are commanded by these old women and the sense of duty and feelings of devotion of the sons for their mother and the '*seba*' performed by the daughters-in-law. None of the young students could comprehend why people would actually enjoy old age as the old women described seemed to be doing or why anyone would try to give up rather than cling on to the pleasures of life. They seemed quite baffled by the idea of renunciation so inherent to getting old in South Asia. At another level, while they appreciated the sense of devotion and duty exhibited towards parents in India, they all agreed that such was not the case in the USA.

I tried to make sense of the rather opposed construction of old age in the two cultures and attempted to connect this to the cosmological perceptions underlying them. The life cycle in South Asia is conditioned by the concept of *ashramas*, each stage is marked by its separate value and lifestyle. The first stage of *brahmacharya* enjoins a person to devote himself to learning and abstain from all worldly pleasures, the second stage of *grihasthya* is the stage when a person marries, sets up a household and raises children. This is also the stage when one can enjoy the physical pleasures, including that of sex. The third stage is of *vanaprastha*, or retiring from this worldly existence, this is the time to withdraw, to reflect on the spiritual dimensions and generally to give up on all those things considered appropriate while one is a householder. Translated into cultural language, this is the time when one's children are grown up, married and may be grandchildren are also born. In earlier times, old people would retire into the forest but remain as advisors to the children, withdrawing but not completely dissociating. The last stage, not undertaken by everyone, is that of *sanyas* or complete withdrawal from the world. In addition to this, there exist the notions of rebirth and the illusory nature of relationships in this world. Thus, each time the soul takes birth, the present relationships are forgotten and new ones formed. In other words, what is very important to us while we are living is only an illusion, a *Maya*.

While reflecting on how life is actually carried on, even in contemporary times, I found that without being conscious of it, we have in South Asia incorporated the four ashrama concept into our life cycle. The separation of stages is still largely followed, students devote their time to learning, they are not expected to get married and even parents do not expect their offspring engaged in studies to have children. Students are also supported by the parents by and large, at least it is expected by everyone concerned that it is the duty of parents to educate the children. In other words, the stages of brahmacharya and grihasthya are still conceptualized as different stages of life. In the USA, on the contrary, I found that no such separation is either expected or normative. As soon as they reach the age of about 16 or when they get a driver's license, boys and girls are mostly expected to support themselves, pay for their own education and are also free to live as they like. There are many who have children while engaged in even undergraduate studies, many marry young, many girls are teen aged mothers (both married and unmarried), and because they are not supported by their parents, they do not feel much obliged to support the parents in old age.

But more importantly, the cultural value regarding old age is very different. Unlike South Asians conditioned by the philosophy of rebirth, the Judeo-Christian traditions advocate a single identity for all humans, something that they retain till apocalypse or the end of time. Also, there is only one birth and one identity and one has to make the best of it. The capitalist consumerist culture has added to the existing world view in making old age unattractive, putting a premium on youth and early achievement, by the principle that the earlier you achieve the farther you can rise. At the same time, the idea of giving in to old age does not exist; it is preferred to go on and on. In other words, life is not viewed as transitional but a monolithic construction of achievement where childhood is being cut shorter and shorter, as children grow up precociously and are rewarded for doing so (one sees it also in popular culture such as the Home Alone movies) and old age is deferred forever. The more one can pack into one life one must try to do it. Old age is not something that happens to everyone but only to the underachiever, for the high achiever, there is no old age; in other words, there is no chronological ageing but only increasing failure to achieve. Thus, ageing icons, such as Hugh Hefner, continue to proclaim their youth by getting married at the age of 80-plus to a woman 60 years younger. For both men women hanging on to youthful looks (by every artificial means available if possible), never accepting that one is getting old, never expressing the desire to withdraw are the proclamations of a successful life. But these are of course very culture specific and apply only to a certain kind of people with celebrity status. Many others may accept ageing gracefully although in the western societies, looking young is always a preferred value.

This analysis is not being made for any kind of value judgment. Each point of view is situated as I have explained in a particular kind of cosmology. While in traditional societies, such as in India and Japan, old age is rewarded with respect, and people rely on their younger generations, in the western societies, individuals are supposed to be responsible for themselves and like to remain independent rather than rely on the younger generations. Being youthful is a sign of accomplishment and one would like to hold onto it forever. Those who become actually old in this set-up, therefore, command no respect, as age in this perspective does not bring wisdom but only senility. In India, on the contrary, age has always been equated with wisdom and treated with respect. Yet, we find that with increasing influx of western capitalist culture, the security of ageing with the assurance of being taken care of by the children is getting eroded. At least in some elite sections of the society, especially those driven by the so-called corporate culture, age is being given a similar interpretation as in the west. With increasing health care and health awareness, people are increasing their lifespan well above what existed in pre-independent India. Here again, there are interesting implications of gender roles and ageing. Men, who were having power and respect in the public space become domesticated when they are older and 'retired'. Many times they are forced into domestic roles such as taking care of grandchildren or even doing household chores. Under these circumstances, they tend to lose prestige. But older women on the contrary continue to do more or less what they have been doing. They may retain control over the kitchen and domestic life. Thus, women often find ageing easier to cope with than men. However, much depends on the occupation and class status of the family. A wealthy patriarch may retain status, even if partially withdrawn from public life. An older woman may find herself superseded by a more educated daughter-in-law who may claim greater knowledge in spite of being younger. Thus, generational gaps are getting a new meaning as the technology and economic transformations are taking place at a rapid pace.

Even in the rural areas, the elderly no longer command the same status as they did earlier, especially in the field of political/economic power. Modern education and the new job market have left the elderly with lesser resources than their children. There are many new technologies in which the younger people are more expert than their elders. At the same time, the globalization of the world and economic and social mobilities are putting a pressure on the existing value systems, and a disjunction is seen at times on the interface between the cosmology that remains largely unchanged and a value system that is changing more rapidly. More than traditional values, the global economic and occupational structures are changing. Even if the elderly remain emotionally connected with the younger generation, the latter may not able to provide physical support to the parents as much as they may like to do so. Thus, in a country such as India, while children still respect and value their parents and elders, because of demands of career and work, they may not be able to take as much care as they would have liked to (Dandekar, 1986; Kumar, 1997; Willigen, Chadha and McDonald, 1999).

In the west, there is no disjunction between the societies, the values and the world view so that the social infrastructure is adapted to take care of the elderly, and the state provides the security that is not provided by the family and children (Lamb, 2002). The values are such that the people learn to provide more for their own future than that of their children. In India, on the contrary, the state is not expected to take care of the elderly, and the family, especially sons, is held morally responsible to take care of the parents. In such a situation, one is dependent on personal affection and relationships, rather than upon the impersonal state or voluntary institutions. The failure or non-existence of any such personal support may leave the elderly with no support (Prakash, 1999). Paying heed to the changing circumstances, a degree of social support and governmental support for the elderly is now becoming imperative for the large number of people who will be the elderly generations of India. While it is important to retain the world view and values that are part of the Indian identity, recognizing changing circumstances and new needs is an imperative that cannot be overlooked.

# Conclusion

In this chapter, we have discussed the social and cultural aspects of ageing. It becomes apparent through the above discussion that social/cultural variables, such as age at marriage, division of labour in the society, education, gender relations, economic status, occupation and power relations, are all in some way or the other factors that both influence the manner in which age and ageing are perceived as well as the actual process of ageing of people. For example, taking the case of North Americans, as discussed by Cruikshank (2009), not only do people value being youthful even in older age, they have the means and the technology to do so. We must remember that plastic surgery, artificial means to remain young as well as access to very nutritious diet and exercise are aspects of modern American, affluent ways of life. Such means may not be available to poorer sections of the people, even in the USA itself, but they too will have the same values. In other words, a poor American will also value being youthful looking and healthy, even at an advanced age but may not have the economic power to do so. Similarly, there may be a gender-based bias also, as Cruikshank (ibid.) points out that in the USA, women are more bound by their biological age, that is menopause than are men, who, if they are rich and powerful may project themselves as young for a much longer time.

In India too, we find that to some extent, the bias against the poor and women exists in matters of ageing. Women are more bound to their biological ages than men. We have many examples of men marrying women much younger to them, as men are expected to remain young and not be biologically limited. Similarly, the poor age must faster than the rich because of their hard life and lack of proper food. But in India, as of now, there is no particular virtue in trying to be young when someone is old, socially and biologically. People will not appreciate older people who imitate young people, but respect those who age gracefully. There is respect and appreciation for older people and their positions within the family and their wisdom in public life. In India, women gain highest status as mothers, and therefore there is no cultural barrier to accepting old age. Also, as we have seen the entire concept of the passage of time and of age as a concept, varying across cultures too. Thus, to sum up, we find that cultural and social factors affect both attitudes towards ageing as well as the psycho-cultural variables that actually affect the process of ageing.

# References

Channa, S.M. (2002). The life history of a Jad woman of the Garhwal Himalayas. *The European Bulletin of Himalayan Research, 22,* 61–80.

Cruikshank, M. (2009). *Learning to be old* (2nd ed.). Lanham, MD: Rowman & Littlefield.

Dandekar, K. (1986). *The elderly in India.* New Delhi: SAGE publications.

Harraway, D. (1988). Situated knowledge: The science question in feminism and the privilege of partial perspectives. *Feminist Studies, 14*(3), 575–599

Hofer, S.M. & Sliwinski, M. (2001). Understanding ageing. *Gerontology, 47,* 341–352.

Kakar, S. (1982). *Shamans, mystics and doctors: A psychological inquiry into India and its healing traditions.* Delhi: Oxford University Press.

Kampchen, M. (2012, July 29). The order of things. *The Sunday Statesman,* p. 6.

Kumar, V. (1997). Ageing in India—An overview. *Indian Journal of Medical Research, 106,* 257–264

Lamb, S. (2000). *White sarees and sweet mangoes: Ageing, gender and body in North India.* Berkeley: University of California Press.

———. (2002). Love and ageing in Bengali families. In D.P. Mines & S. Lamb (Eds), *Everyday life in South Asia* (pp 56–68). Bloomington: Indiana University Press.

Mead, Margaret. (1949). *Male and Female.* New York: New American Library.

Mujahid, G. & Siddhisena, K.A.P. (2009). *Demographic prognosis for South Asia: A future for rapid ageing.* Bangkok: The United Nations Populations Fund.

Munk, K. (2011). Baby in a bowl and other Stories: Socialization in astrological narrative. In A.W. Geertz & J.S. Jenson (Eds), *Religious narrative, cognition and culture* (pp. 291–302). UK: Equinox.

Prakash, I.J. (1997). Women and ageing. *Indian Journal of Medical Research, 106*, 396–408.

———. (1999). *Ageing in India* (prepared for WHO). Bangalore: Bangalore University.

Scheffler, I. (1982). *Science and subjectivity*. Indiana: Hackett Publications.

Staples, J. (2011). At the intersection of disability and masculinity: Exploring gender and bodily difference in India. *Journal of Royal Anthropological Institute* (NS), *17*, 545–562.

Turner, V. (1967). *The forest of symbols: Aspects of Ndembu rituals*. Ithaca: Cornell University Press.

Ulin, R.C. (2001). *Understanding cultures: Perspectives in anthropology and social theory*. Cambridge: Blackwell Publishers.

Willigen, J.V., Chadha, N.K. & Mc Donald, J. (1999). Culture and ageing. *Social Change*, SAGE, *29*(1), 21–31.

# Section V

## Positive Ageing: Outlook and Approaches

# 12

# Bridging Inter-generational Gap through School Education

*A.M. Khan*

## Introduction

The wide gap in the 'ideology of living', feeling and thinking, particularly among young children and older persons, is a matter of great concern for the well-being of the elderly. Scholars such as D' Souza (1982), Gangrade (1999), Khan (2008) and Singh (1999) argued that the status of the elderly was very high in the pre-industrial social order. These scholars have also pointed towards a deteriorating status of the elderly in contemporary India. They are of opinion that the status of the elderly in contemporary India has transformed drastically. The position of Indian elderly till the colonial period reveals a somewhat continuous pattern. In the ancient period, the religious scriptures of the time invest high status in elderly patients. The elderly wielded considerable authority in this period. During the medieval period, there is a proof of the continuity of the earlier status quo, but at the same time, there are hints about the poor condition of elderly widows and even a compulsion to commit suicide among the elderly. The early colonial period with its patriarchal family pattern gives a clear edge to elderly persons in the society. While control over family property ensured their dominance in the family, the joint family system, based on patriarchal authority where the eldest male member was the head of the family, ensured a higher social position of the elderly. In the community, the village and religious affairs, the senior most member of the family represented the family. In India, after the independence, the elderly are in a transitional phase, similar to the tumultuous phase the English and the American elderly went through in the 19th century and the early parts of the 20th century. Apart from the changes in their role and the status due to rapid urbanization, modernization and industrialization, the aged as a separate category have become distinct due to their unique problems hitherto unrecognized. This has made the policymakers sit up and devise strategies to address the problems of the elderly. National policy for older persons (NPOP) 1999 has been developed with a view to address the problems of the elderly.

With the upcoming of the industrial revolution, education and development of a different nature, the structure of the society changed. Urbanization emerged rapidly. Today, a lot of people are migrating to cities for growth and development, because modernization of the world has opened enormous opportunities for the people. More than anything, population growth was visualized as a threat to development. Planners in countries, particularly those which are known today as developed nations, initiated population control policies through education and medical technology. The child population decreased along with progress in education and modernization; and most of these countries were able to raise the quality of life, directly contributing to longevity. Today, the size of older population in such countries is highly parallel to the advancement of development. Such demographic changes have completely altered the structure and function of the family and the role of family members. Many nations lost the glory of family as institutions of living. Today, in such countries, the elderly are suffering greatly with the problems of loneliness and depression. The developing nations including India are also on the same road. In urban families, issues such as marital disharmony, separation, divorce, intergenerational differences and conflicts are reportedly increasing in Indian families (Sooryamoorthy, 2012). With enormous efforts of controlling population growth, the child population is declining and the population of older people is rapidly increasing. In fact, the growth rate of elderly population is almost three times more than the general population. The family structure is also taking a new shape (Census of India, 2001).

Khan (2008) identified four major pillars of elderly care, which are gradually falling down. These are: (a) Social recognition of older people, (b) role of seniors in decision-making, (c) cultural traditional breakdown of family status and (d) family socialization process. Radical changes in the institution of family, structurally (size) and functionally (dynamics of interpersonal relations), migration, modernization are playing incredible role. Housing space, unprecedented engagement of children in studies, TV viewing, enormous hobbies such as, dance, music, games and host of creative activities appear to play a significant role in deciding the children's interaction with the family, particularly with the grandparents. The socialization process appears to be deprived of quality interaction with older parents. The flow of communication with these people in the family is gradually becoming rare. The overall family environment is not what elderly people envisaged during the years of productivity when they were the master of the house. Quite often, they keep on boiling internally between what they had imagined about the family, family members, their behaviours, actions and decisions. While they are ageing, in the absence of power, they cannot control directives and decisions rather just face and digest the bitter experiences of life, cursing more of self rather attributing others. They are internally forced under the influence of family environment causing the life's ambivalence, distress, which significantly contributes to loneliness and depression. In the Indian context, child and old differences are explained under the theory of the generation gap. The values and behaviours in day-to-day life are incongruent between children and old. Liberals argue that the modern way of living is an inevitable reality; children need to be provided a free and fair environment with full autonomy in their development. Without contradicting the stands of liberals about the modern values, there is a dire need of inculcating human values that provide a scope of living in the healthy environment, which includes physical, social, psychological and spiritual dimensions that provide a healthy ground for healthy ageing. Vienna's declarations strongly recommend that the best and the only alternative of elderly care is family, because unprecedented demographic transition world over, particularly in the developed nations, at the moment has challenged the existing model of elderly care that is fully dependent on State resources. More than 64 countries have already gone far below the replacement level of fertility, and their population above 60 is increasingly growing with fast speed. Such countries are suffering from the lack of quality care of older people. Developing countries including India are not going to be an exception. Rather, in the developing countries, the problems are going to be worse because of the simple reason that the developed nations have taken nearly 135 years to reach the present level of elderly population; and contrary, the developing nations will hardly take 35 years to reach that level. If one tries to understand the strength of each nation in terms of their existing national resources, the picture of developing countries becomes gloomier. Therefore, the State-centric model of elderly care, which was considered as an ideal, is not going to survive in the 21st century. In this context, children in contemporary period need to be placed into a developmental framework that can help them to develop sensitivity towards older people, regardless of whatever lives they wish to live. The institution of the strong family needs to survive and flourish, regardless of inevitable modern forces of development, globalized in nature, and it can be guaranteed with suitable scientific interventions at the level of educational institutions across the world.

The traditional family structure is rapidly becoming nuclear. So, the base for the care of the elderly is crumbling for three reasons: (1) caregivers are migrating away from the places where the elderly reside, (2) values related to elderly care are deteriorating and (3) the concept of individualism is growing and the sense of community is declining. A large number of people living in the mega cities without a strong family base and with modern lifestyles are desperately in need of someone who can perform the job of caregiver for the elderly.

# Traditional Family Versus Modern Family

The joint/extended family as the best place for the elderly care appears to be a reality of the past. Based on some inherent changes in the dynamics of relationships, the family could be classified into 'traditional family' and 'modern family. The people in dissimilar types of families have different sensibilities and do not share the same attitudes towards the care of the elderly. Feelings about care for the elderly vary from family to family, depending on its size and types. Some characteristics of 'traditional family and modern family' are listed in Table 12.1. These present a dichotomous picture. Older people in both the categories carry the mindset of the traditional family and younger ones think in terms of the modern family. So, there is a clash of beliefs; incidences of abuse of the elderly emerge out of such a generation gap. Moral,

**Table 12.1**

*Characteristics of the traditional family and modern family*

| Traditional family | Modern family |
|---|---|
| All family members do not assert equally | Everybody asserts equally and justifies their individual standing on all family issues |
| Someone is identified and recognized as authority for taking decisions (head of household) | No one is recognized as an authority |
| Generally, as a head of the house, he/she commands authority in the family | Tendency of imposing authority on each other is discouraged |
| Adherence to the family traditions is stronger value | Individual freedom and choice are key characteristics |
| Joint kitchen, joint celebration and joint action are highly desirable | Sharing with each other is not an essential feature |
| Arguments on every matter are not desired | There is full argumentation, everyone possess freedom and personal choice |
| Freedom for free style of living is completely restricted | Free style of living |
| Absence of free flow of emotions | There is a complete flow of emotions |
| Adjustment as a basic feature in the family is most essential | Absence of adjustment |
| Mutual care and concern are commonly shared values | Highest priority to 'self-care' and 'self-concern' |
| There could be many more characteristics | |

religious and social compulsions for the care, respect and dignity of older persons are a dying phenomenon in today's market-oriented consumer society. In addition, migration and the insecurity of physical space are major threats to the care for the elderly. One can simply expect elderly care from children only through social and legal safeguards, so caregivers should know about and make use of such safeguards.

The purpose of citing these as an example is simply to clarify that modern family values are not friendly to quality care of the elderly. All the salient features of traditional and modern families cannot be crystallized here. However, the dichotomy between traditional and modern families on certain features is apparent. In the context of the characteristics listed, the issues of joint and nuclear families, however, get diluted or become more compelling. It is quite possible that the joint family may not carry forward the essential characteristics of traditional family because of the on-going crises in the social systems, resulting in deterioration in the values of elderly care. Spontaneity in the expression of emotions without caring about the feelings of others is becoming a very common feature in the society. It is quite possible that the members living in the joint family possess some important characteristics of modern family and vice versa. Rather they may depend more on some features of the modern family. It appears that structural changes in the family per se are perhaps a secondary issue. The main issue is whether the nuclear family encourages some of the healthy features of the traditional family or has it completely embraced the values of the modern family? The care of older persons would remain intact if some of the healthy characteristics of both the types of family values survive and encouraged socialization through the process of family and social contracting to social ideological perspective.

## Shift from Family to Self

Modernization and industrialization made their impact on the family structure and gave genesis of the consumerist society. The productivity and contents of modernity mould the relationships gradually. The dynamics of the interpersonal relations are changing their colour rapidly. The concerns for individual freedom and individuality have become the major feature of the modern family system. The obsession for self is becoming a major characteristic of the modern society. The self as a main driving force of the behaviour is becoming a central focus. 'Self' other than 'family-self' seems to be a new phenomenon emerging in the society. Individualized self is a part of the modernization process, whereas the family-self is a reflection of old traditional joint family where thinking, values and behaviours are usually according to the family traditions. People moving faster to modernity have realized constraints of living in the larger joint family, which demands considerable adjustment and control of the individual's interest. The individual freedom does not find a place in the significant family decisions. Area such as education, marriage, lifestyle and general behaviours and values are the main areas of conflict between younger and older.

Under unprecedented circumstances, the process of disintegration of the joint family system started way back in both rural and urban areas.

It is found that within a year of marriage, new couples prefer to have a separate and independent place to live; such changes are happening rapidly in both rural and urban areas. The separation undoubtedly causes physical distance, but it does not necessarily kill the sentiment towards family members completely. That is why the culture of earners sending money orders to the family living in the distant rural area survives and it is a dominant feature of migrant people. In the urban areas too, different forms of communication and support are available. However, all these are likely to change soon due to the growing intergenerational conflict. The younger generation looks to be strongly supporting the consumerist culture, which is really western in nature and fairly hostile to the total care of the elderly. There is a substantial difference between eastern and western cultures. In the eastern culture, the family and community is the centre of behaviour, whereas in the western culture, 'individuality' is a major thrust.

The whole of Asia has carried the tradition of a strong joint family system. In such a system, decision-making is generally governed by family norms. The younger members are not allowed to take individualistic decisions in several dimensions of life, and if they disobey, they are heavily penalized. For example, *gotras, varnas,* caste and religion are special features of the traditional joint family system. Thousands of girls sacrifice their educational and developmental needs. Because they are married without their consent, their schooling is stopped. The community as a larger base works through the family situation. The individual's desires and aspirations are not a priority. It is the family and cultural identity of a person that plays the vital role. Contrary to these cultural traditions and practices, the nuclearization of the family grew along with the development-oriented educational curriculum. Some other compelling forces of the family have pushed people into the nuclear family. Younger generations, however, find some characteristics of the traditional family suffocating and prefer to live alone with their own desires.

The Westernization has been a threat to the traditional and cultural heritage of interpersonal relations and care of older people in developing countries. New generation growing with transitory identity is at great risk. They easily get moulded into new values loaded with characteristics of the modern family system. It does not cement the bondage between young and old generation. The Westernization is becoming a way of life for younger one. It is posing threats to the elderly, as they are failing to retain the base of strong cultural identity. They have rather fallen into the trap of the younger generation. They complain to younger generations for some apparent changes, which they never expected. The younger generation is crazy for a new culture, which is individualistic. The possibility of cultural transition is greater, because the society at large is becoming critical to its own hegemony and not clears to its own cultural values. Either we desire or not, institutional care is likely to emerge as an alternative to home care. It would simply get strengthen in the future. The market forces are simply studying. Builders would come out with enormous variations, larger to smaller, simple to complex system, offering the package of institutional care of different nature. Some builders have already gone for a huge complex of old-age colonies.

The world after post-industrial period has been continuously gaining enormous achievement in different areas. It is equally loosing enormous 'heritage of humanity' and peace. So, we have entered into 'development zone with minimum peace and maximum violence of varied nature', which is continuously spreading throughout the world. Its roots are deeply embedded in modern generation and its perspective of development, modernization, globalization, industrialization and consumerist cultures. The threats to the healthy ageing and elderly abuse of varied nature are also part of the same process.

## Growing Challenges of Ageing

Old age is a growing section of the population and simultaneously it flashes images of miseries, which are socially and culturally learned phenomena. 'Elderly' and 'ageing' are two different concepts, one refers to a section of the population and another one is a process of becoming older. The period of onset of ageing is scientifically difficult, researches are going on. The impression is that it is deeply determined with contours of the country, region and culture. A wide variation in longevity across the world speaks that the biological processes of ageing work in tandem of social, cultural, economic and climatic forces that determine different images of old-age cross-culturally. The secret of healthy ageing lies in scientific understanding of these forces, images of ageing and managing them by scientific interventions.

The major changes in the future would be scarcity of family care of the elderly because of fast growing globalization and industrialization, and it would accelerate the process of migration of earning members within the country and outside the country. This is already resulting in a peculiar situation where elderly persons are left alone. The number of such elderly is going to increase tremendously, and the probability of parents accompanying the sons as earners is minimum because of various reasons and most probably, there will be no change on this part due to a wide generation gap on one hand, and on the other hand, scarcity of space in the migrated place, both physically and psychologically. It would be rampant phenomenon and the organized 'community care' would be the only answer, which at present is hardly evident.

# Denial of Naturalness of Ageing

The age-specific behavioural dispositions are primarily natural and universal. But the perception towards such dispositions is culturally and socially governed. Therefore, behavioural disposition needs to be studied from the angle of individuals as well as the society. Individual's dispositions are always judged by the society. And individual learns and relearns within the frame of society's normative behaviours. In the process of learning and de-learning, individuals generally extinguish such behaviours that do not serve their motive to gain and reinforce those that serve them. The definitions of child, youth and old in the society are equally governed by gain and loss continuum. Why societies deny the vulnerability of natural ageing as only burden unlike vulnerability of children? Why naturalness of ageing is not construed in its real and natural perspective? Why truth of ageing is denied for the elderly? Why the elderly themselves cannot take up ageing as natural part of life and the art of living is the proximity of naturalness. Why cannot society engineers design systems that facilitate the process of healthy ageing? Why economist cannot calculate the economic requirement of vulnerable section which is a real necessity in our society. Old-age planning has never existed and the elderly have been basing their old age on the shoulders of their sons. Today, the family support is gradually diminishing under the existing model of development. Why government cannot take up the responsibility of vulnerable elderly, either destitute or not, create systems to look after basic needs of every elderly. Longevity should not be allowed to prove as a curse and sin. Each stage of life has its own behavioural disposition. For example, the child is a child, no matter what group, region, culture, society and religion he or she belongs. And childhood behavioural dispositions are very much hailed in the society everywhere. But the same behaviour if displayed during the youth becomes condemnable and unacceptable cross-culturally. Every stage of life from childhood to old age, therefore, has its social and cultural definitions in every society, regardless of its differences in chronological characteristics. The deviation, however, is not acceptable. If some youth acts like an old person, he or she is not considered normal and vice versa. So, what is that makes the elderly vulnerable? The answers can be sought in the mindset of the society regarding the different stages of life.

## Active Ageing

Generally, in every society, behavioural dispositions of child, adult and youth are accepted. However, it is not with the older persons. Why does such a paradox in the society exist? What is the implication of such paradox to the older persons? It appears that the positivity and negativity towards old age are deeply embedded into productivity. Non-productive person is seen negatively and vice versa. In every society, individuals from childhood to old age are defined within a fix frame of productivity at present as well as in the future. For example, children's productivity will refer to career building to ensure productivity in the future. The expectations and hopes are set out accordingly in the family. The moment hopes are lost and expectations are shattered, the definition about individuals also changes. And sometimes, the parents disown some grown-up children when their hopes and expectations attached to the child are lost. Quite often, family breakdown takes place due to such reason and grown-up children (e.g., married or unmarried) opt for separation. Sometime, sons themselves disown the parents and demand for partition and distribution of property as per social and legal practices prevailing in the society. The phenomenon of productivity, therefore, is a key to determine the status of the individuals, group and the society. For example, a lot of negligence and discriminatory practices are followed in the case of girl child. This too appears to be closely associated with productivity and non-productivity. Discriminatory treatments are followed simply out of a feeling of loss in productivity. The girls are generally perceived as a 'source of draining the resources' of the family. In other words, the family and the society do not perceive the productivity of girls. Loss of expectations and productivity in the society not only reinforces the psychology of indifference, it rather aggravates indifferent behaviours and unwanted social evils, such as family violence, gender bias, old-age brutalities, neglected care of older persons, etc.

## Care During Oldest Stage of Life

A most crucial situation emerges during the last stage of life when the increasing decay of the body itself becomes a major cause of problems. It is a stage of natural vulnerability. It refers to the crippling status of body organs, individuals become helpless and lose the capacity of carrying out activities of daily life. This stage requires the physical presence of caregivers, their complete devotion and services. Nuclearization of the family is detrimental to elder care, so more resources are required to provide quality care. It places an extra burden on the family. This is a stage where medical and emotional care is of utmost importance.

The failure in carrying out this burden itself generates abuses of various natures. For families already suffering due to economic and housing constraints, the care of the old in the city becomes an unwanted burden that affects them psychologically, socially and economically. Even those who are economically well off are gradually losing the mindset (i.e., state of mind) for the care of frail parents and grandparents. In such cases, longevity becomes a curse to individuals and the family as a whole in the absence of services from formal caregivers, who are not available at the moment. The parents generally develop some expectation with regard to their care in day-to-day life of the family members. In case of unfulfilment of these expectations, parents feel frustrated. It hits the satisfaction level of the elderly. It also becomes a source of conflict and quarrels. We do not have any research on these aspects: what could be a profile of expectations, how much these expectations are fulfilled in day-to-day life and whether such expectations really contribute to some chronic diseases.

The crisis of care for the elderly is associated with many happenings in the family. In big cities, school going children are over-burdened, they are running frantically in pursuit of education, they are becoming intolerant, inpatient, spontaneous in gratifying their needs. They hardly find time for quality interaction with grandparents, even if they are living with them. They are not getting guidance to develop deeper sensitivity for grandparents in the family as well as at school. The quality of interaction and communication between young and old is gradually changing its colour, and the psychological satisfaction of both is declining from what it used to be when children spent more time with the family. Similarly, mother and father, if employed, are most of time outside the reach of older people. They are obviously more concerned for themselves and their children, and their aged parents remain ignored. In big cities, it seems marginalization is emerging as a reality of modern life. How such a development is viewed by aged parents and young children is an important issue. If elders were to mentally accept reality as they did when younger, perhaps the sense of loneliness and marginalization would not cause any problem. But if they do not accept it as a reality of modern times, they are likely to suffer emotionally, and it is likely to affect the dynamics of relationships. Growing conflicts obviously result in indifference, neglect and abuse.

## Intergenerational Gap

There is clear evidence of the intergenerational gap between child and old. Researches have been conducted; the reflection of two researches is discussed here. Intergenerational relationships are interactions between individuals of different generations, thousands of people who share similar but not identical experiences by the virtue that they are born, living and dying within a common historical period. Family is that thread that links multiple generations together through a system of shared beliefs, norms, values and cultural traditions. Within a family, these intergenerational ties are conceptualized as a lineage bridge between the children, parents and grandparents.

In a traditional Indian society, elder people lived within the multigenerational extended family, comprising one or more adult, children, grandchildren and other kins. The aged in these societies enjoyed an unparalleled sense of honour, legitimate authority within the family or community, had decision-making responsibilities in the economic and political activities of the family and were treated as repositories of experience and wisdom. The elderly acted as a link between traditions and customs and were responsible for enforcing them in day-to-day life. There was a division of labour within the family and the aged had an important role to play, making their life meaningful. The elders in the intergenerational lineage played the role of historian, providing information about the cultural and familial past, that of a role model whom the youngster could follow, of a mentor who could guide the young with their valuable experiences and who cared for the king in crisis (Chadha, 2004).

Over 30 years of research has documented that the parent–child relationship is important for both children and parents throughout the life course. Family members are the principal source of emotional support and socialization for their elderly members. It has also been pointed out that intergenerational ties have an important therapeutic role during a family crisis. In the modern Indian society, where most of the parents are busy pursuing their career, grandparents play an important role in caring for the third-generation grandchildren. In addition to the family, better health and education among older people in urban Asia have led to more intergenerational bonding in the extra familial context (Thang and Mehta, 2012), and at the same time, realizing that the family's traditional role of caregiver to the elderly and its solidarity is being subjected to various economic, social and psychological strains. It is necessary for the government to initiate policies and programmes that support, protect and strengthen the family, so as to enable it to continue responding to the needs of its elderly members.

Some of the common conversations heard among elders and kids are: Kids feel that their grandparents are to be shunned. Senior citizens feel they should be treated with respect, welcomed and be entertained by the company and conversation, even it is just some petty small talk. The news articles suggest that a generation gap exists when it comes to using online services. While the younger generation has expressed impatience with the older generation's slowness to adopt the latest online product, the older generation is bewildered by young people who choose to publish their private information on the Internet. The frustration expressed among generations is considered a new generation gap. It is seen as a generational shift. The older generations, coached by their parents that privacy has value, do not always understand the attraction of such remarkable social networking tool such as MySpace, Skype or YouTube. As for the younger generations, they see these tools as fun and necessary, a quick means of getting an answer to a question. They do not view the tools as a malignant force guided by the suggestion, 'Sure, the cell phone is annoying, but is it annoying *enough*'? So, while the older generations discover social networking tools and imagine the tug of a small hand on a pant leg, those who have grown up using new technologies search the globe for friends, contacts and merchandise, for them, lack of privacy is not so much an annoyance as part of the marketing package (Zook, 2007). Technology has also impacted the family to much extent. Some find it useful to stay connected with family members as they can fulfil work, school and other responsibilities. However, others report that an increasing time spent on television watching, playing electronic games and communicating via social media has resulted in reduced personal contact among family members, and hence diminished relationships.

To overcome the unprecedented and rapid demographic transitions leading to the crisis in the lives of millions of people, there is an urgent need to start action on several fronts. As a part of a long-term approach, young children attending school need to be given the priority of sensitization towards old-age care and they should be sensitized to several issues carrying long-term implications for them. The older people also need to be prepared on several fronts, which they never expected to happen in their life the way it is happening. The youth of today need special, comprehensive knowledge of short- and long-term planning in all the dimensions of life, such as social, emotional, health, economic and old-age planning. The crisis of old-age care and elderly abuse will become deeper if the ongoing changes in some of the most desirable values related to the care of older persons are not restored. The present thrust, however, does not address these issues at micro level. Nor has the NPOP taken care of many micro dimensions of ageing that are affecting their day-to-day life under the influence of market forces emerging as a boom of globalization and sector reform.

There is a need to bridge the growing gap between child and old at three levels, as depicted in the Figure 12.1: the child level, the youth level and the old-age level. Thrust at each level varies, so the strategies. The best place to mould children and teach them to treat elders with

**Figure 12.1**

*Diagrammatic presentation of short- and long-term interventions in different stages of life*

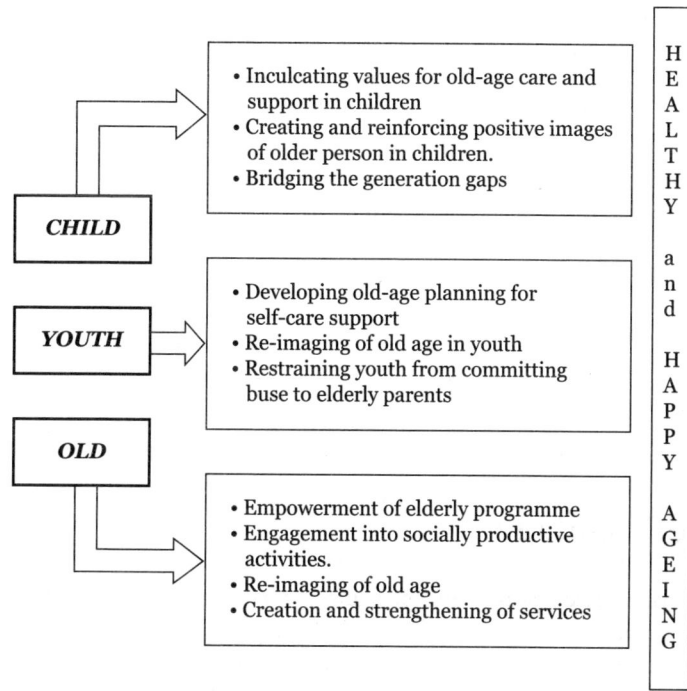

sympathy, care and love is the school. Andrew Shue, a famous American film star, says: 'I created an organization (when I was in high school) to help senior citizens. How many high school kids are out there helping senior citizens?' They are not many. As a part of 'moral instruction', class children may be shown how to help senior citizens. The school may give away prizes for the best student who cares for his grandparents. Local Senior Citizen Associations can institute such prizes by funding the same. During the annual day of the school, Children may be encouraged to take a suitable pledge that all through their lives, they will be 'senior friendly' and helpful. Boy scouts and girl guides may be given special exercises in helping older people: Helping them cross the road in a busy junction, running small errands, accompanying them to the hospital, help them get into buses, etc. School Magazines may encourage small articles or stories that talk about intergenerational gap and the importance of talking to elders kindly.

Senior Citizens Associations and non-governmental organizations (NGOs) working for seniors and elders can do a lot in bridging the generation gap. The senior citizens Association can adopt a school. 'Senior Citizens Forum' in Secunderabad, for instance, has adopted a school where the parents are poor. Whenever members of this Forum go on picnics or tours, some half a dozen kids from the school are also taken along, free of cost. This brings about unimaginable benefits, as it enhances the perception of senior citizens among children, teachers and parents. Senior citizens can engage the children in the school by telling stories about culture, mythology, history, etc. They can also volunteer as teachers, supplementing regular teachers. As stories attract children, this voluntary engagement is likely to improve relationships. Indirectly, they may pick up stories where kids are appreciated for caring about their elders.

# Methodology

A pilot research project on 'bridging the gap between child and old' was carried out by the author of this chapter. A short intervention programme was applied among 500 children from Kendriya Vidyalayas in the age range of 10–16 years during 2009–2010. The children were from class 6 to 11. The focus of the intervention was first to get the views about the existing pattern of interaction of children with grandparents and their perceptions towards them. During interaction with the children, 'family values loaded contents' were shared and significance of interaction with the grandparents was highlighted. The contents of the interventions are as follows:

Step 1  Close interaction with the children.
Step 2  Listing out expectations of grandparents as perceived by children.
Step 3  Time that children spend with grandparents.
Step 4  Deliberation on values related to old-age care.
Step 5  Post deliberation question answer sessions.
Step 6  The feedback session has revealed some important information.

# Findings and Discussion

Many children said, 'we hardly get time to spend with grandparents.' Sometimes, parents discourage, 'don't waste time, they have lived their lives, you have to grow, do hard work,' these are the words of some parents. Some children said, 'we have never been told by parents to take care of grandparents or spend some time with them.' While watching TV, 'we don't like them to join us.' 'Some grandparents keep on insisting something repeatedly which we don't like.' Some said, 'we never thought of celebrating their birthday, taking them out, giving some presents as we do with our own friends.' Some said, 'We never thought of asking about their health, their preferences, liking for food, desire for going anywhere and so on.' Several feedbacks like this suggested lack of sensitivity on the part of the children and their real concern for the care of older people. Close interaction with the children revealed that children are mostly ignorant of expectations of grandparents from them and they were not explained by the parents. Interaction has made the majority of the children highly motivated and they asked, 'what is that they should do for grandparents in day to day life.' The interaction has generated a great desire and concern among the children for continuous interaction with grandparents, even if the parents do not encourage.

Step 7: In the last, the actions initiated after feedback are: (1) Taking pledge to strengthen interaction with grandparents; (2) children taking a moral pledge to spend some time with grandparents, more time on Sunday and holidays; (3) celebrating birthday of grandparents; (4) sitting together with grandparents before TV for some time; (5) helping grandparents in social networking, going outside; (6) spending a little time in park, wishing before going to school and (7) meeting grandparents after the school.

As a part of pilot project; contact with some old persons was established and effort was made to list out expectations of grandparents as perceived by them, time that children spend with grandparents and general behaviour of family members. This exercise has revealed that any interventions minus grandparents are likely to suffer, and therefore grandparents have to be part and parcel of intervention programme. After the programme, some of the schools started 'grandparent's day' in which grandparents were called in the school along with children.

With a lot of activities, this has opened a wonderful platform for old people speak in public and play with children.

As a follow-up, some schools invited experts for 2-hour orientation of the teachers. The programme started with individual introduction, sharing their views about intergeneration, the relation between child and old. Teachers being in middle age shared their conflicting views. Some of them said, 'grandparents are barriers, they spoil children.' Whenever family discipline is applied to children, they take shelter of grandparents. Some of the teachers shared that quite often there is heated argument with grandparents simply on matters related to the child. From this minor pilot study, glaring picture that emerged is revealing that the most valuable treasure of the family is getting lost simply in the absence of quality interactions among the family members. Educational institutions, particularly at the schooling level, while providing an environment for developing cognitive map for the children can play a significant role by sensitizing the children about the core values of elderly care. Children with the given orientation in the school can play a wonderful role in minimizing the differences among the family members and their own gaps with grandparents. These small experiments need validation in the country as well as cross-culturally under suitable quasi-experimental design. It looks that the cost-effective intergenerational bond could be strengthened simply by making it a 'part of children's education. The follow-up with the old people also revealed that they need to redefine their expectations in the context of changing reality of life with which the family member's live.

We need to visualize healthy ageing from a life course perspective. Every child has to place under the strong foundation where he/she inculcates and assimilates values of elderly care.

The response to revolutionary transition in the demographic structure at the moment is centred to the ageing policies. The pace of further development from policies to the programmes is facing resistance of varied nature. In other words, policy planners, programme developers and important government personnel at different levels who have been working on different mode and mindset for the last few decades have yet to realize the kind of society that country is going to have as a result of changes in demographic structure. They are more obsessed with the problems and programmes that they have been carrying on and for which they have been trained. It appears that mindset is a major barrier, and therefore we need to develop strategic plans to sensitize these people to the gravity of the problem that the world is likely to face as a result of rapid growth of the population of older people. Governments, civil societies, other stakeholders and family members need to build and support stronger connections across generations in order to improve the well-being and the quality of life of all generations. Intergenerational solidarity continues to be the primary foundation for personal and social securities, and hence for better human bonding. The policies and programmes need to reinforce the interconnectivity of the generations. Societies need to facilitate human contact and interactions in order to expand intergenerational solidarity (Cruz-Saco and Zelenev, 2010).

## Concluding Remarks

The intergenerational issue has to be viewed from the perspective of children as well as the elderly. The gap could be managed successfully if the children attending schools are given sensitization about the life of the elderly and their expectations from the family members. From the discussion with the children, it was evident that they completely lack an input of elderly care in their socialization process, especially by the parents. The parents, particularly mother as reported by a number of children, are more concerned about the schooling performance, and some of them are of the view that children get spoiled by the old grandparents. Children after getting sensitization felt their responsibility and were curious to know what role they could play to make the elderly happy. This small experiment suggests that elderly care needs to be included in the education system itself and different strategies of reinforcing the relations between young and old and reducing the intergenerational gap could be developed and utilized. In view of global demographic and economies shift, there is a need for supporting the relationships between and among generations in families and societies.

## References

Census of India. (2001). New Delhi: Office of the Registrar General, Government of India.

Chadha, N.K. (2004). Building society through intergenerational exchange. *Indian Journal of Gerontology, 18*(2), 227–236.

Cruz-Saco, M.A. & Zelenev, S. (2010). *Intergenerational solidarity strengthening economic and social ties* (p. 2). New York: Palgrave Macmillan.

D'Souza, V. (1982). Changing social scene and its implications for the aged. In K.G. Desai (Ed.), *Ageing in India*. Bombay: TISS.

Gangrade, K.D. (1999). Emerging conception of ageing in India: A socio-cultural perspective. In A.P. Bali (Ed.), *Understanding greying people of India*. New Delhi: Inter-India publications.

Khan, A.M. (2008). Emerging challenges of ageing: Role of civil society. In R.N. Kapoor & T.M. Dak (Eds), *Population ageing and development in India*. Udaipur: Institute of Social Development.

Singh, D. (1999). Day centres and home for aged. In A.P. Bali (Ed.), *Understanding greying people of India*. New Delhi: Inter-India publications.

Sooryamoorthy, R. (2012). The Indian family: Needs for a revisit. *Journal of Comparative Family Studies, 43*(1), 1–9.

Thang, L.L. & Mehta, K. (2012). Conclusion: Grandparenting in contemporary Asia: Change and continuity. In K.K. Mehta & L.L. Thang (Eds), *Experiencing grandparenthood: An Asian perspective* (pp. 145–158). Netherlands: Springer Publisher.

Zook, G. (2007). *Technology and generation gap*. Available at: www.IIrx.com/features/generation gap.html.

# 13

# Technology Support in Active Ageing

*Usha Dixit and V.C. Goyal*

## Introduction

The UN Secretary-General, Ban Ki-Moon, while celebrating the 'International Day of Older Persons' on 1 October 2009 with the theme *'Celebrating the 10th Anniversary of the International Year of Older Persons: Towards a Society for All Ages'* stressed on international commitment to the United Nations towards promotion of *policies that will enable older persons to live in an environment which enhances their capabilities, fosters their independence, and provides them with adequate support and care as they age* (Secretary-General Message, dated 28 September 2009).

There is a constant increase in the number and proportion of older people living in their own homes as a result of limitations in mobility, dexterity and mental capacity (Varghese and Patel, 2004; Furlan and Fehlings, 2009; Krishnamachari, Mario and Thomas, 2010). As per the recent reports, more than a billion people are estimated to have some or other form of disability, that is, about 15 per cent of the world's population based on 2010 global population estimates (WHO, 2011). Of these, the World Health Survey estimates that 110 million people (2.2%) have very significant difficulties in functioning, while the *Global Burden of Disease* estimates that 190 million (3.8%) have 'severe disability' conditions, such as quadriplegia, severe depression or blindness (WHO, 2009).

It is projected that elderly population of the world will cross the 1 billion mark by the year 2020 (WHO, 2000; Dobriansky, Suzman and

Hodes, 2007). Projections indicate that India's population above 60 years will be double in size between 2001 and 2026, and the elders will account for 12.17 per cent of overall population in 2026 (GoI, 2011). The National Population Commission in India has estimated that the population of the elderly (age group 60 years and above) is expected to grow from 71 million in 2001 to 173 million by 2026. There has been a steady rise in the share of elderly population (aged 60 years or above) in the total population over the decades. As against 5.6 per cent in 1961, the proportion goes up to 7.4 per cent in 2001. For males, the rise was more modest from 5.5 per cent to 7.1 per cent, while for females, there had been a steep rise from 5.8 per cent to 7.8 per cent during the five decadal censuses from 1961 to 2001. With massive increase in older population and ageing people, unprecedented challenges are found in the field of health care, infrastructure support, the quality of life, etc.

Many older people wish to remain in their own homes, as they are faced with slow deterioration in their abilities. Most of the time, they are fit enough to retain their independence but sometimes, they need help as they are more vulnerable to chronic diseases. This shift in ageing population tends to have a profound impact on economic, political and social conditions of the country. Thus, the demographic change will require utilization of vast resources towards support, care and treatment of older persons in order to promote their healthy and independent living. In India, a wide divergence exists with respect to the situation of the aged people in various societies, cultures and regions. The needs of the elderly are distinctive and mostly relate to their health, comfort, dignified living, psychological well-being (including recreation and social networking), meaningful occupation (with or without economic gains) and security aspects. Older persons, therefore, need much more than just medical care, which needs an inter-disciplinary approach integrating medicine with the other functions.

There are initiatives by the government to tackle the issue in a holistic manner, with a focus on the overall well-being of older persons that include their social, emotional, psychological and physical well-being that contribute towards supporting comfortable and dignified living. The Ministry of Social Justice and Empowerment (MoSJE) is considered to be the nodal ministry under the Government of India to deal with the issues related to elderly people in India. The ministry has a programme called 'Integrated Programme for Older Person (2008)', which is a central sector scheme to improve the quality of life of the older persons. The National Institute of Social Defence (NISD) under MoSJE is engaged in the development of programmes in the field of old-age care. Under a project called the 'National Initiative on Care for Elderly (NICE)', areas of interventions have been identified with the objective of ensuring active, healthy and dignified life for older persons. These broad areas of intervention, as outlined in the NICE project, are: *Financial security*—food security for needy elderly and income-generating programmes through non-governmental organizations (NGOs); *health care and nutrition*—geriatric care facilities, expansion of medical care network, special health care facilities for disabled and destitute elderly; *shelter*—provision of subsidized housing in public rural housing schemes, design and facilities sensitive to the needs of the older persons; *education*—assistance to develop outreach programmes for interacting with older persons; *welfare*—non-institutional services to strengthen coping capacity of older persons, catering the needs for social interaction, recreation and other activities and *protection of life and legal safeguards*—services to strengthen a sense of security and providing timely help, design of public transport for easy entry and exit. Under the above-mentioned NICE project, a 1-year postgraduate diploma course in Integrated Geriatric Care is conducted to develop a cadre of skilled personnel at managerial and supervisory level to meet the demand for providing skill-based, field-oriented, trained personnel in old-age care. The course covers subjects such as Gerontology, Public Policy and Planning, Clinical Geriatrics, Geriatric Management, Psychology and Counselling, Research Methodology.

The Ministry of Science and Technology (Government of India) initiated a new programme in 2007 on 'Technology Interventions for Elderly (TIE)' to create an enabling environment for the elderly. The TIE programme was evolved through a series of consultations involving various stakeholders (geriatric specialists, designers, architects, social scientists, senior citizens, etc.). The interventions attempted under the TIE programme include design and development of assistive/enabling devices, designs of homes and use of information and communication technology (ICT) in networking, recreation, entertainment, health and nutritious food.

Government of India has provided useful information for elderly people under 'Senior Citizen Corner' at 'Pensioner's Portal' (http://india.gov.in/citizen/senior_citizen/). Information available on the portal include health care (health ailments and treatment, medical insurance, drug search, health calculators, medical consultation, aids and appliances with list of manufactures/suppliers); travel benefits (in buses, trains and flights); government policies and schemes; pension scheme and details; financial assistance/incentives; recreational/ educational centres; old-age homes; city helplines; pilgrimage and tourism destinations and advice on do's and don'ts for senior citizens.

Police departments in many states have initiated efforts for security of the senior citizens in different localities of the city/town. Apart from the beat constable, duty officer of the area as well as SHO of police station visits homes of senior citizens. Banks are offering various schemes for benefit of the senior citizens. Among these is a 'Senior Citizens Savings Scheme (SCSS), 2004' for persons who have attained the age of 55 years or more, but less than 60 years. Presently, 24 nationalized banks and one private sector bank are authorized to handle the SCSS, 2004. Under this scheme, deposit attracts interest of 9.3 per cent per annum and can be made for 5 years, which can be extended by 3 years. Another useful scheme is 'Reverse Mortgage Scheme', which provides a source of additional income for senior citizens who own self-acquired house property in India for any personal expenses, house repairs, etc. The loan is secured by the way of equitable mortgage of residential property. Banks are also offering special travel loans (e.g., Desh Videsh Yatra Loan of the Bank of Baroda) to senior citizens to help them make it to the places they have always dreamt of. In an effort to help senior citizens to secure jobs post-retirement, the Nightingales Medical Trust (NMT), an NGO, organizes job fair in Bengaluru. Called 'Jobs 60 +—You Are Never Too Old to Retire', it seeks to bring dignity to the lives of senior citizens, who are not getting any regular income and are financially insecure. The job fair provides a platform for needy senior citizens and socially conscious companies to come together for mutual benefit. A large number of senior citizens from different backgrounds (e.g., engineers, technicians, supervisors, administrators, teachers, accountants, data entry operators) participate in such job fairs.

Active ageing allows people to realize their potential for physical, social and mental well-being throughout the life course and to participate in the society, while providing them with adequate protection, security and care when they need. Through strategically planned technology interventions, including development, field trials and dissemination, the technologies can be made accessible, affordable and adaptable to the specific needs of elderly people. This chapter tries to capture some of these new frontiers and suggests a roadmap for future activities in providing technology-based support for care of the elderly in Indian context.

# Technology for the Elderly

The use of technology to support independent living and promote independence of older persons is mentioned in recent government policy documents (e.g., National Policy on Older Persons, 1999). There exists a vast scope of technology interventions for welfare of elderly people in the country so that the technologies are accessible, affordable and adaptable to the specific needs (Goyal and Dixit, 2008a and b; Kumar, Dixit and Goyal, 2009).

## Health and Nutritious Food

With advancing age, health also deteriorates and the aged become weak and susceptible to different kinds of health problems. In order to lessen the effects of ageing, technology interventions help utilizing the available resources and culturally appropriate competing needs of the society. For example, elderly individuals are more likely to use their medication appropriately if the labels and instructions are printed in their native language. Medication organizer, automatic pill dispenser, portable health diagnostic kits and equipment are some examples of technology development in the field of health care. Malnutrition is a serious problem among older people. The regular intake of sufficient and nutritious food is required for the aged to sustain their bodies, which will require development of culturally appropriate nutritional recipes for elderly people. Well-designed education material (guidebook, self-help booklets and hand-outs) can help to enhance the knowledge and skills of older adults pertaining to the nutritional care—promotive, preventive and curative, in various forms such as awareness modules on nutritious foods, fitness activities, traditional medicines, nutrition-based eating habits, etc. (Pasricha and Thimmayamma, 2005; Puri and Khanna, 2009). Technology can play an effective role to understand the strategies for communicating health messages and awareness on healthy lifestyle behaviours. The city of Reno in partnership with the State of Nevada Food Commodity and Distribution programme has launched the Senior Farmers' Market Nutrition Programme funded through a US Department of Agriculture grant. This programme provides eligible low-income seniors with vouchers to use at accredited farmers' markets throughout the community. Also, there are other programmes, such as Washington State programme, helping seniors to purchase produce that is locally grown.

## Special Designs

Many older persons require specialized goods and services, making them a distinct and often disadvantaged group of consumers. This also requires special designs, catering to the special needs of the elderly based on an understanding of the elder groups and their requirements, preferences (Scherer, 2002), including the language, cultural and other contexts, which may be different from those of the dominant culture of the country or region they are in (Parette, Huer and Scherer, 2004). In some countries, this has given rise to well-defined markets for older persons (*Demibileck and Demirkan, 2004*). The quality of life of the older persons is often dependent on the adequacy of their living conditions. The use of enabling devices and home modifications for eliminating barriers in the homes of older persons is becoming more common, as health care professionals and building contractors gain expertise in these areas (Goyal and Dixit, 2008c). Examples of such useful items include designs for kitchens (adjustable height storage racks, counters and cupboards, finger protector, utensils with finger bump grips or hand straps, jar opener), bathrooms (raised seats, grab bars, non-skid rugs or mats), stairs (stair glide, ramp), doors and windows (door wedge, lever doorknob handles), electric fittings (remote control/voice-activated switches for electric lights), domestic appliances, furniture designs, safety alarms, video intercoms, bed rails, mobile phone with one-touch call facility, cordless speaker phone with large buttons, etc. Physical disabilities of the elderly often make it hard to get dressed and undressed. The design of clothing for the elderly requires attention to bodily changes from ageing in order to facilitate and raise the quality of life. Season-specific and need-specific materials and designs are especially required for the elderly. Emerging technologies help development of special clothing for the elderly that are aesthetically attractive, comfortable, made of non-allergic textile fibres and are durable. The conventional footwear design many times prohibits optimal biomechanical function of the foot, causing majority of foot, leg and back problems, which leads to a host of painful symptoms in case of elderly users. Specially designed footwear improves the comfort and performance (e.g., wide fittings, soft leather uppers, lightweight shoes, Velcro fastenings, stretchy uppers, washable shoes and slippers).

The public transport services/vehicle systems need to be robust for catering the needs of the elderly and disabled people (Karim and Nwagboso, 2004). It has been reported that older peoples' vision deteriorates, particularly at night, reducing the ability of older people to read signs and to see objects such as pedestrians in low light. Their sensitivity to visual motion decreases, increasing detection failures and making traffic gap judgments less accurate (Stamatiadis, Tayor and Mckelvey, 1990; Mitchell, 1997). The developments of advanced technologies and their application to road transportation include computing, sensors, communications and controls, and have been in use for some time in various countries (Suen, Mitchell and Henderson, 2003). These include: (1) advanced traveller information systems with navigation systems for route guidance information, advance warning of junctions and lane changes, blind spot obstacle detection; (2) advanced vehicle control and safety systems helps to avoid collisions, improve visibility at night, assist with the longitudinal and lateral control of the vehicle and assist with speed control; (3) non-contact smart cards to pay fares in buses; (4) buses with on-board display of the name of the next stop and stop request buttons within reach of seated passengers; (5) snooze alarm while driving; (6) an electronic memory to reset seats, steering and mirrors, and monitoring of vehicle condition and (7) in-vehicle signs, warnings for traffic signals and rail intelligent cruise control crossings.

## Old-age Homes/Retirement Township

In India, some builders have constructed exclusive townships and homes (e.g., in Pune, Bangalore, Chennai, Mumbai, Coimbatore, Bhiwadi and Jaipur) for elderly people by incorporating many of technology features. The concept of retirement resorts or complexes is gradually emerging as the most viable option among the senior members of the society who are financially independent. They want to live with dignity and have secure life. Townships and residential colonies exclusively for senior citizens are now coming up in the country where they can relocate and spend the sunset of their lives without bothering about paying electricity bills, cooking and getting prompt medical care. Some of the addresses and details of such home/townships are given below.

1. **Dignity Lifestyle** is a project by Dignity Foundation for active and productive living for the senior. Dignity Lifestyle Township Neral, Matheran main Road, Village Mangaon, District Raigad Maharashtra (www.dignitylifestyle.org/index.htm)
2. **Classic Kudumbam** is a specially designed retirement community in a green and pollution-free environment. Classic Kudumbam Classic Farms Road, Off: Old Mahabalipuram Sholinganallur, Chennai (www.kudumbam.com)
3. **Ashiana Utsav** Unit No. 4 and 5, 3rd Floor Plot No. D-2, Southern Park Saket District Centre, Saket New Delhi and Ashiana Bageecha Shopping Complex Bhagat Singh Colony Bhiwadi, Rajasthan (www.ashianautsav.com/utsav-web/index-0.htm)
4. **Athashri** has been designed around the unique requirements of the senior citizen (Pune, India, http://www.pscl.in/index_1.html)
5. **Riverdale Consortium** is India's first and finest senior living community at Cochin, Kerala benefits of all the social, recreational and cultural opportunities (Kandanad Cochin, Kerala, www.riverdaleresorts.com/index.htm)
6. **LICHFL Care Homes Ltd.**, a retirement village at Bangalore promoted by the LIC Housing Finance Ltd. (LIC Housing Finance Ltd.,15/1, 2nd Floor, Hayes Centre, Hayes Road, Bangalore-560025, Website: www.lichfl.com)
7. **Golden Nest Senior Commune** is Pune's first commune designed for senior citizens and a joint venture by Vascon Engineers Pvt. Ltd. and Manisha Constructions. (www.goldennestindia.com)
8. **The NEST** is a residential complex outfitted with handrails at strategic locations throughout the complex including toilets, kitchens, and gardens, etc. and bathroom fitted with shower seats while the flooring laid using anti-skid tiles, furniture with round

edges, emergency alert systems, etc. (Flamingo 52, Aakriti Eco-city, E -8, Extension, Bawadiakalan, Bhopal, Website: www. theaakritigroup.com)

9. **OASIS–Senior Citizen Communes** (Dalal House, Kondhwa Khurd Pune, www.oasisseniorcommune.com).

10. **Senior Care Comfort homes**—Soundaryam, Santhosham and Shenbhagam at Coimbatore and Serene Adinath at Chennai (Covai Property Centre (India) Pvt. Ltd. Damu Nagar, Puliyakulam Main Road, Coimbatore, Tamilnadu, www. covaiprop.com)

In Sweden, the government has adopted the 'Ageing in Place' policy and has developed a special programme for adapting the elderly housing (Brick, 2011). In 1998, Denmark changed its policy to stop building old-age institutions and instead build residential units for the elderly without steps, with suitable accessibility and the possibility of receiving round-the-clock services. Similar system of support and services available within the community with housing adaptation and the development of technological systems in different countries such as Italy, United Kingdom, Spain, Japan, Canada, The United States and Israel (Brick, 2011). Australia offers its elderly home and community care services, aged care packages, National Aboriginal and Torres Strait Islander Flexible Aged Care Programme and has developed 'Apartments for Life model' by The Benevolent Society (TBS), which offers older people the chance to purchase housing in their local community to meet the support requirements needed to enable them to age in place (Bartlett and Carroll, 2011). Public-supported long-term care insurance programmes for senior citizens are functional in Netherlands, Israel, Germany, Austria and Japan. The US-born Foster Grandparents Programme has been replicated in a number of other countries, while hospice care for the terminally ill migrated abroad from Ireland and the United Kingdom (Nusberg, 2009).

## Assistive and Enabling Devices

The technologies provide needed support and assistance in everyday life to both disabled and frail/ailing elderly, covering various needs, for example, medical and daily activities, such as personal care, housework and leisure activities. Age–related changes often negatively affect our health and independence, thus increasing the need for assistance. Faced with gradual deterioration in their abilities, many older people wish to remain in their own homes. For these individuals, use of 'assistive technology' makes a difference between retaining their independent quality of life and self-respect. Due to the growing numbers of the elderly who wish to stay independent in the community, assistive and enabling devices are becoming natural choice of these users. Assistive technology is defined as any equipment or system that assists people who have difficulties, due to infirmity or disability, in carrying out everyday activities. It covers simple items such as walking sticks, bath seats and grab rails, as well as electro-mechanical equipment (e.g., powered wheelchairs), electronic aids (e.g., digital hearing aids and environmental controls) or equipment used by carers, such as lifting aids. A variety of such devices are available for needy people (see, for example, Goyal and Dixit, 2009; Kumar et al., 2009). Developments in emerging fields such as robotics could also benefit older people with cognitive impairments as well as those with physical disabilities.

Under the TIE programme of the Ministry of Science and Technology, a mobile eldercare unit (MEU) was supported in rural areas of Himachal Pradesh in 2009 to meet the variety of needs of elderly people, for example, health needs by promotion of health care and wellness activities through screening and providing medical facilities at their door step and to rehabilitate elderly people physically, socially, economically and psychologically. The MEU provided preventive, promotive and curative health care through a combination of different systems of treatment, including timely detection of chronic diseases and motivating people to adopt a healthy lifestyle. The MEU served as good info base for availability of elderly specific resources and facilitated preparation of comprehensive database both for research and for quality control purposes.

## Home-based Technology Support

*Daily Activities at Home:* Starting from simple safety devices in kitchen (e.g., finger protectors, gas leakage detectors, tin openers), the use of technology in safety devices can be noticed in, for example, shock prevention in electrical/electronic gadgets, fire alarms, door security intercoms, skid-free floors, ramps, unobtrusive entrances and exits, fall protection devices, diapers for elders with health problems, etc.

*Home Monitoring Systems:* A 'smart home' is a residence equipped with technologies that enhances safety of elders at home and monitors their daily activities. The features in the home are automated, where enabling devices can communicate with each other through a communication network. For example, devices and sensors control lighting, smoke detectors, door entry systems, locks, water outlets, as well as visual and tactile signalling devices.

Wireless networks, fast internet connections, smart digital sensors and gadgets have provided the necessary capabilities for round-the-clock monitoring of 'smart homes'. Through a network of such smart sensors and data collection and transmission electronics, it is possible to collect environmental, behavioural and biological data for elderly inmates. With use of such sensors (e.g., motion sensors), it is possible to watch for abnormal behaviour, sleeping patterns, use of toilet, kitchen, etc. The system establishes the person's normal routine so that it can quickly detect when there are changes to these routines. When something abnormal happens, alerts are automatically sent via phone or email to the predefined addresses of the caregivers. It is also possible to monitor activities, for example, if the stove has been left on, medicines have been taken from the dispenser, food taken from the refrigerator/oven, etc.

The Swedish government is known to support the development of products and services that can assist elderly people and their relatives in everyday life through testing of the new technology for the elderly in their homes (alarm unit with GSM backup, mobile phone designed for the elderly and wireless home care safety system). The other examples are: 'Robot Nurses' in Japan and 'Flo-robot' in Pittsburgh being used to provide assistance in activities such as cleaning, assisting patients from wheelchairs and onto beds, etc. (Chris and Gavan, 2000), and use of telemedicine and remote monitoring systems in home-based care (The Economist Intelligence Unit Limited, 2009). Robots with affective-response capability have recently entered the market. Japan pioneered this field a decade ago through the development of robotic pets, and further research in this direction has taken place in Europe (Heerink, Kröse, Evers and Wielinga, 2010). More recently, company such as Alderbaran Robotics (France) has introduced human-form 'android' robots such as 'Nao' that are responsive to voice, eye gaze and gesticulation (Normie, 2011). Presently, many national/ international ageing-in-place technology collaborative projects focused on development of robots that are in progress. Examples are Multi Purpose Mobile Robot for Ambient Assisted Living (FLORENCE), Knowledgeable Service Robots for Ageing (KSERA) and Multi-Role Shadow Robotic System for Independent Living (SRS). [Available online http://www.ûorence-project.eu, http://ksera.ieis.tue.nl, http://srs-project.eu].

Monitoring of activities can be extended to daily health checks, for example, home instrumented with devices to measure heart rate, temperature, nutrition, etc. Such technologies are currently available, and also being developed, that will not only permit monitoring of the physiological status of an individual, but will also permit observation and knowledge of the psychological, cognitive and behavioural health of an individual. As older people have different types of disabilities, different types of assistive devices and services are available to help overcome such disabilities. For example, accessibility to public facilities by the elderly, such as shopping centres, hospitals, leisure centres and cultural attractions/recreational travel and other day-to-day facilities, is important. Assistive technologies are available that can help the elderly to get into and out of their vehicles and drive more safely. Adjustable mirrors, seats, and steering wheels, power wheelchair, wheelchair lift, or stair elevator, etc. can reduce their dependence on others. The European Commission through its 'Seventh Framework Programme' has directed substantial funds to support collaborative research by international consortia developing applications for older citizens, using brain–computer interface (BCI)-controlled environments. Such projects include the control and reduction of neurological tremor, such as in Parkinson's and multiple sclerosis sufferers (Grimaldi and Manto, 2010), and a means for emotional expression, social interaction and environmental control for victims of cerebral trauma and stroke (Navarro, Weber and Wermter, 2011).

Older Adults Technology Services (OATS) has spearheaded the USA's largest and most successful municipal technology initiative for senior citizens in New York city in partnerships with over 40 community organizations. The OATS provide intensive, multi-week trainings to senior citizens at home and in community technology laboratories on topics ranging from computer basics to health research and workforce skills. This service typically works in low-income, minority communities in partnership with neighbourhood organizations that serve vulnerable populations. These programmes have achieved national recognition as a model for engaging, training and supporting older adults to use computers and broadband access to improve their health, social engagement, access to services and the quality of life (OATS, 2009). Israel is a leading developer of sophisticated telehealth technology, such as remote cardiac monitoring. A variety of gerontechnology research programmes are carried out in Israel, both in the public and private sectors. Research carried out at the geriatric medical and rehabilitation centres in Israel has resulted in many quality-of-life enhancing technologies for older peoples in the area of stroke rehabilitation, therapeutic treatments for Parkinson's and Alzheimer's diseases and effective management of decubitus (Normie and Brick, 2009). In Israel, Yad Sarah offers a range of services to help the elderly to age in their homes, such as distress call buttons, occupational therapy for the housebound, transportation for the disabled, loan of medical, rehabilitative and technological equipment, etc. (Brick, 2011).

## Networking

The elderly suffer loss of primary network of relations, largely on account of abandonment by their children or on account of neglect by their family members. Networking assumes importance in such cases by which older persons can not only create recreational avenues for themselves but also organize pooling of skills and resources available at different places. Secondary social networking can be achieved through peer group interaction within the old persons' residential complexes or with neighbourhood groups, day care centres, senior citizens associations, etc. Tertiary network of relations, for examples, systems of governance and development programmes, can also be tried for constructive engagement. Activities such as mixing and linking of generations at special and diverse occasions, and for example through ICT-based gadgets, can prove beneficial to address this isolation and loneliness. Geographical information system-based resource mapping provides a useful tool for pooling of information and resources useful to the elderly.

A Chandigarh-based NGO *DadaDadi* is using short message service (SMS), 24×7 helpline and other web-based technologies to ensure the safety of elderly people living alone in the city. Another example includes '*Senior Citizens Initiative at Facebook*' that provides much desired social networking among the elderly. Such sites cater to the needs of senior citizens to battle loneliness, get news and information, play games/ work on puzzles and share life online with a group of like-minded people in their age bracket. Datta (2008) provides an overview of the HelpAge India's efforts in establishing elder's helplines in India. Older persons have a wealth of experience and knowledge that they have gathered in their lifetime (Dixit and Goyal, 2011). An exchange network based on specific knowledge bases, such as Third Age Universities, can value the experiences of the elderly and can also be useful in recounting their career paths to children in schools. The Universities of Third Age (U3As) are self-help, self-managed lifelong learning cooperatives, with no full time work for older people, providing opportunities to share learning experiences in a wide range of interest groups and to pursue learning not for qualifications, but for fun. WorldU3A is an international forum whose purpose is to encourage international understanding and contacts for all active retired people everywhere. It does this through its Internet activity and publishes two monthly newsletters—Signpost and U3A Patrika (http://worldu3a. org/signpost/). 'U3A Patrika' is a newsletter of the Indian Society of Universities of the Third Age (http://u3aindia.org/patrika/index.htm), which provides useful information for older people in Asia in general and India in particular.

## Recreation and Entertainment

Community-based and recreation-oriented programmes for the elderly will help them to develop a sense of self-reliance, community responsibility and creative use of their time, keeping in view the therapeutic value of recreation (Rauterberg, 2004). Also, participation in entertainment activities has proved to be helpful for the maintenance of cognitive skills (Luciano et al., 2006). Memory games and specially designed video games are available for people with difficulty in concentration or thinking. For example, 'Brain Age' (known in Japan as brain training), a new brain-training game for the elderly from Nintendo Co., played on the company's hand-held DS console is a package of cerebral workouts aimed at the over-45s that claimed to improve mental agility and even slow the onset of dementia and Alzheimer's disease (McCurry, 2006). Khoo et al. (2006) developed 'Age Invaders', an interactive game, to allow elderly people to play together in a physical space with grandchildren, while parents could participate through the Web.

Development of an 'Infotainment package for Elderly' could well serve a utility for community-based, recreation-oriented programmes that include music (classical/instrumental); reading material (traditional books, magazines and newspapers); elder brain age games/amusement game; travel guide; songs, poems, plays, stories, spiritual programmes, folk dances; VCDs on traditions, historic movements, pilgrimage and tourist places, folk and religious songs, fitness programmes, etc. Some countries have local government exercise programmes for elderly people, such as exercise classes for people with Parkinson's disease and osteoarthritis in Palm Coast, (Florida), the city of Beachwood (Ohio) has swimming, gentle-on-joints exercise, tai chi, yoga, reflexology and a golf league, town of Northborough (Massachusetts) offers strength training/exercise as well as line dancing at its senior centre (available online www.n4a.org/pdf/MOAFinalReport.pdf)ý. The Senior-Friendly Business Programme, an initiative of the Moncton Mayor's Seniors Advisory Committee in partnership with Downtown Moncton Centre-ville inc. (DMCI), Canada, claims to provide friendly quality services and facilities to elderly people (Available at www. moncton.ca/Residents/Seniors/Senior_Friendly_Business_Program and seniorjournal.com/Travel.htm) dedicated to seniors provides latest information on wide categories. For example, Senior Citizen Travel and Leisure—The Centres for Disease Control and Prevention released the online version in August 2013 of the 2014 edition of *CDC Health Information for International Travel*, commonly known as the 'Yellow Book' to help international travelers stay healthy when in foreign lands (www.cdc.gov/travel). A unique vacation concept 'Look After Me' launched in Rotorua in July 2011 and founded by award-winning Rotorua scientist, writer and performance poet Julia Charity, designed especially for senior travellers across New Zealand. The 'Look After Me' website is a 'virtual hotel' providing hosts with a 'hotel-in-a-handbag' that connects senior travellers with authentic Kiwi hosts to create a unique and memorable travel experience (Available online at www. lookafterme.co.nz.).

# Conclusion

Modern scientific and technological advancements have opened up new possibilities for elderly care to support comfortable and dignified living and active ageing of older persons. Capabilities of modern technologies coupled with traditional knowledge systems play a vital role in utilizing vast available resources for benefit of the elderly at affordable cost. With the use of assistive/enabling devices, the elders can look forward to safe and secure living, both inside home and outdoors. Such devices reduce dependence on the caregivers and facilitate independent living for the elders. Community living concept is gaining acceptance in India, at least in urban areas where affordability is improving. Assistive technologies can play vital role in such community living places. Even existing old-age homes, day care centres, etc. can be retrofitted or remodelled with technology products. The success of technology applications for the elderly depends to a great extent on the policies and programmes that promote healthy ageing and provide means of dignified living. Of course, the technology systems must be reliable and simple in operation and maintenance, otherwise elders try to avoid it or discard it, once a fault occurs. The challenge for the future is to ensure that people will be enabled to age with dignity and continue to participate in their societies as citizens with full rights. Some of the technologies mentioned in this chapter can easily be implemented through combined efforts of government, voluntary or NGOs and industry. Associations and federations of elderly peoples can be important vehicle for propagation of such technology interventions.

# References

Bartlett, H. & Carroll, M. (2011). Ageing in place down under. *Global Ageing: Issues and Action*, 5(2), 25–32.

Brick, Y. (2011). Ageing in place. *Global Ageing: Issues and Action, 7*(2), 5–14.

Chris, T. & Gavan, Q. (2000). *The design and technological feasibility of home systems for the elderly: Research project report* (p.33). Belfast: The Queen's University.

Datta, A. (2008). Elder's helplines—HelpAge India's response to an urgent need for distress intervention. In S. Bhatia, M. Cherian & J.R. Gupta (Eds), *Protection of life and property of senior citizens in India*. Navi Mumbai: All India Senior Citizens' Confederation (AISCCON).

Demibileck, O. & Demirkan, H. (2004). Universal product design involving elderly users: A participatory design model. *Applied Ergonomics, 35(4), 361–370.*

Dixit, U. & Goyal, V.C. (2011). Traditional knowledge from and for elderly. *Indian Journal of Traditional Knowledge, 10*(3), 429–438.

Dobriansky, P.J., Suzman, R.M. & Hodes, R.J. (2007). *Why population ageing matters: A global perspective* (pp. 1–32). Washington, DC: US Department of State, U.S. Department of Health and Human Services, National Institute on Ageing, and National Institutes of Health.

Furlan, J.C. & Fehlings, M.G. (2009). The impact of age on mortality, impairment, and disability among adults with acute traumatic spinal cord injury. *Journal of Neurotrauma, 26*(10), 1707–1717.

GoI. (2011). *Situation analysis of the elderly in India*. New Delhi: Central Statistics Office, Ministry of Statistics and Programme Implementation, Government of India.

Goyal, V.C. & Dixit, U. (2008a). R&D and institutional infrastructure issues for assistive and enabling technologies for elderly people in India. In S. Bhatia & V.C. Goyal (Eds), *Assistive technologies for senior citizens in India*. Navi Mumbai: All India Senior Citizens' Confederation (AISCCON).

———. (2008b). Technology for safety and protection of elderly. In S. Bhatia, M. Cherian & J.R. Gupta (Eds), *Protection of life and property of senior citizens in India*. Navi Mumbai: All India Senior Citizens' Confederation (AISCCON).

———. (2008c, July 11). Role of technology in housing needs for senior citizens. *Symposium on challenges facing senior citizens: Shelter, health care and protection of life and property*, CII, Chandigarh.

———. (2009, February 27). Assistive and enabling technologies for elderly in India. *International congress on gerontology and geriatric medicine* AIIMS, New Delhi.

Grimaldi, G. & Manto, M. (2010). Neurological tremor: Sensors signal processing and emerging applications. *Sensors. 10*, 1399–1422.

Heerink, M., Kröse, B., Evers, V. & Wielinga, B. (2010). Relating conversational expressiveness to social presence and acceptance of an assistive social robot. *Virtual Reality, 14*,77–84.

Karim, N.A. & Nwagboso, C. (2004). Assistive technologies in public transport: Meeting the needs of elderly and disabled passengers. *Proceedings of International Conference on Information and Communication Technologies: From Theory to Applications* (19–23 April). New York: IEEE Press.

Khoo, E.T., Lee, S.P., Cheok, A.D., Kodagoda, S., Zhou, Y. & Toh, G.S. (2006). Age invaders: Social and physical inter-generational family entertainment. *CHI '06 extended abstracts on human factors in computing systems.* pp. 243–246.

Krishnamachari, S., Mario, V. & Thomas, T. (2010). Prevalence of health related disability among community dwelling urban elderly from middle socioeconomic strata in Bangaluru, India. *Indian Journal of Medical Research, 131*, 515–521.

Kumar, P., Dixit, U. & Goyal, V.C. (2009). Assistive and enabling technology needs of elderly people in India: Issues and initial results. In S. Bhatia & V.C. Goyal (Eds), *Assistive technologies—towards home-based elder care* (pp. 978–993). Ambala Cantt.: Associated Book Service.

Lawrence, N. 2011. Technology for ageing in place. *Global Ageing: Issues and Action (International Federation on Ageing (IFA), 5*(2), 45–51.

Luciano, G., Mariano, A., Giacinto, B., Malena, F., Francisco, I. & Lisa, P. (2006) Cognition, technology and games for the elderly: An introduction to ELDER GAMES Project. *PsychNology Journal, 4*(3), 285–308.

McCurry, J. (2006, March 7). Video games for the elderly: An answer to dementia or a marketing tool? *The Guardian*. Available at http://www.guardian.co.uk.

Mitchell, G.G.B. (1997). *Intelligent transportation systems (ITS) applications for improving transportation for elderly and disabled travelers* (TP 12925E). Montreal, Canada: Transportation Development Centre, Transport Canada.

Navarro, N., Weber, C. & Wermter, S. (2011). Real-world reinforcement learning for autonomous humanoid robot charging in a home environment. *Lecture Notes in Computer Science: Vol. 6856. Towards Autonomous Robotic Systems* (pp. 231–240).

Normie, L.R., & Brick, Y. (2009). The technological response to accessibility in Israel: Accomplishments, challenges, and opportunities. In S. Bhatia & V.C. Goyal (Eds), *Assistive technologies—towards home-based elder care*. Ambala Cantt.: Associated Book Service.

Normie, L. (2011). Technology for Ageing in Place. *Global Ageing: Issues and Actions, 7*(2), 45–52.

Older Adults Technology Services (OATS). (2009). *Response to request for information: Broadband initiatives program and broadband technology opportunities program*. Available at www.ntia.doc.gov/legacy/broadbandgrants.

Parette, H.P., Huer, M.B. & Scherer, M. (2004). Effects of acculturation on assistive technology service delivery. *Journal of Special Education Technology, 19*(2), 31–41.

Pasricha, S., & Thimmayamma, B.V.S. (2005). *Dietary tips for the elderly* (p. 30). Hyderabad: National Institute of Nutrition.

Puri, S. & Khanna, K. (2009). *Dietary guide for healthy ageing* (p. 74). Delhi: Institute of Home Economics.

Rauterberg, M. (2004). Positive effects of entertainment technology of human behaviour. In R. Jacquart (Ed.), *Building the information society* (pp. 51–58). Toulouse: Kluwer Academic Press.

Scherer, M.J. (2002). Editorial, the change in emphasis from people to person. Introduction to the special issue on assistive technology. *Disability and Rehabilitation, 24*, 1–4.

Secretary-General, SG/SM/12500, OBV/812. (dated 28 September 2009). Department of Public Information, News and Media Division, New York. Available at: http://www.un.org/News/Press/docs/2009/sgsm12500.doc.htm.

Stamatiadis, N., Tayor, W.C. & Mckelvey, F.X. (1990). Accidents of elderly drivers and inter-section traffic control devices. *Journal of Advanced Transportation. 24*(2), 99–112.

Suen, S.L., Mitchell, C.G.B. & Henderson, S. (2003). Application of intelligent transport systems to enhance vehicle safety for elderly and less able travellers. *Transportation Development Centre Transport Canada*. pp.386-394. (Paper Number 98S2-O-03). Available at www-nrd.nhtsa.dot.gov/pdf/Esv/esv16/98S2O03.PDF.

The Economist Intelligence Unit Limited. 2009. *Healthcare strategies for an ageing society* (pp.1–31), Philips (Ed.), fourth report in a series of four Commissioned.

Varghese, M. & Patel, V. (2004). The graying of India: Mental health perspective. In S.P. Agarwal (Ed.), *Mental health. An Indian perspective 1946–2003* (pp. 240–248). New Delhi: Elsevier.

WHO. (2000). Social Development and Ageing: Crisis or Opportunity?, Special Panel at Geneva, pp.1–12.

———. (2009).World Health Survey Geneva, 2002–2004. Available at http://www.who. int/healthinfo/survey/en/.

———. (2011). *World report on disability* (WHO/NMH/VIP/11.01, pp.1–24). Geneva: World Health Organization.

# 14

# Ageing Well and Way Forward

*Renu Tyagi and Tattwamasi Paltasingh*

## Introduction

The elderly in India constitute a heterogeneous group with variations in demographics and diverse needs, ranging from health and family care, socio-economic support to safety against crime and mistreatment, etc. Disintegration of the traditional joint family system and increasing Westernization have adversely affected the situation. In India, both the share and size of elderly population are increasing over time. There are 98 million citizens of 60 years and above in India. This figure is projected to raise from 5.6 per cent in 1961 to 12.4 per cent of total population by the year 2026. About 65 per cent of the aged depend on others for their day-to-day maintenance. Less than 20 per cent of elderly women and majority of elderly men are financially independent (Nandan, 2012). More than half of elderly men are found with sickness with a high concentration in the urban areas. Most of the programmes for the elderly such as old-age homes, day-care centres and mobile Medicare units, managed by the non-governmental organizations (NGOs) or funded partially by the government are urban based, expensive and that often ignore the elderly residing in the rural areas. Isolation is recognized as an increasing trend among elderly population (CSO, 2011).

The ageing process is unavoidable and inevitable, but one can pass through this stage of life with a positive approach that can help in confronting the challenges concerning old age. Positive ageing is a lifelong and personal process that cannot be achieved in isolation from others. There are a number of important prerequisites for positive ageing. A wider recognition of heterogeneity of elderly population is one of those requirements. Little attention is being paid to the significant proportion of the elderly hailing from different culture and regional background. It is important to assess the degree to which older people are considered as equal participants in the society. Learning how to cope with morbidity and mortality is an essential part of living that must be learned throughout life and not just in old age. Acceptance of ageing is an important prerequisite for positive ageing and a major factor in combating negative attitudes to ageing. Regarding the work participation, there are difference of opinions and theoretical perspectives. While there is a general appreciation that older people are discriminated against in the labour market, many people also believe that older people should give way to younger people in this field. This view directly and indirectly challenges their equal right to be self-fulfilled through participation in the labour force. Freedom from disability should be the central determinant of the well-being of older people and it need to be emphasized. Associations between low burden of diseases and healthy cognitive function support longevity as well as successful ageing (Paulson, Bowen and Lichtenberg, 2011). Measures to assist incapacitated older people and their caregivers are important and need to be strengthened. The identification and promotion of such measures must therefore be a priority in any campaign for positive ageing. Old age can be taken as time of creative development when one has enough time to pursue interests, overlooked in earlier stages of life. Continued physical and social activities supplement positive living and positive ageing (Doyle, Mc Kee and Sherriff, 2010). Intergenerational contact provides wider prospects for older people to share their knowledge and experience with younger people. Such sharing helps older people to establish their rightful place in the society. Promoting positive attitudes to ageing among vulnerable categories of older people, such as the frail elderly, those in institutions, the mentally and physically challenged, should be given due attention. Physical activity, social network, friendship, development of coping skills, the importance of experience, knowledge should be promoted to facilitate positive ageing.

In this chapter, different challenges confronted by elderly population have been broadly discussed under two broad categories, that is, 'socio-economic deprivation and disparities' and 'increasing crime against the elderly'. This is followed by a section on safety initiatives and legal support for socio-economic support and crime against the elderly. The next section highlights the hope and possibilities despite the challenges, giving emphasis on the relevance of positive ageing. The elderly may visualize their life with dignity that is beyond violence and poverty and this makes focus of the next section. The chapter concludes with some relevant recommendations and suggestions.

# Challenges Confronted

Biological, economic, emotional and interpersonal facets of ageing influence the well-being of individuals in different ways. Changing traditional family values, family structure, mobility of the younger generation and changing role of women have adversely affected the elderly care (Kapoor and Kapoor, 2004; Khan, 2008). The elderly in India, no doubt, confront a large number of socio-economic issues and challenges including insufficient income, declining health, meagre social security, changing social roles and recognition, and more serious issues such as crime against the elderly and elder abuse, etc. Modernization and urbanization, despite the claim of better infrastructure and comfort to the citizens, have added more segregations, isolations and frequent occurrences of crimes, creating more vulnerability to the elderly (Patel, 2005). One cannot ignore these contradictions in day-to-day life. The next section has highlighted two major issues, that is, challenges in the socio-economic sphere that deprive many elderly to proper care and resources and giving them the feeling of isolation and rejection. The other major issues include the untold stories of many senior citizens as some of them become the victims of physical and mental torture at domestic level as well as by the outsiders who do not hesitate to do any kind of heinous crime against them for instant financial benefit.

## Socio-economic Deprivation and Disparities

Economic, health and social insecurities are increasing among the elderly in India (World Bank, 2001; Ramamurti, 2003), and women are more vulnerable than men to experience poverty in old age (WHO, 2002;

NSSO, 2006). In India, the majority of the elderly work in the informal sector with low levels of wages and poor working conditions that has placed the aged in a state of deprivation and vulnerability (HelpAge International, 2002). Various types of pressures associated with poverty include: making ends meet, poor housing, fear of crime and declining physical health that may further leads to poor emotional well-being. Social interaction may become limited due to declining mobility and increased chronic illness among elderly population. Consequently, they become more vulnerable to crime (Khan and Handa, 2006; Das, 2009; McCormick et al., 2009).

Social isolation is a widely recognized challenge for elderly population in both developing and developed nations. More than 60 per cent of the aged in the Organisation for Economic Co-operation and Development (OECD) countries are in social isolation despite of being economically well off. Social isolation often accompanies health risks (Alam, 2007). Poor health among the elderly lead to financial dependency, loss of autonomy, reduced social contact and loneliness. In developed countries, there exists 'compression of morbidity' resulting in delay in chronic illness associated with ageing (WHO, 2002; Kinsella and Phillips, 2005). However, in India, it is indicated that the gain in life expectancy is going to be accompanied by increased years of poor health due to chronic diseases, and hence 'expansion of morbidity'. Most of the elderly across the globe are deprived of health care and protection (WHO, 2006), and these deprivations get aggregated in the developing countries (HelpAge International, 2006).

## Crime and Mistreatment

Crime and mistreatment against the elderly have received global attention and influenced the ageing population ranging between 60 and 85 years and even more in all respects. However, there is very limited database in India with regard to the incidence and rate of elder neglect and crime against the elderly. One of the main reasons for increasing mistreatment of the elderly is negative and stereotyped attitude towards the older people. As long as older people are devalued and marginalized by the society, they will suffer from loss of self-identity and remain highly susceptible to mistreatment and neglect. The fading joint family system in India, fear of crime or loneliness are mostly responsible for an increasing number of the elderly shifting to the old-age homes. Crime against the elderly has been featured in many daily newspapers at regular interval that includes the issues such as robbery followed by murder, attempt to murder, causing severe injuries, etc. Some of these deaths take place in mysterious manner where the offender is untraceable (*The Sunday Express*, 2009; *Hindustan Times*, 2013; *ToI*, 2008, 2012; TNN, 2014a, 2014b, 2014c). Some of these crimes are not reported as well due to lack of detailed database in official compilations, which points to insufficient focus on the issue (The Hindu, 2013). There is a sharp increase in crime rates against the elderly from 7.6 per cent in 2003 to 8.8 per cent in 2007 at the national level. The crime rate for mega cities has also increased (24,709) in 2007 as compared to that in 2006 (21,861), that is, an increase of 13.0 per cent in just one year with more female victims as compared to the males (Mangoli and Tarase, 2009). The cases of crime against the elderly are reported more in urban areas (77.58%) than rural areas (22.42%). Majority of the crimes are committed during the daytime and the majority of the victims belong to the age group of 61–65 years (Table 14.1). The incidents of murder

**Table 14.1**

*Distribution of crime against elderly*

| Nature of crime | % of the cases |
|---|---|
| Murder | 44.71 |
| Attempt to murder | 71 |
| Theft | 12 |
| Hurt | 8.24 |
| Robbery | 8.82 |
| Kidnapping | 3.53 |
| Cheating/Fraud | 6.47 |
| Mistreatment | 5.29 |
| Chain snatching | 6.47 |
| Others | 7.65 |
| Total | 100 |

*Source*: Mishra and Patel (2013).
*Note*: The percentage has been calculated out of the total 170 cases reported in newspapers.

are higher than any other types of crimes and prevalent in both urban and rural areas (Patel, 2013; Mishra and Patel, 2013).

About 32,496 elderly have been murdered and 5,836 cases of not amounting to murder and kidnapping have been reported all over India from 2001 to 2010 (NCRB, 2010). Senior citizens often become victims of the crimes and mistreatment committed by their domestic helpers, members of their families and relatives. The academicians and the policymakers have begun paying attention to the crime against the elderly (Das, 2009; Rufus and Shekhar, 2011). Different kinds of elder abuse including verbal abuse (60%), physical abuse (48%), emotional abuse (37%), economical abuse (35%) and neglect (20%) have been reported (Help Age India, 2011). The major types of crimes faced by the elderly are murder, attempt to murder, hurt, kidnapping, dacoit, robbery, burglary, theft, cheating, criminal breach of trust, etc. (GESS, 2009). Most of the crimes against elderly are either never reported or under reported; however, in all communities and across all sections of the society, they are on rise (Khan and Handa, 2006). The elderly constitute a vulnerable group and are easy targets for criminals, resulting in an increasing number of crimes against the elderly (Das, 2009). In a study conducted in metropolitan cities, it is reported that the crime and violence against the elderly are highest in Mumbai, followed by Delhi and then Kolkata (Table 14.2).

The breakdown of traditional joint family to nuclear families has added to increased crime rate against the elderly today. Rapid urbanization and modernization processes have made a substantial impact on family and community values, and the generation gap has widened, making the youngsters more individualistic than before (Dannefer and Western, 2010). The elderly are confronting the challenges of insecurity, loneliness, weak intergenerational bonding, lack of safety and family care (Patel, 2005). The existing literature and evidences speak volume on challenges confronted by elderly population and lack of preparedness in tackling the issue. This challenge can be confronted and eradicated by sensitizing younger generation and making stronger laws and policies. It is important to identify the policies that can ensure right to life of every citizen of the country, most importantly through proper enactment of relevant laws and right provisions. For instance, the Atlantic provinces of Canada, Israel and a number of states in the United States have legislation for the mandatory reporting of abuse of the elderly (Binstock and George, 2006).

**Table 14.2**

*Incidence of cognizable IPC crime against senior citizens in major cities*

| S.No. | Types of crime | No. of cases registered from 2003 till June 2008 in | | |
|---|---|---|---|---|
| | | Delhi | Mumbai | Kolkata |
| 1. | Murder | 108 | 43 | 8 |
| 2. | Culpable homicide not amounting to murder | 6 | 1 | 2 |
| 3. | Attempt to murder | 16 | 11 | 15 |
| 4. | Grievous hurt | 62 | 73 | 33 |
| 5. | Hurt | 39 | 250 | 126 |
| 6. | Kidnapping and abduction | 8 | 7 | 3 |
| 7. | Dacoity | 4 | 10 | 1 |
| 8. | Robbery | 62 | 59 | 24 |
| 9. | Burglary | 212 | 806 | 37 |
| 10. | Theft | 635 | 2693 | 531 |
| 11. | Criminal breach of trust | 11 | 104 | 21 |
| 12. | Cheating | 89 | 1014 | 96 |
| 13. | Others | 718 | 1477 | 363 |
| | **Total** | **1,970** | **6,548** | **1,260** |

*Source*: GESS (2009).

# Addressing Welfare and Safety of the Elderly: Initiatives and Legal Support

In the Indian Constitution, the directive principle under Article 41 highlights the role of the State for the right to work, to education and to public assistance in old age, sickness and disablement. The Entry 24 of the Concurrent List of Seventh schedule is also directly related to welfare of elderly persons. This provision empowers both the Central and State governments to enact laws and policies for the welfare of the elderly. The Sections 125–128 of Criminal Procedure Code 1973 are enacted to provide maintenance against those persons who neglect or refuse to maintain their dependent wives, children and parents who are unable to maintain themselves. Under section 20 (3) of the Hindu Adoption and Maintenance Act 1955, applicable for Hindus only, maintenance is provided to aged or infirm parents.

Both male and female children are under legal obligation to maintain their aged and infirm parents. Further, the obligation is personal and independent of possession of any property. According to Section 3 (b) of the Act, maintenance includes in all cases, provision for food, clothing, residence and medical attendance and treatment. Where such parents have more than one child, they are entitled to maintenance from any one or all.

Indian Parliament has passed a bill, that is, 'The Maintenance and Welfare of Parents and Senior Citizens Act 2007', as an effective measure towards elder care. The objective of the Act is to provide more effective provisions for the maintenance and welfare of parents and senior citizens guaranteed and recognized under the Constitution. The new legislation makes easy and cost-effective provisions for claiming maintenance that includes food, clothing, residence, medical assistance and treatment. This legislation promises to make claims of the maintenance speedier (the cases will be disposed in a maximum of 90 days). The Bill contains an appropriate mechanism to provide need-based maintenance to parents and senior citizens of 60 years and above. The Bill provides for setting up of a tribunal in every district for helping the elderly in distress. Besides the penal provision, the law also empowers to the tribunals to disinherit the children, if the senior citizens desire so. It even empowers the tribunal to make a monthly allowance during the proceedings. It also provides for establishment of old-age homes in all districts. Once the person is convicted, no further appeal against the punishment could be made in regular courts. The governments of Maharashtra, Goa and Himachal Pradesh have such legal act for senior citizens. Unfortunately, most other state governments have not considered any legal interventions for safeguarding the interests of older persons. Few states have some other general statutory provisions for older persons under certain conditions. For instance, the Madhya Pradesh government initiated the MP Act No. 26 of 1976 that provides legal aid and legal advice to weaker sections including older people. The legal interventions are a powerful tool in addressing elder abuse issues. The Maintenance and Welfare of Parents and Senior Citizens Act, 2007 (No. 56 of 2007) is the only specific legislation in India on elder abuse, and this is often covered under criminal law or by laws dealing with property rights, civil rights, family violence and mental health. However, several instances of abandonment of parents have come to notice in metros.

India has a well-developed system of succession laws that governs a person's property after his death. Indian Succession Act 1925 applies expressly to Wills and Codicils made by Hindus, Buddhists, Sikhs, Jains, Jews, Parsis and Christians. The Muslim Personal Law is applied to Muslims and they are not governed by the Indian Succession Act, 1925. Different laws that deal with the concept of 'Wills' are: The Indian Succession Act 1925; The Hindu Succession Act 2005; The Muslim Personal Laws and The Indian Registration Act 1908. Hindu Succession Act, 1956 and some provisions of the Indian Succession Act mainly govern Hindus, Buddhist, Sikh and Jains. The Mohammedans are mainly governed by their Personal Law. Indian Succession Act, 1925 is applicable to others, that is, Christians, Jews, Parsis and the person whose marriage is solemnized under Special Marriage Act, 1954. The Hindu Succession Act makes a distinction between male and female in deciding the manner of distribution of their estates. Devolution of the property of a Hindu male dying intestate is governed by section 8 and that of distribution of property of Hindu female dying intestate is governed by the Sections 15 and 16 of the Hindu Succession Act, 1956. Apart from these acts, various states of India have their own amendments of Hindu Succession Act 1956, according to the local customs. There is nothing to prevent a Hindu male from bequeathing his entire property to a stranger. The Muslim male cannot will away more than one-third of estate, and two-thirds of the property must be divided among the family members in the shares as laid down in the law. A Muslim wife cannot be dispossessed. The widow gets a definite share. The male heirs, sons get twice the share of daughters. The Code of Criminal Procedure, 1973, in Section 125 (1) (2) recognizes the right of parents without any means to be supported by their children having sufficient resources. However, 'maintenance' under Section 125 of the Code of Criminal Procedure, 1973 has not been defined, which gives scope to the 'fair' completion of the case and suitable grant of maintenance for maintaining an adequate and appropriate standard of living as per the status of the older parent, while in settlement of some disputes, liberal interpretation of maintenance has been adopted in the courts (Bakshi, 2000).

The Government adopted the National Social Assistance Programme (NSAP) in 1995 for the welfare of the elderly in the unorganized sector. In 2007, the Government renamed the pension programme as 'Indira Gandhi National Old Age Pension Scheme' (IGNOAPS). However, several challenges such as identification, coverage and delivery regarding the pension schemes (NSAP, 2011) are found to be the limiting factor to disburse the pension. The private insurance market for the elderly is still in an infancy stage in India. Productive and lifelong participative involvement of the elderly may be considered in the absence of a universal pension programme for them. The productive ageing can include work for money or satisfaction. However, the type of work should be as per the capability and the choice of the senior citizen. The western concept of 'productive ageing' referred to formal work for remuneration. However, the Asian perspective of productive ageing includes productive and participatory approach (Butler and Gleason, 1985). Productive and participatory ageing not only empowers the elderly but it also supports healthy and quality ageing. There is need to work towards better economic participation of the elderly to facilitate care for growing numbers of older Indians (Bloom, 2011).

## Protecting the Elderly in India: Policy Reflections

The Indian Government, on 13 January 1999, approved a National Policy for Older Persons (NPOP) to empower elderly persons. The policy recognizes older persons as a valuable resource and propagates the cause for their empowerment. The NPOP, 1999, identified education, shelter, health care, nutrition, financial security, protection of life and property, etc. as important areas of intervention for the welfare of the elderly. The NPOP recognizes elder abuse, influencing the type of living arrangements of elderly population in the country. The family ties in India are strong with majority of older persons living with their sons or are supported by them. The working couples find the presence of old parents emotionally bonding and of great help in managing the household and caring for children. However, the policy acknowledges that the position of the majority of older persons has become vulnerable due to various forces such as shortage of residential space in urban areas, high rents and higher cost of living, etc. In order to implement the recommendation of the NPOP, a National Council for Older Persons (NCOP) has been constituted by the Ministry of Social Justice and Empowerment in 1999. As per the policy, various voluntary organizations and associations of older persons have been supported for providing protective services to older persons through helpline services, legal aid and other measures. Further, it has directed the police to keep a vigil on older couples and more specifically those living alone. However, a lack of political will and inadequate funds for the schemes have led to partial implementation of NPOP. The National Programme for the Health Care of Elderly (NPHCE), developed by the Ministry of Health and Family Welfare, addresses separate and specialized comprehensive health care to the senior citizens at various levels (NPHCE, 2011). However, an effective implementation of the programme to bring quality improvement in the health of the elderly remains a challenge. The 'Draft National Policy for Senior Citizens, 2011' has highlighted the elderly concern with some more gravity. The policy covers the concept of productive ageing as an important area for intervention that further aims to create avenues for continuity in employment and/or post-retirement opportunities. In addition, it envisions creating Directorate of Employment to find re-employment for the elderly and reviewing of the age of retirement in view of increasing longevity. As per 2011 policy, the abuse of the elderly and crimes against senior citizens, especially widows and those living alone and disabled, would be tackled with the help of community awareness and policing (GoI, 2011). Social isolation, lack of support and stress increase risk of morbidity and mortality from chronic conditions. Yet, strategies to increase opportunities for social participation have not been emphasized in current policies. In view of continuing erosion of values and the institution of family, there is a need of strong, consistent policies to strengthen the Indian family system. A forward-looking policy for older age can promote successful ageing from middle age onwards, rather than simply aiming to support elderly people with chronic conditions (Bowling and Dieppe, 2005). Despite of increasing incidences and frequency of crime against the elderly, there is no exclusive policy to combat such serious issues. Developing an exclusive policy for this critical emerging issue, that threatens the safety of the senior citizens, should be the focus of the government policies concerning elderly population.

## Instilling Positive Ageing: Beyond Violence and Poverty

There has been a gradual shift in interest among the gerontologists to accept the ageing process and associated changes. There has been an emerging trend in the literature as well as the policy dialogues that have highlighted the positive contributions of the elderly (Bali, 1999;

Batra, S. (2004). Social components of active ageing: A comparative study of engaged and disengaged women after retirement. *Research and Development Journal, 10*(1), 12–20.

Binstock, R.H. & George, L.K. (2006). *Handbook of ageing and the social sciences.* San Diego, CA: Associated Press.

Bloom, D.E. (2011). India's baby boomers: Dividend or disaster. *Current History, 110*(735), 144–149.

Bowling, A. & Dieppe, P. (2005). What is successful ageing and who should define it? *British Medical Journal, 331*(7531), 1548–1551.

Butler, R.N. & Gleason, H.P. (1985). *Productive Ageing: Enhancing Vitality in Later Life.* New York: Springer Publishing Company.

Chen, H. (2009). Successful ageing amongst older people needing care: International comparisons seeking solutions. *Social and Public Policy Review, 3*(1), 1–16.

CSO (Central Statistics Office). (2011). *Situation analysis of the elderly in India.* New Delhi: Ministry of Statistics and Programme Implementation. Government of India.

Dannefer, D. & Phillipson, C. (2010). *The SAGE handbook of social gerontology.* London: SAGE Publications Ltd.

Das, P.K. (2009). Crimes against elderly: A critical analysis. *Helpage India–Research and Development Journal, 15*(2), 21–33.

Doyle, Y.G., Mc Kee, M. & Sherriff, M. (2010). A model of successful ageing in British populations. *European Journal of Public Health, 10*, 1–5.

Fried, L.P. (2004). A social model for health promotion for an ageing population: Initial evidence on the experience corps model. *Journal of Urban Health, 81*(1), 64–78.

GESS (Group for Economic and Social Studies). (2009). *Rising Crime against Elderly People and Responsibility of Police in Metros.* New Delhi: Ministry of Home Affairs, Government of India.

Glass, T.A. (2003). *Successful ageing: Brocklehurst's textbook of geriatric medicine and gerontology* (6th ed.). London: Harcourt Health Sciences.

GoI. (2011). *National Policy for Older Person, Help Age India report.* New Delhi: Ministry of Social Justice and Empowerment, Government of India.

*Hindustan Times.* (2013, January 19). Year of sensational crimes against the elderly. (New Delhi).

HelpAge India. (2011). *Elder abuse and crime in India.* New Delhi: HelpAge India.

HelpAge International. (2002, 2006). *Poverty not pensions.* Available at: www.helptheaged.org.

Jamuna, D. (2007). Intergenerational issues in elder care. In K.L. Sharma (Ed.), *Studies in gerontology—intergenerational perspective.* New Delhi: Rawat publication.

Kapoor, A.K. & Kapoor, S. (2004). *India's elderly: A multidisciplinary dimension.* New Delhi: Mittal Publications.

Khan, A.M. (2008). Emerging challenges of ageing: Role of civil society. In R.N. Kapoor & T.M. Dak (Eds), *Population ageing and development in India.* Udaipur: Institute of Social Development.

Khan, A.M. & Handa, S. (2006). Case studies of elder abuse—roots and bases of interventions. *Journal of the Indian Academy of Geriatrics, 2*, 21–27.

Kinsella, K. & Phillips, D.R. (2005). Global ageing: The challenge of success. *Population Bulletin, 60*(1), 1–40.

Mangoli, R.N. & Tarase, G.M. (2009). Crime against women in India: A statistical review. *International Journal of Criminology and Sociological Theory, 2*(2), 292–302.

McCormick, J., Clifton, J., Sachrajda, A., Cherti, M., McDowell, E. (2009). *Getting on: Well-being in later life.* London: The Institute for Public Policy Research.

Mishra, A.J. & Patel, A.B. (2013). Crimes against the elderly in India: A content analysis on factors causing fear of crime. *International Journal of Criminal Justice Sciences, 8*(1), 13–23.

Nandan, T. (2012). *More elderly women than men in India by 2050: A report.* New York: United Nations Population Fund.

NCRB (National Crime Record Bureau). (2010). *Crime in India 2012 Compendium.* New Delhi: Ministry of Home Affairs.

NPHCE (National Programme for Health Care of the Elderly). (2011). *Operational guidelines for national programme for health care of the elderly.* New Delhi: Government of India.

NSAP (National Social Assistance Programme). (2011*). Annual Reports 2005–06, 2006–07 and 2010–11.* New Delhi: Government of India. Available at: http//: www.nsap.nic.in.

NSSO (National Sample Survey Organization). (2006). *Morbidity, health care and the condition of the aged,* (Report No. 507). New Delhi: Ministry of Statistics and Programme Implementation, Government of India.

Patel, A.B. (2013). Effect of crime on the wellbeing of the elderly: A content analysis study of Indian elderly. *International Journal of Criminology and Sociological Theory, 6* (2), 1138–1149.

Patel, T. (2005). *The family in India: Structure and practice.* New Delhi: SAGE publications.

Paulson, D., Bowen, M.E. & Lichtenberg, P.A. (2011). Successful ageing and longevity in older old women: The role of depression and cognition. *Journal of Ageing Research, 9*(12), 680–687.

Ramamurti, P.V. (2003). Empowering the older persons in India. *Indian Research and Development Journal, 9*(2), 5–9.

Rani, K. (2004). The aged: Need love and protection. *Social Welfare, 16*(7), 6–7.

Rebok, G.W. (2004). Short-term impact of experience participation on children and schools: Results from a pilot randomized trial. *Journal of Urban Health, 81*(1), 79–93.

Rufus, D. & Shekhar, B. (2011). A study on victims of elder abuse: A case study of residents of old age homes in Tirunelveli district. *Help Age India-Research and Development Journal, 17*(3), 29–39.

*The Hindu.* (2013, June 15). Elders need a fair deal.

*The Sunday Express.* (2009, July 5). News line (New Delhi), p. 1.

Tierney, J.P., Grossman, J.B. & Resch, N. (2000). *Making a difference: An impact study of big brothers, big sisters.* Philadelphia, PA: Public/Private Ventures.

TNN. (2014a, April 18). 70-year-old woman murdered in flat in Mumbai.

———. (2014b, April 27).Four get life term for dacoity, elder's death.

———. (2014c, April 30). Senior citizen found gagged, murdered.

*The Times of India.* (2008, April 10). Denied porn on PC, youth kills granny.

———. (2012, March 21). Elderly woman found strangled at home. (Lucknow), p.3.

UN. (2002). World Population Ageing 1950–2050. New York: United Nations Department of Economics and Social Affairs Population Division.

WHO. (2002). *Active Ageing: A policy framework action.* [Online]. Available at http://whqlibdoc. who.int/hq/2002/WHO_NMH_NPH_02.8.pdf

———. (2006). *What are the public health implications of global ageing?* [Online] Available at http://www.who.int/features/qa/42/en/index.html

World Bank. (2001). *India: The challenge of old age income security. Finance and private sector development:* South Asia region (Report No. 22034). Washington DC: World Bank.

Zedlewski, S.R. & Schaner, S.G. (2006). *Older adults engaged as volunteers: The retirement project perspectives on productive ageing.* Washington, DC: Urban Institute.

# About the Editors
# and Contributors

## Editors

**Tattwamasi Paltasingh** is an Associate Professor at Sardar Patel Institute of Economic and Social Research, Ahmedabad.

**Renu Tyagi** is an Indian Council of Social Science Research (ICSSR) Postdoctoral Fellow in the area of Social Gerontology at Sardar Patel Institute of Economic and Social Research, Ahmedabad.

## Contributors

**Heemanshu Aurora** is a doctoral fellow in Department of Anthropology, University of Delhi. Her area of interest lies in nutrition and public health domain with specialization in infectious diseases.

**Sanjeev Bakshi** is PhD and teaches statistics at the Ravenshaw University, Odisha. He has worked on the ageing of Indian population at the Population Studies Unit of Indian Statistical Institute (ISI), Kolkata. His current research is focused on the well-being of older adults in India. His areas of interest include population and environment, applied statistics, data analysis and systems science.

**Prerna Bhasin** is Senior Research Fellow, Department of Anthropology, University of Delhi. She is pursuing her doctoral thesis on reproductive profile of women and its correlation among the urban and tribal populations. Her research interests include body composition studies, reproductive health among women, child care and ageing.

**Subhadra Mitra Channa** is PhD and working as Professor in Social Anthropology, University of Delhi. Her interest areas include gender studies, issues on marginalized groups, religion and ecology, border studies, anthropological theory and methodology. She has been a visiting faculty to many universities in India and abroad.

**Anupama Datta** is MPhil from Jawaharlal Nehru University (JNU). Presently, she is serving as Director, Policy Research and Development at HelpAge India. She was trained in Social Gerontology and Policy Formulation, Planning, Implementation and Monitoring of Madrid Plan of Action on Ageing from UN International Institute on Ageing, Malta. She has worked on research and advocacy for the rights of older persons in the country.

**Meenal Dhall** is PhD and presently working as Assistant Professor in Department of Anthropology, University of Delhi. She has been actively working on public health problems, especially obesity and cardio metabolic disease, nutritional status, physical activity and its related health outcome among different populations.

**Usha Dixit** is PhD from Central Food Technological Institute (CFTRI), Mysore and worked as a Postdoctoral Fellow at Tokyo Institute of Technology, Japan. Dr Dixit has contributed towards the development and management of some new scientific programmes such as Technology Interventions for Elderly in addition to many other scientific contributions.

**V.C. Goyal** is PhD from Indian Institute of Technology (IIT), Roorkee and heads the Research Management and Outreach Division at National Institute of Hydrology (NIH), Roorkee. Dr Goyal also served in the Department of Science and Technology, Government of India, New Delhi.

**Anup K. Kapoor** is PhD from University of Delhi. He is presently working as Professor in Anthropology, University of Delhi. He has done extensive research on bio-social anthropological aspects among tribes, caste and ethnic population groups in India. He was the former Vice Chancellor at Jiwaji University, Gwalior.

**Satwanti Kapoor** is PhD from University of Delhi and Post Doctoral Fellow from University of Glasgow and Loughborough University, UK. She is presently working as Professor, Department of Anthropology, University of Delhi. Her research and teaching interests include physiological anthropology, obesity and biology of ageing. She is a member of many national and international bodies and has been a visiting fellow to different universities in India and abroad.

**J. John Kattakayam** is PhD and also the Honorary Director at the Centre for Gerontological Studies, Trivandrum. He is also Former Director, UGC Academic Staff College and Dean, Faculty of Social Sciences, University of Kerala. Besides this, he is also Former Member of Indian Council of Social Science Research (ICSSR) and Former President of Indian Sociological Society, New Delhi.

**A.M. Khan** is PhD and presently Director, Astron Institute of Social Sciences, Delhi. He also served as Professor and Head, Department of Social Sciences, National Institute of Health and Family Welfare (NIHFW), New Delhi. He has specialized in Research Methodology, Health System Research, Social Gerontology, Child Development, Maternal Health and Geriatric Care.

**Pawan Kumar** is working as the Chief Medical Officer in Central Health Services, Delhi. He has also worked as a State Program Officer at National Rural Health Mission (NRHM) and contributed in evaluation of national health programmes. His areas of interest include health care administration, human resource management, public health and health laws.

**N.K. Mungreiphy** is PhD and also a Postdoctoral Fellow in Department of Anthropology, University of Delhi. Her areas of specialization are obesity, physique, biosocial study, tribes and cardio-metabolic health research.

**Aswini Kumar Mishra** is PhD from Nabakrushna Choudhary Centre for Development Studies (NKCCDS), Bhubaneswar. Presently, he is Assistant Professor for Economics in Birla Institute of Technology and Science (BITS) at K.K. Birla Goa Campus. His research and teaching interests include industrial economics, econometrics, social security, poverty, infrastructure and financial inclusion.

**Prasanta Pathak** is PhD and heads the Sampling and Official Statistics Unit. He is also the Member-Secretary, Board of Directors, International Statistical Education Centre, Kolkata. He has worked in areas of health, family planning, action research and operations management, human resource management. His research areas include health, population policy, reproductive health, population dynamism, ageing and HR planning.

**Indumathi Rao** is PhD and Founder Member of Community-based Rehabilitation (CBR) Network for South Asian countries. She has been a member of the National Commission for Persons with Disabilities at the Policy Making Advisory Board of Inclusive Education in National Council of Educational Research and Training (NCERT). Dr Rao also received the Rotherberg Fellowship from the Royal Society, UK.

**Mala Kapur Shankardass** is PhD and works as Associate Professor at Department of Sociology, Maitreyi College, New Delhi. She is a sociologist, gerontologist, health and development social scientist. She is the consultant for United Nations agencies at New York and India office and many national and international organizations.

**Deepali Verma** is Doctoral Fellow in Department of Anthropology, University of Delhi. Her research interest includes public health with a specialization in non-communicable diseases in ethnically and geographically diverse population.

# Index